CIPS STUDY MATTERS

ADVANCED DIPLOMA IN PROCUREMENT AND SUPPLY

COURSE BOOK

Managing Risks in Supply Chains

Printed and distributed by:

The Chartered Institute of Procurement & Supply,
Easton House, Easton on the Hill, Stamford,
Lincolnshire PE9 3NZ
Tel: +44 (0) 1780 756 777
Fax: +44 (0) 1780 751 610
Email: info@cips.org
Website: www.cips.org

First edition October 2012
Reprinted with minor amendments June 2016

Contents

Preface

Welcome to your new Study Pack, consisting of two elements.

- A **Course Book** (the current volume). This provides detailed coverage of all topics specified in the unit content.
- A small-format volume of **Revision Notes**. Use your Revision Notes in the weeks leading up to your exam.

For a full explanation of how to use your new Study Pack, turn now to page xi. And good luck in your exams!

A note on style

Throughout your Study Packs you will find that we use the masculine form of personal pronouns. This convention is adopted purely for the sake of stylistic convenience – we just don't like saying 'he/she' all the time. Please don't think this reflects any kind of bias or prejudice.

The Office of Government Commerce

The Course Book refers several times to the UK's Office of Government Commerce (OGC). The OGC no longer functions in its original form and its responsibilities have been allocated to different areas within the UK Government, principally the Crown Commercial Service (CCS). However, the OGC's publications remain an authoritative source of guidance on best practice in procurement and definitions of terminology. It is perfectly valid to cite the work of the OGC in these areas when answering exam questions.

June 2016

The Unit Content

The unit content is reproduced below, together with reference to the chapter in this Course Book where each topic is covered.

Unit purpose and aims

On completion of this Unit, candidates will be able to appraise a variety of tools and techniques to:

- Establish the level of risk in supply chains
- Recommend ways of avoiding, mitigating or managing those risks.

This Unit is designed to enable candidates to undertake risk analysis and apply a range of appropriate risk management tools and techniques in supply chains.

Learning outcomes, assessment criteria and indicative content

Chapter

1.0 Understand the nature of risk affecting supply chains

1.1 Analyse the main risks that can impact on supply chains

• Definition of risks, hazards, exposure and risk appetite	1
• Positive and negative consequences of risk	1
• Direct and indirect losses	1
• Internal and external sources of risk	1
• Categories of risk: financial, strategic, operational and hazard	1
• Risks from the wider environment: STEEPLE – social, technological (failure including cyber risks and crime), economic, environmental, political, legislative and ethical (labour standards and sourcing aspects)	1

1.2 Analyse the main methods for eliminating corruption and fraud in supply chains

• The nature of fraud in organisations and supply chains, why fraud takes place and different types of fraud	4
• The nature of bribery and corruption in organisations and supply chains	4
• The different types of corruption	4
• Legislation affecting bribery and corruption	4
• The use of ethical codes including the CIPS Ethical Code	4
• Corporate governance including corporate accountability to stakeholders	4
• The Sarbanes-Oxley regulations	4

1.3 Analyse the main operational risks in supply chains

• Contract failure	5
• Financial risks such as currency, supplier cashflow and insolvency	5
• Quality failure	5
• Security of supply	5
• Technology	5
• Logistics complexity	5
• Risks in outsourcing and offshoring	5

3.0 Understand the main processes in managing risk in supply chains

4.0 Be able to propose risk management strategies to mitigate risks in supply chains

How to Use Your Study Pack

Organising your study

'Organising' is the key word: unless you are a very exceptional student, you will find a haphazard approach is insufficient, particularly if you are having to combine study with the demands of a full-time job.

A good starting point is to timetable your studies, in broad terms, between now and the date of the examination. How many subjects are you attempting? How many chapters are there in the Course Book for each subject? Now do the sums: how many days/weeks do you have for each chapter to be studied?

Remember:

- Not every week can be regarded as a study week – you may be going on holiday, for example, or there may be weeks when the demands of your job are particularly heavy. If these can be foreseen, you should allow for them in your timetabling.
- You also need a period leading up to the exam in which you will revise and practise what you have learned.

Once you have done the calculations, make a week-by-week timetable for yourself for each paper, allowing for study and revision of the entire unit content between now and the date of the exams.

Getting started

Aim to find a quiet and undisturbed location for your study, and plan as far as possible to use the same period each day. Getting into a routine helps avoid wasting time. Make sure you have all the materials you need before you begin – keep interruptions to a minimum.

Using the Course Book

You should refer to the Course Book to the extent that you need it.

- If you are a newcomer to the subject, you will probably need to read through the Course Book quite thoroughly. This will be the case for most students.
- If some areas are already familiar to you – either through earlier studies or through your practical work experience – you may choose to skip sections of the Course Book.

The content of the Course Book

This Course Book has been designed to give detailed coverage of every topic in the unit content. As you will see from pages vii–x, each topic mentioned in the unit content is dealt with in a chapter of the Course Book.

Each chapter begins with a reference to the assessment criteria and indicative content to be covered in the chapter. Each chapter is divided into sections, listed in the introduction to the chapter, and for the most part being actual captions from the unit content.

All of this enables you to monitor your progress through the unit content very easily and provides reassurance that you are tackling every subject that is examinable.

Each chapter contains the following features.

- Introduction, setting out the main topics to be covered
- Clear coverage of each topic in a concise and approachable format
- A chapter summary
- Self-test questions

The study phase

For each chapter you should begin by glancing at the main headings (listed at the start of the chapter). Then read fairly rapidly through the body of the text to absorb the main points. If it's there in the text, you can be sure it's there for a reason, so try not to skip unless the topic is one you are familiar with already.

Then return to the beginning of the chapter to start a more careful reading. You may want to take brief notes as you go along, but bear in mind that you already have your Revision Notes – there is no point in duplicating what you can find there.

Test your recall and understanding of the material by attempting the self-test questions. These are accompanied by cross-references to paragraphs where you can check your answers and refresh your memory.

The revision phase

Your approach to revision should be methodical and you should aim to tackle each main area of the unit content in turn. Read carefully through your Revision Notes. Check back to your Course Book if there are areas where you cannot recall the subject matter clearly. Then do some question practice. The CIPS website contains many past exam questions. You should aim to identify those that are suitable for the unit you are studying.

Additional reading

Your Study Pack provides you with the key information needed for each module but CIPS strongly advocates reading as widely as possible to augment and reinforce your understanding. CIPS produces an official reading list of books, which can be downloaded from the bookshop area of the CIPS website.

To help you, we have identified one essential textbook for each subject. We recommend that you read this for additional information.

The essential textbook for this unit is Kit Sadgrove, *The Complete Guide to Risk Management*.

Note on the order of syllabus coverage

The syllabus isolates the **assessment/evaluation of risk**, and the formulation of **strategies to reduce or mitigate risk**, as separate strands of the risk management process, in the final Learning Outcome of the syllabus.

This is a valid approach to defining Learning Outcomes, which (a) recognises that in practice, the knowledge and skills you acquire across the syllabus will eventually be integrated in cross-syllabus problem solving, and (b) follows the process-based approach of the most recent risk management standards.

However, for ease of learning, we have preferred a different order of learning in this Course Book.

We introduce the **main phases of the risk management cycle** 'up front', in the first three chapters, to give you an overview of the whole process – as a framework within which the management of particular categories of risk, highlighted by the syllabus, can be understood in a holistic way.

We introduce **potential mitigation strategies for each category of risk** highlighted by the syllabus, as we proceed – rather than separating coverage of each risk from coverage of its solution or mitigation.

In addition to supporting ease and efficiency of learning, this approach reflects:

- The approach taken by the Recommended Textbook for this module, so that you can more easily integrate your further reading and
- The approach you may be called upon to use in the exam, where the identification, analysis and mitigation of particular risks will form an integrated cycle of decision-making.

Examination

This subject is assessed by completion of four exam questions, each worth 25 marks, in three hours. Each exam question tests a different learning outcome.

CHAPTER 1

Risk Identification

Assessment criteria and indicative content

 Analyse the main risks that can impact on supply chains

- Definition of risks, hazards, exposure and risk appetite
- Positive and negative consequences of risk
- Direct and indirect losses
- Internal and external sources of risk
- Categories of risk: financial, strategic, operational and hazard
- Risks from the wider environment: STEEPLE – social, technological (failure including cyber risks and crime), economic, environmental, political, legislative and ethical (labour standards and sourcing aspects)

Section headings

1. Defining risk
2. The consequences of risk
3. Risk identification
4. Categories of risk
5. Internal risks
6. Risks from the wider environment

Introduction

The management of risk has developed and come to the fore in business thinking over recent years. In particular, risk in supply chains has attracted attention. Factors such as supply base rationalisation, supply partnerships and the development of lean and agile supply chains have increased the dependency of buying organisations on their supply networks. Disruption or variability of supply can have severe consequences for dependent supply chains. In consequence, the considered management of supply chain risk and vulnerability is an increasing requirement – and an important discipline – in modern business.

The first section of this syllabus is concerned mainly with the identification of different types and categories of risk that impact on supply chains. In this chapter we begin with an overview of the terminology used in risk identification (risk and hazard, exposure and vulnerability); and the main categories of risk and consequences of risk.

In Chapters 2 and 3, we complete the basic risk management cycle (covering risk assessment and risk mitigation) – before returning in Chapters 4–6 to examine some of the key categories of risk, highlighted by the syllabus, in more detail.

1   Defining risk

Risk and uncertainty

1.1   **Risk** is defined by CIPS as 'the probability of an unwanted outcome happening'. Probability is the measure of the *likelihood* that a given event or result *might* occur. The International Standard on risk management (ISO 31000: 2009) defines risk simply as: 'the effect of uncertainty on objectives'.

1.2   Any transaction or undertaking with an element of **uncertainty** as to its future outcome therefore carries an element of risk. Uncertainty may arise from:

- *Variability*: a situation where one measurable factor can take one of a range of possible values. The uncertainty arises because there are many possible ways a situation could develop or turn out.
- *Ambiguity:* uncertainty of meaning. The uncertainty arises because the information about a situation could be interpreted in various ways.

1.3   Uncertainty gives rise to risk: situations in which desirable outcomes may *not* occur – and undesirable outcomes *may* occur. **Risk management** involves understanding and analysing the nature of the risk involved; calculating the possibility of the risk event occurring (often by looking at the frequency of similar events occurring in the past); calculating the impact or consequences of the risk event occurring; and developing options to offset or reduce the risk. In other words, risk management is essentially a discipline for dealing with uncertainty. It may be defined as:

- 'The process whereby organisations methodically address the risks attaching to their activities with the goal of achieving sustained benefit within each activity and across the portfolio of all activities' (Institute of Risk Management)
- 'Co-ordinated activities to direct and control an organisation with regard to risk' (ISO 31000)

1.4   Risk is effectively unavoidable. It can never be eliminated from business, but it can be identified and mitigated: either reducing the *likelihood* of a risk event's occurring (eg by placing preventive controls in place) or by reducing the *impact* of its occurrence (eg by having insurance and contingency plans in place).

Risk and hazard

1.5   A 'hazard' may be defined as a 'source of potential harm' (ISO/IEC Guide 51), or a source of danger. A 'risk' is the *probability* (likelihood) that a hazard will in fact cause loss or damage. Sadgrove uses the example of a staircase: the stairs are a *hazard* (a source of potential harm to health and safety) posing the *risk* of an accident (since there is possibility of people falling down the stairs).

1.6   Risk may therefore be defined as 'the possibility that a hazard will cause loss or damage.'

Risk and vulnerability

1.7   The term 'vulnerability' is used to describe:

- *Things or factors that make an organisation more prone to risk*, in terms of either the probability of the risk event occurring, or the impact of its occurrence. In systems risk management (information assurance), a vulnerability is something that makes a system more prone to attack, or more prone to fail if attacked: an area of weakness that can be exploited. In procurement and supply, keeping inventory of high-value, portable, re-saleable items, for example, might be identified as a vulnerability (to the risk of theft). Dependency on a sole overseas supplier, with complex logistics and lack of mechanisms for ethical or quality monitoring, might similarly be a vulnerability (to the risk of quality or compliance failure and reputational damage). Excessively lean supply chains may create a vulnerability to quality failure, supply delays and stockouts (due to the lack of buffer stocks), or a supplier in financial difficulties. Vulnerabilities 'make the risk greater'.

- *The extent to which an organisation is affected by potential vulnerabilities*, or open to risk events occurring. A report by the Cranfield School of Management *(Supply Chain Vulnerability,* 2002), for example, defines supply chain vulnerability as 'an exposure to serious disturbance, arising from risks within the supply chain as well as risks external to the supply chain.' – pg 2

1.8   Since resources for risk monitoring, control and mitigation are typically limited (if not scarce, in today's business environment), the concept of vulnerability is important in supporting the **prioritisation** of risks. It enables managers to focus on areas in which the organisation is most exposed to risk.

Risk and exposure

1.9   'Exposure' in risk management is a technical term, used to refer to the consequence that may be experienced by the organisation, if a specific risk is realised. It is, effectively, the *maximum loss or damage* that can be suffered.

- An **inherent risk** is the exposure arising from a specific risk, before any action has been taken to manage it.
- The term **residual risk** is given to the level of risk remaining after controls and mitigating measures have been applied to the inherent risk.
- The objective of risk management is therefore to arrive at a **residual risk exposure** which is acceptable to the organisation: that is, the worst that can happen – having been constrained by risk controls and mitigation measures – represents a tolerable cost or consequence.

Risk events

1.10   So far, all the terms we have defined have to do with uncertainty, possibility, probability or likelihood. The term 'risk event' is used for the actual occurrence of the possible event: the circumstances in which a hazard, threat or attack does, in fact, cause damage, loss or harm. If the stairs are a hazard, and there is a risk of accident, the 'risk event' is someone actually falling down the stairs.

1.11   Risk events may be of different types, and different degrees of severity, and this sometimes gives rise to different terminology.

- **Shocks** are unanticipated events which cause trauma and disruption to an organisation (such as, arguably, the onset of the Global Financial Crisis or the sudden death of a founding CEO)
- **Crises** are major events (anticipated or otherwise) which threaten to cause significant damage or loss to an organisation, its stakeholders or its reputation. Examples might include a major accident (such as the Costa Concordia sinking), environmental disaster (such as an oil spill), industrial action (such as the grounding of the Qantas fleet in 2011), consumer boycott, product recall or loss of a patent rights lawsuit. Crises are often categorised as: financial crisis (such as short-term liquidity problems or the threat of bankruptcy); strategic crisis (changes in the business environment that call the viability of the company into question); and public relations crisis (negative publicity damaging corporate reputation and credibility). The management of crises (once they actually occur) often requires decisions to be made within a short time frame: in order to reduce uncertainty in such circumstances, organisations often create specific crisis management plans.
- **Disasters** are major natural or human-induced events (anticipated or otherwise) which cause significant damage to the infrastructure critical to an organisation or supply chain, and therefore significant disruption to its operations: war or terrorism, floods, earthquakes, fires and so on. Business continuity planning involves making contingency plans to keep all aspects of a business functioning in the midst of such disruptive events. The term 'disaster recovery planning' is usually given more specifically to the recovery of the technology infrastructure that supports business functions (such as ICT systems).

Risk appetite

1.12   The term 'risk appetite' is used to describe the amount of risk an organisation is willing to bear.

- Some organisations seek out high-risk ventures and investments, in pursuit of correspondingly high returns and opportunities: 'nothing ventured, nothing gained'! Such organisations are said to be **risk-enthusiastic**, or to have a high risk appetite. This profile is broadly typical of newer, smaller entrepreneurial and innovation-focused businesses.
- Others seek to minimise risk as much as possible, with the emphasis on protecting the interests of stakeholders. Such organisations are said to be **risk-averse** or to have a low risk appetite. Risk aversion is a preference for avoiding or minimising risk and exposure. This profile is broadly typical of larger, traditional, bureaucratic and highly-regulated organisations (including public sector organisations, where exposure to audit scrutiny, transparency and policy regulation is said to create a risk-averse culture, especially in procurement).

1.13   The concept of risk appetite can also be illustrated by considering whether risk is viewed as a threat or as an opportunity. (We discuss this concept further in the following section.) The ISO 31000 standard uses the term **risk attitude** to describe an organisation's 'approach to assess and eventually pursue, retain, take or turn away from risk'.

1.14   The organisation may have formally or informally defined **risk tolerances**: a range of values which represent a tolerable or acceptable level of exposure. For example, a buying organisation may define a maximum percentage of its external expenditure on a given category of inputs which will be given to a single supplier, as representing the maximum risk it is willing to take (in terms of dependency, exposure to supplier failure or supply disruption and so on). Similarly, there may be maximum levels of investment (say, as a proportion of the company's revenue or capital) which can be ventured in a single project.

1.15   The definition of acceptable exposure will also depend on the **risk-reward calculation** for a given project, strategy or decision.

- Optimal business opportunities are low-risk and high-reward – but these are not often available. High rewards are often associated with high risks.
- A high-risk, low-reward project is unlikely to be attractive.
- A low-risk, low-reward project may suit a very stable, bureaucratic organisation in a stable environment, but would appear pointless to more dynamic, competitive, growth- and value-seeking organisations.
- Companies can *influence* the level of reward (eg by negotiating higher prices, investment grants, tax concessions and so on) and/or the level of risk (eg by rigorous project planning, forming close supply chain partnerships, taking out insurances, using contractual protections and so on).

1.16   The concept of risk appetite can be considered at three distinct levels within an organisation.

- **Corporate risk appetite** is the overall amount of risk judged to be appropriate at a strategic level. At this level, the Board of Directors will judge the tolerable range of exposure for the organisation and set policies to ensure that those lower in the organisational hierarchy understand their constraints when taking risks.
- **Delegated risk appetite** is the agreed corporate risk appetite that can be cascaded down the organisational structure, agreeing risk levels for different parts of the organisation. A process for *risk escalation* places boundaries of discretion on business units and functions (similar to spend levels in procurement): when a given risk reaches the tolerance level, it may not be accepted without reference upwards.
- **Project risk appetite** falls outside the day-to-day policy and decision-making of the organisation, as projects have their own defined objectives, constraints and decision-making structures. Projects may require different risk appetite choices, to reflect the particular nature (standardised or speculative) of the project.

2   The consequences of risk

Positive and negative consequences

2.1   Despite the common definition of risk by reference to unwanted outcomes, risk offers **opportunity** as well as potential loss.

2.2   Attempting to eliminate all uncertainty or risk may put an organisation in a position of paralysis, where it is unable to undertake uncertain ventures and investments in order to achieve desired outcomes. Innovation is a risk. Entering a new market, or developing a new product, is a risk. But a business would stagnate without such 'gambles'. Lack of risk management can lead to disaster – but at the other end of the scale, excessive caution (or risk aversion) can lead to paralysis, stagnation and missed opportunities. Appropriate **risk assessment** (prioritising risks; assessing exposure; conducting cost/benefit analysis of risks; and so on) is required to steer a middle course which optimises business performance and profitability.

2.3   Moreover, uncertain outcomes can – as gamblers know – be positive as well as negative.

- The term 'downside risk' may be given to uncertainties with negative outcomes. In investment terms, for example, a downside risk is the probability of a security or other investment's decline in value if market conditions change, and/or the amount of loss that could be sustained as a result (the investor's exposure). Downside risk is sometimes also used as a synonym for 'worst case scenario'.
- The term 'upside risk' (or 'upside potential') may be given to uncertainties with positive outcomes, events the outcomes of which are more positive than expected, or a potential 'best case scenario'. In investment, for example, upside risk is the probability that (and the amount by which) the value of a security or other investment may increase beyond forecast levels.

Direct and indirect consequences

2.4   The negative consequences of a risk event may be a direct loss or an indirect (or consequential) loss.

- A **direct loss** is a loss arising directly from a risk event. Direct physical or material loss, for example, includes loss, theft or damage to tangible property or assets, such as deliveries in transit, stock, buildings, vehicles or equipment. Other direct losses would include exchange rate loss, repair or replacement costs and disrupted supply. Such risks will normally be covered by insurances, providing compensation for the value of the loss.
- The term **consequential loss** is used to describe an *indirect* loss resulting from a risk event. As an example, fire in a factory will incur direct loss (of equipment, premises, lost production etc) – but the loss of reputation and goodwill as a result of the disruption to production would represent a consequential loss. Other examples of indirect loss include: expenses incurred in coping with risk events; indirect loss of revenue or profits; lost productivity through labour turnover; compensation and legal costs. Insurances do not usually take into account indirect consequential losses deriving from the claim risk event. (Business interruption insurance is available, however, to extend damage coverage to consequential losses such as extra expenses, rental value, profits and commissions.)

2.5   Indirect consequential loss can have its most severe impact in the form of reputational damage. Supply chain ethical breaches, quality failures, supply disruption, project delays, confidentiality or privacy breaches and other risk events may damage stakeholder goodwill and the reputational equity of the company.

Risk and financial loss

2.6   Sadgrove argues that a wide range of risk events eventually, or consequentially, results in financial loss (Table 1.1) – which is why risk is fundamentally important to the management of businesses and supply chains.

Table 1.1 *The results of uncontrolled risk*

TYPE OF RISK	INITIAL EFFECT	ULTIMATE EFFECT
Quality problem	Product recall; customer defection	Financial losses
Environmental pollution	Bad publicity; customer dissatisfaction and defection; court action; fines	Financial losses
Health and safety injury	Bad publicity; worker compensation claims; workforce dissatisfaction; statutory fines	Human suffering; financial losses
Fire	Harm to humans; loss of production and assets	Human suffering; financial losses
Computer failure	Inability to take orders, process work or issue invoices; customer defection	Financial losses
Marketing risk	Revenue drops	Financial losses
Fraud	Theft of money	Financial losses
Security	Theft of money, assets or plans	Financial losses
International trading	Foreign exchange losses	Financial losses
Political risks	Foreign government appropriation of assets; prevents repatriation of profits	Financial losses

2.7   Other types of loss include reputational loss, environmental loss, and lost opportunities. We might summarise these as in Table 1.2. (We add some possible mitigating actions, for future reference. Generic mitigation processes are covered later in the syllabus, but it makes sense to include them in relation to specific risk categories here.)

Table 1.2 *Key types of loss*

LOSS	IMPACT	SAMPLE MITIGATING MEASURES
Financial (eg if an event causes exchange rate loss, lost profits, added costs, damaged assets)	• Financial losses • Reduced profitability • Reduced viability • Loss of investment	• Insurance • Financial controls • Financial management • Security measures
Reputational (eg from association with illegal or unethical trading, employment or environmental practices, quality or delivery failure)	• Reduced ability to attract quality staff and suppliers • Loss of investor support • Loss of goodwill and influence • Devaluation of brand equity • Increased scrutiny	• Proactive issues management • Crisis management plans • Ethical and quality policies and policy monitoring and review • Supplier monitoring and management
Environmental (eg disruption of supply by natural forces; increasing resource scarcity; escalating resource prices; 'polluter pays' penalties; costs of environmental repair)	• Reputational damage • Environmental degradation • 'Polluter pays' penalties • Costs of adjustment • Pressure group resistance	• Environmental risk and impact analysis and monitoring • Environmental policy and controls
Health and safety (eg costs of sickness benefits, lost production, higher insurance premiums, litigation, compensation, employee turnover)	• Lost productivity • Costs (eg repair, penalties, compensation, higher insurance) • Reputational and employee relations damage	• H&S policy and rules • Communication, training • Risk cycle • Culture of safety • Protective equipment etc • Insurance
Lost opportunity (eg risk aversion or cost focus leading to low investment and innovation, non-synergistic relationships)	• Lost return on investment • Lost opportunity for improvement or synergy • Lost sources of ideas, supply or revenue	• Support entrepreneurs • Raise delegated risk appetite • Culture of acceptable risk

The relevance and priority of risk management

2.8   All businesses are subject to uncertainty and risk. However, formal risk assessment and management or mitigation will not be a priority for all organisations – depending on factors such as their exposure and their risk appetite. The larger and more complex the business and its supply chain, and the more dynamic and uncertain its environment, the more it will benefit from systematic risk management.

2.9   Risk management may be particularly beneficial (or necessary) for organisations with: multiple sites (owing to logistical complexity); overseas or global operations; different processes; complex supply chains and networks (not under the direct control of management); large enough size that no one individual can monitor and 'stay on top of' the range of hazards; older premises and work sites (posing potential health and safety and compliance risks); a dynamic product and supply environment (posing newly emerging threats); and/or a highly regulated industry, such as aviation or financial services (with a high degree of compliance risk).

Benefits of effective risk management

2.10   Sadgrove argues that 'companies tend to introduce risk management in response to outside factors such as scandals, legislation or regulation (for example, Stock Exchange reporting requirements). They are less likely to introduce risk management because it will help the corporation produce better results'.

2.11   However, a business case can be made that proactive and systematic risk management brings the following benefits:

- Avoids or minimises costs incurred by risk events, shocks and crises (eg by avoiding litigation and damages; theft or misuse of funds; loss or destruction of assets and so on)
- Avoids or minimises costs incurred by failure to demonstrate risk mitigation (eg by enabling reduced insurance premiums)
- Avoids disruption to production and revenue streams (eg through loss of data or assets, supply failure, logistics disruption, technology failures and so on)
- Secures supply, by mitigating supply chain vulnerability
- Protects market share (eg by managing marketing, brand-related and reputational risks; avoiding technological obsolescence; avoiding theft of competitive intellectual property; and so on)
- Supports business and supply chain resilience: enabling business continuity and disaster recovery
- Safeguards the key human resources of the organisation from pain, suffering, insecurity and distress (which, quite apart from humane considerations, impact on their motivation, morale and performance)
- Enables the organisation to attract and retain quality employees, suppliers and network partners (eg by avoiding a damaged employer brand and reputation, avoiding loss of morale due to accidents and litigation)
- Helps management objectively to decide which risks are *worth* pursuing (in order to seize opportunities) and which should be avoided – allowing higher risk opportunities to be successfully pursued (while mitigating their downside risk)
- Improves the quality of strategy-, policy- and decision-making (by encouraging environmental monitoring, risk awareness, analysis of processes and supply chains)
- Improves organisational and supply chain co-ordination (by encouraging cross-functional and cross-supply-chain communication on risk issues)
- Improves stakeholder confidence and satisfaction (eg in regard to corporate governance, the protection of consumer and shareholder interests, and the equitable sharing of risks through the supply chain).

3   Risk identification

3.1   The processes of risk identification and analysis are effectively concerned with identifying all the potential things that *might* go wrong with an activity – or sources of risk – and estimating the probability of their happening. If a risk is not identified, it cannot be evaluated and managed. Risk identification is a formal process within risk management that seeks to identify potential problems or areas of uncertainty.

Techniques for risk identification

3.2   Risk identification is often an inexact discipline, as it relies on people's awareness and experience of potential risk areas. Initial risk identification may involve a combination of the following activities.

- Monitoring of published academic research results and reports by risk consultants
- Environmental scanning and corporate appraisal (STEEPLE and SWOT analysis)
- Horizon scanning (identifying future developments that may introduce new opportunities and risk)
- Monitoring risk events in benchmark organisations
- Market intelligence gathering and management information systems
- Critical incident investigations (investigating the causes of major or unexpected variances or problems with contracts or projects)
- Scenario analysis (eg using computer models or spreadsheets to model the effect of changes in variables, or the consequences of actions)
- Process audits (checking the effectiveness of quality management, environmental management, performance management and other processes)
- Periodic checks and inspections on health and safety, quality, maintenance (etc)
- Examining project plans, supply chain maps etc for identifiable vulnerabilities
- Conducting formal risk assessments (for high-value projects or activities in volatile environments, and identified vulnerabilities)
- Consulting with key stakeholders and industry experts: using brainstorming, survey questionnaires, workshops; and visual ideas-capture tools such as mind-maps, Ishikawa (cause and effect) diagrams, decision trees, supply chain maps and so on.
- Employing third party risk audit and risk management consultants (as discussed in Chapter 12)

In an exam case study, of course, you will mainly have to *recognise* potential contractual risks (such as the categories discussed in this chapter) from available data.

3.3   Risk identification should be an ongoing process, as the organisation's contractual risk profile may continually change, presenting new risks or turning slight risks into potential crises (eg if they attract media or regulatory scrutiny). A comprehensive list of identified risks should be compiled in a **risk register** (discussed below) for major contracts.

Internal and external sources of risk

3.4   Organisations face risks, hazards and vulnerabilities in both their internal and external environments. The main difference between the two is that internal risk can to a large extent be controlled by managerial action, while external risk factors are largely *uncontrollable*. They can be anticipated and planned for, but the variables which create the risk are largely beyond the organisation's direct control.

3.5   The risk environment of a given organisation (or procurement and supply function) can be seen as a series of concentric circles: Figure 1.1.

Figure 1.1 *Sources of risk*

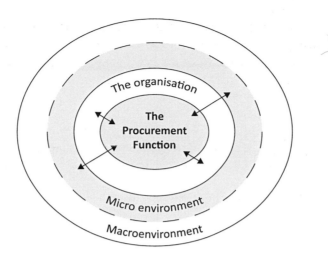

- The **internal environment** of the organisation includes its structures and relationships; its various functions and personnel; its style or 'culture'; its strategic objectives and plans; systems and technology; policies, rules and procedures; communication flows; premises, plant and equipment; and so on.
- The immediate **operating or micro environment** of the organisation includes the customers, suppliers and competitors (connected stakeholders) who directly impact on its operations.
- The general or **macro environment** incorporates wider factors in the market and society in which the organisation operates: industry structure, the national economy, law, politics, culture, technological development and natural resources. It also includes the organisation's relationships with secondary stakeholders (including the government, media, interest and pressure groups, communities and the 'public' at large.)

3.6 Supply chain management activity will be strongly *influenced* by factors in all three 'tiers' of the environment: from internal procurement procedures, to supplier changes, to national contract law or international commodity prices. In turn, a procurement function has a measure of *influence* or control over risks in:

- The *internal* environment (most obviously, by managing the flow of materials into and through the organisation, and the formulation of procurement policies and procedures) and
- The *micro* environment (most obviously, by seeking to manage supplier behaviour and relationships, and by contributing to the organisation's competitive advantage).

3.7 The *macro* environment, however, is *not* generally within a buying organisation's direct control. It will merely seek to anticipate, identify and manage emerging threats and opportunities, to its own advantage – and, ideally, more efficiently and effectively than its competitors. The procurement and supply function is particularly important in this context, because buyers – by means of their contacts with the external supply market – span the boundary between the organisation and its environment. The marketing and corporate communications functions performs a similar role by means of their contacts with external customers and other 'audiences'.

3.8 Each environmental 'circle' can therefore be a source of risk. We will survey some sources of internal and external risk in Sections 5 and 6 of this chapter.

Supply chain mapping

3.9   A useful tool for risk and vulnerability identification is the mapping of the supply chain or value stream. Research from Cranfield University (*Creating Resilient Supply Chains*) argues that a systematic approach is needed to identify business, supply and contractual risks arising from failure within the supply chain, at some point in the flow of value towards the customer, or at some 'linkage' point in the chain.

3.10   Supply chain mapping is a technique that provides a time-based representation of the process involved as goods, materials, information and other value-adding resources move through the supply chain. The map (eg a network diagram or flowchart) shows the time taken at the inter-connection (linkage) and movement points within the chain. This enables organisations to determine:

- The inter-connecting 'pipeline' of suppliers through which value-adding elements must travel to reach the end-user
- The transport links by which value-adding elements are passed from one 'node' to another in the chain
- The amount of work in progress and inventory stockpiled at each stage in the pipeline
- The time it would take to source replenishment from various points in the pipeline in the event of disruption.

3.11   The Cranfield researchers argue that the information gained from such an analysis can assist in identifying areas of contractual and supply risk, and planning actions such as the following.

- Consulting and collaborating with supply chain partners to manage areas of identified vulnerability
- Strengthening relationship and contractual protections at vulnerable linkage points or supplier relationships
- Monitoring and managing first tier suppliers' management of lower tiers of the supply chain, to reduce vulnerabilities at lower tiers
- Determining alternative sources of supply
- Holding additional buffer or safety stocks ('just in case' inventory)
- Formulating contingency plans for alternative transport arrangements in areas vulnerable to disruption

4   Categories of risk

4.1   Risk management systems, and priority risk areas, will vary across sectors and industries. However, any systematic approach to assessing and managing risk will generally involve categorising risks under the following main headings, which will be examined further as we progress through this Course Book.

- **Strategic risks** arise from the vision and direction of an organisation, and the organisation's positioning in a particular industry, market and/or geographic area. Examples of strategic risk include: markets, competitors, technology, the economy, consumer needs, corporate-level legal issues and merger or acquisition risks.
- **Operational risks** arise from the functional, operational and administrative procedures by which organisational strategies are pursued. They relate primarily to an organisation's production or service delivery operations. Such risks might include quality issues, health and safety risks, technology vulnerabilities, transport and logistics, weather events, fraud, suppliers and supply security.
- **Financial risks** arise internally from the financial structure of the business, and externally from financial transactions with other organisations. Financial risks impact on the organisation's ability to trade profitably (or meet public service targets). Examples include: exchange rate and interest rate risk, liquidity and cashflow, profitability and viability, costs and credit.
- **Compliance risks** arise from the need to ensure compliance with laws, regulations and policy frameworks; and the potential damage incurred by exposure of non-compliant or illegal activity by the organisation or its supply chains, including reputational, operational and financial penalties. Examples

include: company law, tax requirements, employment law, environmental regulation, ethics and internal controls.

4.2 Here are some other categories of risk you might come across in your reading.

- **Market risks:** strategic risks arising from factors or changes in the external supply market, such as rising commodity prices, resource scarcity, the pace of technological change, or high or growing supplier power (eg with few suppliers, or supply market consolidation). There may also be product market risk, as a result of falling demand, product obsolescence or competitor initiatives (resulting in loss of competitive advantage).
- **Technological risks:** both strategic and operational risks arising from technology dynamism and obsolescence, systems or equipment failure, data corruption or theft, new technology 'teething troubles', systems incompatibility (eg where buyer-supplier systems need to be integrated) and so on.
- **Supply risks:** both strategic and operational risks arising from supply market instability and resource scarcity; supplier failure (eg as a result of financial instability, excessively 'lean' supply chains or cashflow problems); supply disruption (eg as a result of industrial action, weather events, transport problems or damage to supplies in transit); the length and complexity of supply chains and logistics (long lead times, transport risks); and so on.
- **Reputational risks:** classified as financial and/or compliance risks, arising from exposure of unethical, socially irresponsible or environment-damaging activity by the organisation or its supply chain, potentially damaging the organisation's image, brand and credibility in its customer, investor, labour and supply markets.

Strategic risk

4.3 The terms strategic, operational and project-based risk are often used to categorise risks which affect different levels of decision-making in organisations.

4.4 As we noted earlier, **strategic risks** arise from the vision and direction of an organisation, and the organisation's positioning in a particular industry, market and/or geographic area. Johnson, Scholes & Whittington define strategy as 'the direction and scope of an organisation over the long term; ideally, which matches its resources to its changing environment, and in particular its markets, customers and clients so as to meet stakeholder expectations'.

4.5 Strategic risks therefore include big-picture issues, commonly dealt with at Board level.

- The effectiveness with which an organisation's resources, competencies and direction 'fit' the dynamics and demands of its environment (partly expressed in the effectiveness of the organisation's strategic planning capability)
- The ability of an organisation to compete and maintain competitive advantage in its markets: its distinctive, hard-to-imitate competencies and sources of added value
- The strengths and weaknesses of an organisation's structure, processes, resources, competencies and management, which support or constrain it in the pursuit of its mission and objectives
- The opportunities and threats arising in the external environment, which support or constrain it in the pursuit of its mission and objectives
- The risks presented by environmental changes (including competitor initiatives and changes in customer needs, wants and attitudes)
- The risks presented by organisational decisions to pursue new strategies (which may be beyond current experience, capacity or competence) or strategies with inherent risk (such as outsourcing, single sourcing, global sourcing, innovation, product diversification, entering new markets, entering international markets – and so on)

4.6 Some key areas of strategic risk (and mitigation methods) are summarised in Table 1.3. In addition, there may be technological, environmental or reputational risks arising from particular strategic decisions.

Table 1.3 *Summary of some key strategic risks*

AREA OF STRATEGIC RISK	HAZARDS (eg)	RISK MITIGATION
Commercial risk	Supplier failure, supply chain underperformance, changing supply or customer market conditions	• Environmental monitoring • Product or market planning • Procurement research • Supplier management
Financial risk	Lack of liquidity, increased costs of finance, investment risk, foreign exchange loss, poor credit management, fraud	• Financial management • Investment appraisal • Internal controls • Corporate governance
Directional or competitive risk	Competitor initiative or retaliation; failure of inappropriate strategies; loss of core competencies; damage to brand	• Systematic strategic analysis, choice, review • Apply risk cycle • Competitor research and monitoring • Competitive intelligence gathering and analysis
Developmental risk	*Merger or acquisition*: financial risk, incompatible culture or systems *Strategic outsourcing*: costs, incompatibility, reputational damage, staff resistance	• Strategic analysis, choice • Wide ranging criteria for partner choice • Stakeholder management • Transition planning • Exit strategies
Internationalisation risk	Exchange rate loss; cultural and legal differences; market unfamiliarity; restricted access to markets and networks; increased transport risks	• Currency management • Joint ventures or agencies • Research and risk analysis Insurances • Incoterms

4.7 Strategic decisions should be evaluated using risk management criteria, with the aim of ensuring that strategic plans and choices fall within the organisation's risk appetite. Launching a new product in China, for example, may be considered too great a risk. By entering a joint venture with a Chinese business partner, for example, the risk may be mitigated to an acceptable level of residual risk – although there may be secondary risks (such as being locked into partnership with a potentially incompatible partner...).

4.8 Johnson, Scholes and Whittington *(Exploring Corporate Strategy)* identify three key evaluation criteria for any strategy, as part of the rational strategic planning model.

- **Suitability**. Does the strategy fit the situation identified in the strategic appraisal (environmental analysis and corporate appraisal)? Does it capitalise on the organisation's identified strengths and exploit its core competencies (for competitive advantage)? Does it overcome identified weaknesses? Does it deflect or neutralise identified threats? Does it exploit identified opportunities?
- **Feasibility**. Can the strategy be implemented? Will it work in practice? Feasibility may be measured in various ways (which you might like to think of as an alternative set of 'PEST' factors):
  — **Practical:** does the organisation have the resources to do this? Will it be able to attain and sustain the required level of performance? Will it be able to respond to likely retaliation by competitors?
  — **Economic**: are the financial resources available? Will there be a satisfactory return on investment, at an acceptable level of risk? (This will be analysed by financial analysis and investment appraisal tools, such as breakeven analysis, discounted cashflow analysis, financial ratio analysis and risk analysis.)
  — **Social:** will stakeholders accept and support the strategy – or resist it? (This overlaps with 'acceptability', covered below.)
  — **Technical:** can the strategy be implemented using available or accessible technology (equipment, systems and processes)?
- **Acceptability**. Stakeholders in a strategic decision may include a wide number of groups, whose acceptance may (depending on their power) be required for successful implementation.
  — Will the strategy be sufficiently profitable to meet shareholder expectations?

— Will managers and employees favour or resist the decision?
— What will be the impact on customer satisfaction, loyalty and demand?
— What will be the impact on long-term supply chain relationships?
— What will be the 'external' costs and impacts on the wider community (eg the environment or employment)?

Operational risk

4.9   The operational level of organisational planning and decision-making refers to deploying, controlling and maximising the capabilities of organisational resources in order to meet the aims and objectives of strategic plans. The role of operations is to take inputs (materials, components, labour, finance, data and so on) into an organisation and to transform or convert them into outputs (products, services, information, profits, customer and shareholder value, and so on). Operational objectives concern the delivery of plans, contractual commitments and stakeholder expectations. If these requirements are not met, both commercial and reputational risks may result.

4.10 As we noted earlier, operational risks relate primarily to an organisation's core production or service delivery operations, and related activities such as inbound and outbound logistics, procurement, and quality management. Such risks might include product and process design and quality issues; insufficient (or excess) operational capacity to meet demand; labour or skills shortages, loss of key personnel and/ or employee relations problems (affecting productivity); health and safety risks; security risks (concerning the security of premises, assets and personnel); technology vulnerabilities; issues of logistical complexity and supply security (eg supply disruption or supplier failure); and operational-level financial risks (such as cashflow problems or inability to reduce the cost base).

4.11 A range of operational risks specified by the syllabus is considered in detail, in Chapter 5 of this Course Book, but an overview is provided in Table 1.4.

Table 1.4 *Examples of generic operational risks*

AREA OF GENERIC OPERATIONAL RISK	EXAMPLE RISK MITIGATION MEASURES
Poor cost structure or inability to reduce cost base	• Cost analysis and restructuring • Subcontracting or outsourcing
Insufficient (or excessive) demand for products and services	• Improved demand forecasting and management • Improved customer relationships • Adjusted marketing mix
Supplier or outsource provider failure	• Careful supplier selection, evaluation, monitoring, performance management
Disruption to supply	• Multiple or back-up sourcing • Agile and resilient supply chain management
Disruption to productivity (eg through industrial unrest, equipment failure)	• Preventive and contingency planning • Insurances
Health, safety and welfare issues	• H&S policy, practices, equipment, training, insurances
Inefficient systems, processes and management	• Process audits, benchmarking, BPR or continuous improvement (*kaizen*)

Project risk

4.12 Project risk may be considered a type of operational risk, since projects generally concern the operational implementation of strategic plans. However, projects are often distinguished from 'business as usual' operational processes, as having specific and self-contained objectives, time frames, organisational structures and resource allocations. Project management – and project risks – are the subject of a separate section of the syllabus, and will be explored in detail in Chapters 7–10.

The AS/NZS 4360 risk standard

4.13 Standards Australia published AS/NZS 4360 in 1995, as the world's first risk management standard, which signalled a new maturity in the discipline of corporate risk management. The standard categorises risk under eight risk categories: Table 1.5.

Table 1.5 *Categories of risk in AS/NZS 3460*

CATEGORY	EXAMPLES
Commercial and legal relationships	For example: poorly defined contract terms (failing to mitigate or share risk); dependency on sole suppliers or a narrow supply base; or adversarial relations with a strategic supplier or contractor. Commercial relationships must be managed and monitored in such a way as to develop the mutual interests of both parties, over the long term, supported by regular discussions and minuted meetings on risk issues. In a legal contractual relationship the aim will be to provide a framework that enables the relationship to develop while at the same time defining risk responsibilities and obligations (as discussed in Chapter 11.)
Economic circumstances	Eg interest rate movements and lending policies (affecting cost of finance); economic activity and economic cycles (affecting consumer demand and investor confidence); exchange rate fluctuations (affecting import and export costs); employment (affecting availability and cost of labour); or commodity and energy prices (affecting operating costs). Monitoring of economic indicators, and assessment of their impact on the organisation's risk exposure, should be integrated into risk strategy.
Human behaviour	Eg irresponsible behaviours in regard to health and safety, the possibility of user error in technology or systems, lack of risk awareness in behaviour and decision-making, or deliberate fraud, sabotage and other threats. In a business setting, there are often legislative, policy and procedural controls to ensure that human behaviour is relatively predictable, and constrained within acceptable boundaries, but risks still remain.
Natural events	Eg fire, flood, drought, earthquake, storm, tsunami and similar events (sometimes identified by insurers as 'Acts of God', for which no human being can be held responsible, and over which organisations can exercise little control).
Political circumstances	Eg change of government and government policy (eg supportive of business, protectionist or supportive of free trade); change of political and trading 'blocs' (such as the European Union); cuts in government spending; risks of political instability (civil unrest, war, terrorism); or pressure group and public activism against corporate interests.
Technology and technical issues	Eg vulnerability of information systems and websites to attack (such as viruses, hacking, or distributed denial of service [DDOS] attacks); risks of technological obsolescence; technology breakdown or compatibility issues (coupled with a high degree of dependency); and lack of information assurance measures to protect data and systems.
Management activities and control	Eg lack of limits, constraints or controls (supervision, procedures, rules, checks and audits, authorisations and approvals) to minimise vulnerability; creation of an uncontrolled risk-taking ('macho' or 'gung ho') culture; poor management decision making (eg in relation to projects and investments).
Individual activities	Eg fraud and theft perpetrated by individuals within the organisation or supply chain network.

5 Internal risks

5.1 Internal risks are risks arising in the internal environment of the organisation and/or supply chain: its organisational structure, systems and processes, strategies, policies, governance, technology, management and human resources.

5.2 Examples of internal risks include the following.

- **Human personality factors:** eg over-confidence, carelessness, resistance to rules and policies and so on
- **Cultural values and norms:** eg macho cultures encouraging dangerous 'horseplay' or competitive risk-taking; blaming cultures discouraging disclosure and problem reporting; and so on

- **Group dynamics:** eg risky decision-making by over-cohesive teams (due to 'group think'); poorly functioning teams; lack of leadership
- **Human error and inexperience:** eg lack of training, instruction or supervision; poor flow of job-related information and performance feedback; unclear goals and instructions; and poor performance management (failure to identify improvement and learning needs, and lack of improvement interventions)
- **Business management:** eg uncontrolled costs; poor strategic planning, product and market planning or financial management; poor supply chain relationship management; lack of investment in product development; poor investment appraisal and so on.
- **Malicious activity** eg fraud, sabotage, theft, data theft or industrial espionage, or unethical conduct – facilitated by poor corporate governance, lack of ethics management, lack of support for whistle blowers, and lack of security provisions (eg against theft, computer viruses and hacking and so on).
- **Breakdown of technology, equipment or systems** eg through lack of maintenance, incorrect usage, lack of contingency planning (eg for power failure)
- **Security risks:** eg unprotected or unauthorised access to facilities, unsecured cash, assets or data, attacks on personnel (including kidnapping, ransom and extortion), industrial espionage
- **Lack of internal controls:** eg financial controls, security system, policies and policy reviews, risk monitoring and assessment, internal and external audits, contingency plans
- **Workplace hazards:** risk of accidents and ill health arising from a range of health and safety hazards, including: materials handling; poor ergonomic design; poorly maintained or unhygienic work environments; work-related stress; poorly maintained or incorrectly used machinery; the use and storage of hazardous substances; non-use or misuse of protective equipment; and additional risks to certain categories of employee (such as young workers, pregnant workers, new and temporary workers, or night-shift workers)
- **Poor employee relations:** causing a risk of industrial action, loss of productivity, instability and loss of morale (caused by excessive employee turnover), and difficulties attracting and retaining talent
- **Loss of key personnel and knowledge:** through natural wastage (without succession planning), accelerated wastage (through failure of retention policies), downsizing or outsourcing

5.3 The key point about internal risks is that they should be *controllable* by the organisation, its managerial processes (such as risk assessment, monitoring and supervision) and internal controls (policies, rules, checks and risk management measures). A range of internal risks is considered in Chapters 4–6.

Internal controls

5.4 An organisation's systems of internal controls are designed to manage internal risk. Internal controls facilitate the effectiveness and efficiency of operations and contribute to delivering risk objectives. Internal controls are put in place to manage both internal sources of risk and the impacts of external sources of risk.

5.5 Internal control systems will vary according to the organisation but should cover the following key areas.

- The nature and extent of the risks facing the organisation
- The extent and categories of risk that it is acceptable to bear
- The likelihood of the risk occurring
- The organisation's ability to reduce the incidence and impact on the business of risks that do materialise

5.6 Internal controls are subject to limitations and these limitations should be considered as part of the risk management process.

- Directors and managers are responsible for the establishment, implementation and continuance of internal controls. Although the processes will be the subject of review and auditing it is effective management that ensures successful delivery.

- Internal controls provide reasonable assurance but are not a total guarantee against risk.
- Within any organisation there will be gaps that can be exploited by individuals. Internal controls must be responsive to potential gaps within the system.

5.7   We will discuss this further in Chapter 4, where we explore internal controls in relation to corporate governance.

6   Risks from the wider environment

6.1   The 'open systems' model of organisations emphasises the importance of taking the external environment into account in corporate risk management. Firstly, because an organisation *depends* on its environment as the source of its inputs; the market for its outputs; and a key source of feedback information to identify and assess risk. And secondly, because an organisation also *impacts* on its environment, in the process of taking in inputs and creating outputs (both products, such as goods and services, and 'by products' such as waste, pollution, supplier development or local employment).

6.2   The external environment exerts an important influence on the vulnerability of an organisation and its supply chain, in three basic ways.

- It presents *threats* (such as restrictive legislation, competitor initiatives, technology obsolescence or supply shortages, say) and *opportunities* (such as consumer demand, technological improvements or innovative suppliers entering the supply market). These affect the organisation's ability to compete in its market and fulfil its objectives (strategic risk). Environmental threats and opportunities are key factors in the formation of business – and supply chain – strategies and plans.
- It is the source of *resources* needed by the organisation (labour, materials, supplies and services, energy, finance, information and so on). Environmental factors determine to what extent these resources are, or are not, available in the right quantity, at the right time and at the right price – and what sort of supply chain strategies, policies and practices will help to secure supply.
- It contains *stakeholders* who may seek, or have the right, to influence the activities of the organisation. These include suppliers and their supply chains – and also law makers, regulatory bodies, industry associations and other parties with an interest or 'stake' in supply chain ethics, management and performance. Stakeholders can pose risks to the organisation's strategy and operations, reputation and value.

The STEEPLE model

6.3   A popular tool for analysing external macro environment or supply market factors is described by the acronym PEST (and more comprehensive variants such as PESTLE). The most comprehensive version of this model – specified in your syllabus – is STEEPLE: Table 1.6 . We have chosen some illustrative examples of STEEPLE factors which may be identified as risk factors for organisations and supply chains.

Table 1.6 *The STEEPLE framework*

FACTORS	EXAMPLES
Socio-cultural *(How might changes affect the demands or expectations of customers, suppliers or other stakeholders?)*	• Demographics (age, gender, ethnicity, population movements and so on) affecting demand for goods and services, and the availability of skills • Consumerism and consumer power • Education and skilling infrastructure (affecting the availability and price of skills) • Values (eg re corporate social responsibility and diversity, and shaping the psychological contract) • Attitudes to work, employment equity and employee relations • Cultural differences (impacting on cross-cultural and multi-cultural management) • Gender roles (affecting expectations of equality)
Technological *(Are there opportunities for development – or risks of obsolescence?)*	• Information and communications technology (ICT) developments changing products, business processes (eg e-commerce) • Automation and ICT facilitating workforce rationalisation or downsizing; 'virtual' organisation; outsourcing (through improved communication, integration and control) • Automation and ICT changing job roles and organisation; skill requirements
Economic *(How might changes affect product demand and/or supply and cost of inputs?)*	• The economic strength and stability of the industry or market (eg affecting employment, investment in HR, priority for business survival, sources of competitive advantage) • Rates of inflation, interest and taxation (impacting on disposable incomes, the costs of business finance, pay rates and expectations) • In international supply markets: exchange rates, comparative wages and taxes, freedom of labour and capital movements, trade agreements and so on.
Environmental (or 'ecological') *(Which factors may cause supply problems, compliance issues, market pressure or risk to reputation)*	• Consumer demand and public pressure for eco-friendly products and processes • Law and regulation (and related compliance risks) on environmental issues such as pollution, carbon emissions and waste management • Emerging or local priorities re green 'issues': eg water management, de-forestation, climate change and greenhouse gas emissions • The availability, scarcity and price of natural resources and commodities
Political *(What are the likely implications of policies or changes in policy?)*	• Government policies (eg on international trade, support for business and innovation, public sector spending cuts, or HR policies eg work-life balance, life-long learning and skilling) • Grants and subsidies available eg for employee, supplier or regional development Political risk (eg political or civil unrest or war) in operational regions or supply and labour markets
Legal *(How will the organisation need to adapt policies and practices in order to comply?)*	• A wide range of law and regulation on issues such as: employment rights and obligations; workplace health and safety; equality; working hours; minimum wage; environmental protection; consumer rights and contracts; data protection; and public sector procurement procedures.
Ethical *(Which issues may cause market pressure or reputational risk?)*	• Consumer demand for ethically sourced and produced goods and services (eg fair pricing, supply chain labour standards, avoidance of animal testing, sustainable sourcing of non-renewable resources) • Ethical codes and standards published by buyers and suppliers, professional bodies (such as CIPS), trade unions and pressure groups • Ethical and reputational risk arising from exposure of, or association with, unethical practices in the supply chain • The 'employer brand' of the organisation (the labour market's perception of the organisation as an ethical employer, affecting its ability to attract and retain quality labour).

6.4   This is a useful structure for identifying and categorising sources of risk from the external environment – both in practice and in exam situations.

Financial crisis and supply chain vulnerability

6.5 Many financial risks are likely to be exacerbated by challenging economic conditions – such as the 2008–2009 global financial crisis – and you should certainly reflect on the role of risk management in:

- Managing the downside *and* upside risks of recession (since there may well be opportunities available for resilient supply chains and investors)
- Helping an organisation and its employees to cope with crisis
- Promoting business continuity and recovery.

6.6 The following is a checklist of the kinds of issues raised by macro-economic 'crisis' for risk managers.

- Reduced risk appetite, with the change of focus from long-term competitive advantage to survival of the business and supply chain
- Need to ensure that risk management plans are up to date, to minimise supply disruptions. This requires a full and detailed understanding of key supply markets, as a basis for category strategies.
- Ethical, responsibility and related risk issues of stakeholders (including suppliers) affected by the recession; need to pursue efficiencies, mutual support and relationship-building to support recovery throughout the supply chain
- Critical need to monitor suppliers' financial viability, to protect continuity of supply – facilitated by strong ongoing supplier relationship management, less emphasis on single or dual sourcing arrangements and contingency plans for supplier failure
- Risk of losing core organisational competencies, with down-sizing and outsourcing, erosion of development budgets etc. The need to develop key skills for survival and recovery, as part of business continuity planning (discussed in Chapter 13)
- Increased risk of fraud, as a result of financial pressures (discussed in Chapter 2)
- The need to balance wider stakeholder needs (including social and environmental sustainability, which come at a short-term cost) with the immediate interests of primary stakeholders (shareholders) and need for economic survival. There may be a dilemma for firms seeking to introduce CSR and sustainability, where this is constrained by cost pressures.
- Negotiation and employee relations risks of redundancies, pay freezes, restructuring, recovery planning and so on
- Potential opportunities (upside risks) of economic downturn: weaker businesses failing, leaving survivors in a stronger competitive position; procurement professionals raising their influence as a result of business partnering and bottom-line contribution.

6.7 An article in *Supply Management* ('Beyond low prices', 28 May 2009) helpfully divides recession risk response measures into strategic and tactical responses: Table 1.7.

Table 1.7 *Recession risk response measures*

	ACTIONS	TOOLS AND TECHNIQUES
Strategic	Update supply chain risk management plans	Risk analysis Risk response plans
	Understand changes in main supply markets	Five Forces (competitive environment) STEEPLE analysis
	Communicate with key suppliers	Shared demand planning Joint cost reduction Financial analysis
Tactical	Support supplier cashflow	On-time payment Early payment discounts Online negotiation of discounts
	Ensure quality does not drop	Increase inspections on delivered goods Discuss quality problems with suppliers Consider QA visits to suspect suppliers
	Best price for suitable categories	Eg using e-auctions, leverage negotiation
	Manage price fluctuations	Lock in low prices with fixed-price dealings in rising markets Use escalation and de-escalation clauses

The international business environment

6.8 With the increasing globalisation of business, organisations now need to view risks on different levels.

- Local – the immediate or micro-environment surrounding the company
- Regional – the area where the organisation interfaces with many of its stakeholders
- National – the country in which the organisation operates
- International – the other countries to which the organisation markets its products and services, from which it sources its supplies, and in which it may have operational sites (or 'offshore' outsourced operations)
- Global – the wider global environment of economic activity, trade, communication, political structures (such as the UN or World Trade Organisation) and issues (such as global warming or sustainable development). The greater the extension and integration of an organisation globally, the greater its need for broad and continual risk monitoring.

6.9 An international or global trading environment introduces a new range of risks to an organisation's local, regional and national risk profile.

- **Country risk** – the risk that a particular country (in which the organisation has suppliers, customers or operations) may seize assets, lack currency for payments, suffer political or economic instability, impose import and export quotas or tariffs, or be subject to widespread corruption in trade dealings
- **Payment risk** – difficulties ensuring that foreign buyers make payment (addressed by using risk-managed methods of payment such as letters of credit and bills of exchange)
- **Currency and exchange rate risk** – dealing in a range of different currencies in a fluctuating exchange rate environment (addressed by using risk-managed strategies such as forward exchange contracts or negotiated common currencies)
- **Transit and logistical risk** – the risk that goods may be lost, damaged, deteriorated over long-distance supply lines (generally addressed by packing and transport strategies, insurances and incoterms to allocate risk and liability)
- **Legal and contractual risk** – the risk of contracts being ambiguous, unenforceable or disputed, owing to differences in legal regimes, inadequately defined legal jurisdictions, failure to provide for international arbitration of disputes and so on (generally addressed by contractual measures such as the use of standard contract terms and arbitration clauses).
- **Compliance and reputational risk** – the risk of association with compliance, quality, ethical or

environmental failures by suppliers and network partners, owing to differences in standards, and the difficulties of compliance monitoring.

The competitive environment

6.10   The competitive environment is not explicitly mentioned in the syllabus, but competitor activity clearly represents a major external environmental threat to an organisation's brand positioning, market share, profitability and share value. It therefore presents a major source of strategic risk.

6.11   Professor Michael Porter *(Competitive Advantage)* developed an influential framework which argues that the extent of competition in an industry – and therefore its attractiveness or potential profitability to any given player within it – depends on the interaction of five forces in the organisation's industry environment: Figure 1.2.

Figure 1.2 *Porter's five forces model*

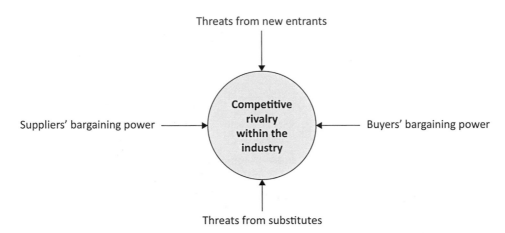

6.12   The changing dynamics of the competitive environment, in each of these five dimensions, requires continual monitoring to guard against unanticipated strategic risk.

Saunders's model of environmental factors

6.13   A model devised by Malcolm Saunders (Figure 1.3) gives a more integrated perspective on external factors impacting on organisations and their supply chains. Such a model may be used as a framework for systematic environmental scanning and monitoring, in order to identify strategic risks.

Figure 1.3 *Saunders's integrative model of environmental factors*

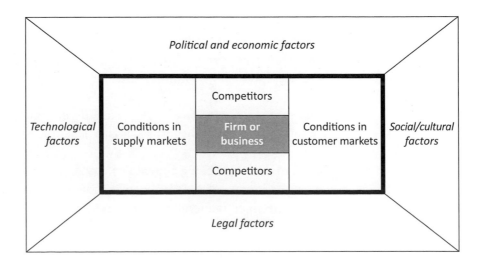

Chapter summary

- Risk is defined as 'the probability of an unwanted event happening'. Different organisations display different levels of tolerance for taking risks (ie different 'risk appetites').
- Uncertainties with positive outcomes are referred to as 'upside risks'.
- Risks may give rise to both direct losses and indirect (or 'consequential') losses.
- A first stage in risk management is identification of risks from both internal and external sources.
- A major classification of risks distinguishes between strategic, operational, financial and compliance risks.
- Internal risks can arise from many sources (such as human personality factors, cultural values etc). An organisation's system of internal controls should be designed to manage such risks.
- There are also many sources of external risk, and use of the STEEPLE model can help in identifying them.

Self-test questions

Numbers in brackets refer to the paragraphs where you can check your answers.

1   Define risk management. (1.3)

2   Explain why different organisations may have different risk appetites. (1.12)

3   What is meant by 'consequential loss'? (2.4)

4   List benefits of effective risk management. (2.11)

5   List techniques for identifying risks. (3.2)

6   What are the benefits of supply chain mapping in relation to risk? (3.10)

7   Distinguish between strategic risks and operational risks. (4.1)

8   List examples of operational risks and possible mitigation strategies. (Table 1.4)

9   List examples of internal risks. (5.2)

10   What areas relating to risk should be covered by an organisation's internal control system? (5.5)

11   In what ways does the external environment exert an influence on an organisation? (6.2)

12   What additional risks arise in the context of international trading? (6.8)

CHAPTER 2

Risk Assessment

Assessment criteria and indicative content

 Analyse the use of probability and impact assessments to manage risks in supply chains

- Methodologies for assessing the probability and impact of risk
- Vulnerability assessments
- Collating statistical evidence of risks
- The use of probability theory
- Assessing the probability of events using the normal distribution
- The binomial and Poisson distributions

 Develop a risk assessment and a risk register to mitigate risks in a supply chain

- The use of templates for risk assessments and risk registers
- Completing risk assessments and risk registers
- Engaging stakeholders in the development of risk assessments and registers

Section headings

1. Risk and vulnerability assessments
2. Qualitative tools and techniques
3. Statistical (quantitative) tools and techniques
4. Risk registers
5. Involving stakeholders

Introduction

In this chapter we move on from risk identification to the next phase of the risk management process: risk assessment. In this phase, the probability and impact of an identified risk is evaluated – and, where possible, quantified, as the basis for prioritising efforts to either reduce the likelihood of the risk occurring or to reduce the impact of the risk event if it does occur.

We also introduce an important tool in the management of risk: the risk register. Although this is used at all phases of risk management, it is an essential tool in the recording, monitoring and review of risk assesments.

In Chapter 3 we will complete our overview of the risk management cycle, by discussing risk management strategies: ways in which the information about risks (gathered during risk identification and assessment) can be used to reduce the organisation's residual risk and exposure.

1   Risk and vulnerability assessments

Risk assessment

1.1   **Risk identification** identifies all the potential things that can go wrong with an activity. **Risk assessment** is the appraisal of the probability and significance of identified potential risk events: in other words, asking 'how likely is it and how bad could it be?'

1.2   As we saw in Chapter 1, risk is often quantified using the basic formula:

Risk = Likelihood (probability) × Impact (adverse consequence)

- **Risk likelihood** is the probability of occurrence, given the nature of the risk and current risk management practices. This may be expressed as a number between 0 (no chance) and 1 (certainty) or as a percentage (100% = certainty), a score (1–10) or a rating (low–medium–high). The more likely the risk event is to occur, the higher the overall level of risk, and the higher priority risk management will be.
- **Risk impact** is the likely loss or cost to the organisation or the likely level of impact on its ability to fulfil its objectives. The severity of impacts may be quantified (eg in terms of estimated cost or loss), scored (1–10), or rated (low–medium–high).

1.3   High-probability events may not be subject to approaches which minimise the risk of the event occurring. Instead, resources may be applied to minimising their impact. Low-probability events may not be worth the allocation of resources. However, if they are high-impact, contingency and recovery plans may need to be made, so that the organisation can respond effectively to the event if it occurs. A catastrophic outcome with a low likelihood of occurrence may be of more concern than a minor outcome that is highly likely.

Vulnerability assessment

1.4   A vulnerability assessment is the process designed to identify, quantify and prioritise areas in which a system, organisation or supply chain is particularly 'open' to risk or attack. In other words, it is a form of risk assessment specifically designed to identify weak spots in the risk profile. 'A vulnerability analysis serves to categorise key assets and drive the risk management process' (United States Department of Energy).

1.5   Vulnerability assessments are often performed on systems such as IT systems, energy and water supply systems, transportation and logistics systems and communication systems – both within single businesses, and for large regional or national infrastructures. For the purposes of this unit, you might also think of assessing the vulnerabilities or 'weak spots' in supply chains and supply chain processes.

1.6   A vulnerability assessment would typically include four basic stages.

- Listing or cataloguing the resources (assets and capabilities) in a given system
- Assigning a quantifiable value, score or rank order of importance to those resources
- Identifying the vulnerabilities or potential threats to each resource
- Planning to mitigate or eliminate the most serious vulnerabilities for the most valuable resources

1.7   The term 'vulnerability assessment' is also used to describe the disaster management process of assessing threats to the population, infrastructure and environment. Lövkvist-Andersen *et al* (*Modelling Society's Capacity to Manage Extreme Events*) argue that: 'Classical risk analysis is principally concerned with investigating the risks surrounding a plant (or some other object), its design and operations. Such analysis tends to focus on causes and direct consequences for the studied object. Vulnerability analysis, on the other hand, focuses both on consequences for the object itself *and* on primary and secondary consequences for the surrounding environment. It also concerns itself with the possibilities of reducing such consequences and of improving the capacity to manage future incidents.'

1.8 Sadgrove suggests a basic template for a **vulnerability audit**: Figure 2.1

Figure 2.1 *Template for vulnerability audit*

TYPE OF HAZARD	VULNERABILITY ('LOW' TO 'HIGH')	PRIORITY ('LOW' TO 'TOP')	ACTIONS (TO REDUCE VULNERABILITY)	COST $
Quality				
Environment				
Health and safety				
Fire				
Security				
Fraud				
Finance				
IT				
Marketing				
Buildings				
HR				
Other				

2   Qualitative tools and techniques

Risk probability/impact matrix

2.1 A simple risk or impact assessment can be performed by using a matrix or risk map on which threats and hazards can be plotted according to (a) the likelihood of their happening and (b) the seriousness of their effect if they do happen: Figure 2.2.

Figure 2.2 *Risk assessment grid*

	Impact/effect on organisation	
	Low	High
Likelihood of occurrence Low	A	C
High	B	D

2.2 Taking the segments of the grid one by one:

- Segment A will contain events which are not likely to happen and would have little effect if they did: say, a power failure at all suppliers' factories at once, when they all have emergency back-up generators. Given the low level of impact, the organisation can safely *ignore* such factors as low-priority.
- Segment B will contain events which are relatively likely to occur, but will not have a major effect: say, an exchange rate fluctuation, if the organisation is not heavily exposed by international sourcing. The appropriate response is to *monitor* such factors, in case the situation changes and the impact may be greater than expected.
- Segment C will contain events which are not likely to happen, but will have a big impact if they do: say, failure of suppliers of critical requirements, or natural disasters (such as earthquake or tsunami, in areas not generally prone to such events). The appropriate response is to draw up a *contingency plan* to minimise the impact, in case the event occurs: perhaps having a back-up source of supply,

and insurance. Where the risk can be mitigated without undue cost, this should be considered: one example, is the small risk of air disaster wiping out the senior management team – for which reason, many organisations have policies against 'key people' travelling together (as well as 'key person' insurance).

- Segment D will contain events which are both likely to happen and serious in their impact: say, the emergence of a new technology that will alter the supply market. The appropriate response is to *respond* to the perceived threat or opportunity, including it in strategic analysis and planning.

2.3 Sadgrove develops the risk mapping approach, using simple, qualitative categories for the severity of impact (Insignificant, Minor, Serious, Catastrophic) and the probability of occurrence (Very unlikely, Improbable, Quite probable and Certain/Very probable). Risks can then be plotted on a simple grid: Figure 2.3. The diagonal line represents the level at which risks may be considered broadly acceptable or unacceptable – or high priority (above the line) and low priority (below the line) for risk management.

Figure 2.3 *Qualitative risk matrix*

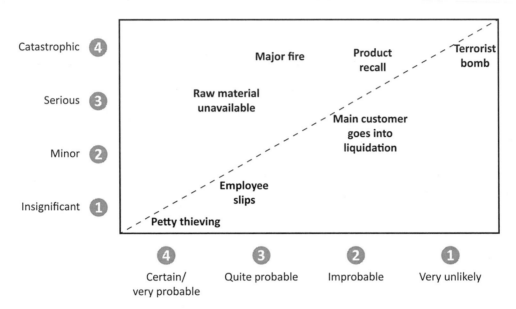

Risk scoring

2.4 Other risk matrix tools seek to quantify the risk. Karlof & Lovingsson *(An A–Z of Management Concepts and Models),* for example, suggest a simple risk matrix based on the *probability × consequence* formula. Probability is expressed as a percentage and consequences are expressed as a number from 1 to 10 (1 being a negligible consequence and 10 being a catastrophic consequence). For example, in appraising a contract to outsource the information technology function, some of the key elements of risk may be identified as follows.

Element of risk	Probability	Consequence	Risk level
Systems failure	20%	10	2.0
Staff strike	80%	6	4.8
Teething problems	30%	4	1.2

2.5 This analysis may be used in several ways.

- Staff strike carries the highest risk, so this may be a priority for management action (eg gaining assurances from the supplier on employee relations negotiations, conducting an employee communications and consultation campaign and so on)
- There may be set tolerance levels for consequence, however, so that (say) action must be taken on

all risks with a potential consequence of over 7: systems failure would therefore be the priority for management action (eg ensuring that contingency plans and back-up systems are in place).

- The various elements of risk may be mapped on a graph: Figure 2.4. This enables decision guidelines to be set: no action required for 'acceptable' levels of risk; risk management required for 'moderate' risk levels; and risk avoidance or elimination for 'unacceptable' levels.

Figure 2.4 *Risk analysis matrix*

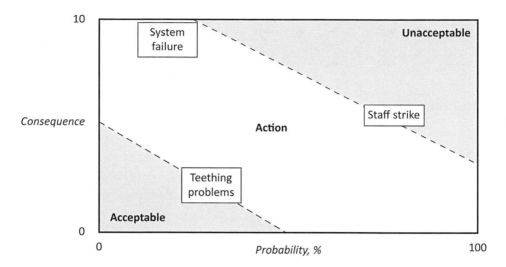

2.6   Another risk scoring approach would be simply to allocate numerical scores for likelihood, from very low (1) to very high (5), and impact from insignificant (1) to catastrophic (5), say. Mike Brooks *(Accountancy, January 2007)* suggests definitions for such scores: Table 2.1.

Table 2.1 *Scoring likelihood and impact*

SCORES FOR LIKELIHOOD	SCORES FOR IMPACT
1 Has never happened in this industry	1 Would have no discernible effect
2 Has happened in this industry but never in this group	2 Would cost 10% of this business unit's net assets if it happened
3 Has happened in this group but never in this business unit	3 Would wipe out this business unit if it happened
4 Happens occasionally in this business unit	4 Would cost 10% of group net assets if it happened
5 Happens frequently in this business unit	5 Would wipe out the group if it happened

2.7   The combined score (*likelihood score* × *impact score*) will range from 1 to 25.

- A risk score of 6 or less (low level of risk) would not justify mitigating action – and any existing controls should be reviewed to ensure they are not disproportionate.
- A risk score of 8–12 (medium level of risk) should trigger a review of existing controls, and may require the implementation of additional controls: cost-benefit analysis should be used to assess the pay-off between reduced risk and the cost of achieving it. The risk score should be reviewed annually, in case of escalation.
- A risk score of 14–20 (high level of risk) should trigger a review of existing controls, and mitigation planning: the issue may need to be escalated to a higher level or risk committee. The risk score should be reviewed at quarterly intervals.
- A residual risk score of 21 or above (maximum risk) should be a priority for high-level mitigation or avoidance planning, and should be continuously reviewed.

Quantifying impact

2.8   We will look at statistical techniques for quantifying the probability of risk in the following section. However, the consequences, severity or impact of risk can also be partially quantified, by creating severity definitions and categories. Sadgrove recommends a Scale of Impact definition, which defines 'catastrophic', 'serious', 'minor' and 'insignificant' impacts for a range of identified risks. For example:

	Catastrophic	Serious	Minor	Insignificant
Lost revenue	Over $10m	$1m–$10m	$0.1m–$1m	Less than $0.1m
Health and safety	Death	Major injury	Minor injury	Trip/slip

And so on . . .

Scenario analysis and planning

2.9   A 'scenario' may be defined as 'an outline of future development which shows the operation of causes' *(Chambers English Dictionary),* or 'an internally consistent view of what the future might turn out to be – not a forecast, but one possible future' (Porter, *Competitive Advantage).* Scenario analysis involves the asking of 'what if?' questions to try to anticipate the consequences of decisions and actions. What if the price of raw materials were to double? What if we were to lose our two biggest customers? What if the internet were to crash? What if Greece were to exit the Euro?

2.10   In a nutshell, scenario analysis involves:

- Using brainstorming or facilitated group workshops to stimulate the identification of issues and possibilities (both positive and negative) in the business or supply chain, industry or market, or wider external environment
- Describing or computer-modelling (using spreadsheets or more complex modelling software) the key variables in a scenario
- Altering selected variables (according to 'what if?' questions) and observing the effect (a) on other variables and (b) on the overall outcome
- Creating best, most likely and worst case scenarios to measure impacts.

3   Statistical (quantitative) tools and techniques

Collating statistical evidence of risks

3.1   A key technique for evaluating the probability of occurrence is to extrapolate from *historical statistical data* to predict the likelihood of future occurrences. In the case of risk assessment, the occurrences of a risk event in the past may be a good guide to the likelihood of its future occurrence. Risk assessors will be interested in a range of historical risk data, including the circumstances in which risk events occurred, and what mitigating or preventative measures were (or were not) in place at the time. However, particular attention will be given to quantifiable, statistical data such as the frequency and cost of occurrence.

3.2   Statistical sampling will often be used. In many cases, the total 'population' of data may be large, and it would be impractical to collect and collate all possible data. Instead, analysts will select a carefully structured sample for use. Provided that the sample is representative, data can be extrapolated from the sample to draw valid conclusions about the wider population.

3.3   To use a risk assessment example, a company may be interested in the likelihood of a new product being regarded favourably by consumers, to minimise its marketing risk. By carrying out market research among a representative cross-sectional sample of consumers, it can estmate the likely response of the wider market.

3.4 In order for statistically valid conclusions to be drawn from a sample, the sample must be of sufficient size, and representative of the wider population (ie not sampled from a particular geographical region or demographic group, which might distort the results).

3.5 Statistical data on risks can be gathered from a wide range of sources.

- Published reports, statistical digests and online databases cataloguing and analysing risk events (eg business failures, the performance of various classes of investment, industrial accidents, environmental impacts and so on)
- Published risk monitoring reports and assessments for various categories of business risk
- Statistical surveys of stakeholder groups
- The organisation's records and documents (risk registers, accident and incident reports, quality failure reports and so on).

Using probability theory

3.6 The general concept of probability is an everyday one: we all speak in general terms of whether it is likely to rain today and how unlikely we are to win the lottery. The use of probability theory as a quantitative tool aims to add a numerical scale of measurement to ideas such as 'very unlikely' or 'quite likely'.

3.7 By convention, the measurement scale ranges from 0 (impossible) to 1 (certainty): 0.5 therefore represents an even or 50: 50 chance.

3.8 If there are **m** equally likely outcomes to a trial, **n** of which result in a given outcome **x**, the probability of that outcome – symbolised as P(x) – is n/m.

For example, if an unbiased die is thrown in an unbiased way, each of the scores 1 to 6 is equally likely. The probability of an even number being thrown can be calculated as follows: $P(\text{even}) = \frac{3}{6} = \frac{1}{2}$. (Three of the six outcomes are even numbers: 2, 4 and 6.)

3.9 Where events are **mutually exclusive** (that is, one event precludes the other): then P (A and B) = 0. However, the probability that either A or B will occur is the sum of the separate probabilities of each occurring: P (A or B) = P (A) + P (B). So your probability of throwing a 6 or a 1 on your die is: $\frac{1}{6} + \frac{1}{6} = \frac{2}{6} = \frac{1}{3}$.

3.10 Where events are **independent** (that is, one happening or not happening does not affect whether the other happens or doesn't happen), then the probability of both A and B occurring is the product of the separate probabilities: P (A and B) = P(A) x P (B). As an example, say a delivery contains 12 components of which 4 are defective and the rest are OK. $P(\text{defective}) = \frac{4}{12}$, while $P(\text{OK}) = \frac{8}{12}$. The probability of drawing two OK components (if you replace the first before the second is selected) is calculated as follows.

P (component 1 OK) = $\frac{8}{12}$; P (component 2 OK) = $\frac{8}{12}$

P (component 1 and 2 OK) = $\frac{8}{12} \times \frac{8}{12} = \frac{2}{3} \times \frac{2}{3} = \frac{4}{9}$ (or 0.44).

Probability distributions

3.11   There are three main probability distributions: Table 2.2.

Table 2.2 *Probability distributions*

TYPE	FOCUS	EXAMPLE APPLICATIONS
Binomial distribution	The probability of discrete events with only two outcomes (p or q: eg success or failure, has or doesn't have a particular attribute, answer is yes or no, event will or won't happen). P(p + q) = 1 So if p = ½ , q = 1 − ½ = ½	• Probability of a batch containing defects or non-defects; x or more/less-than-x defects • Customers buying or not buying a brand. • Success or failure of a project; delivery on time or late.
Poisson distribution	The probability of a discrete event (p) within a continuous stream of events or tests (n). Should be applied when there is a small probability of the event occurring in a single test, and a very large number of tests.	• Quality control: defects (or non-defects) within eg a length of cable or time period. • Risk assessment: problems occurring, or success/failure within a given time period.
Normal distribution	Ranges of possibilities, and how likely they are to occur, based on: continuous historical data, formed into a frequency distribution, diagrammed as a histogram.	'If defects are normally distributed, calculate the probability that defects are between 3 and 7 (tolerance level) per delivery.'

Decision tree analysis

3.12   Decision tree analysis is a technique for coping with a series of decisions, each one having a variety of possible outcomes. The decision tree maps the various combinations of decisions and outcomes in a structured way. By estimating the probabilities of the various possible outcomes, and assigning monetary values to them, this map improves the visibility of decision-related risks, and enables managers to select the optimal decision options.

3.13   As an example, suppose a company is considering the production of a new consumer item with a five-year product life. To manufacture the item requires the building of a new plant. Management has identified three options.

- Option A is to build a large plant now at a cost of $1m. If market conditions are good (probability 70%), the company can expect an annual profit from the new product of $350,000 for five years. If market conditions are poor (probability 30%) there would be a loss of $75,000 in each of the five years.
- Option B is to build a small plant now at a cost of $550,000. If market conditions are good, we profit by $200,000 per year; if market conditions are bad, we make a loss of $25,000 per year.
- Option C is to wait for a year while more information is collected. If the resulting information is unfavourable (probability 20%), management would abandon the idea. If it is favourable (probability 80%) management would build either the small or the large plant, and again would face either good or poor market conditions thereafter.

3.14   The position is shown in Figure 2.5. The squares represent decision points: points at which managers must make up their minds on how to proceed. The circles indicate the possible outcomes that may ensue: market conditions may be good or poor; information received under Option C may be favourable or unfavourable. The financial outcomes depend both on the decisions taken and on the circumstances that prevail afterwards.

Figure 2.5 *A simple decision tree*

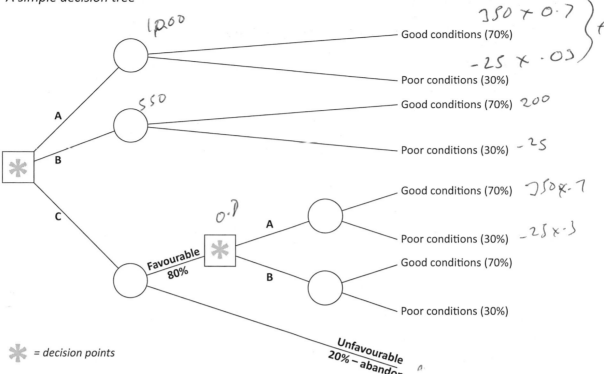

✳ = decision points

3.15 Using the estimated probabilities and the estimated cashflows arising from each outcome it is possible to evaluate the expected value of each option. In general, management will choose the option with the most profitable expected value (though of course there are many non-financial considerations that should not be overlooked in such a decision).

3.16 In the above example, we have not performed the mathematics, because it would take us well beyond your syllabus. In practice, decision trees are nowadays invariably produced using appropriate computer software so that manual calculations are never necessary.

3.17 Decision tree analysis may be useful where specific supply management issues or project decisions can be reduced to a set of mutually exclusive (either/or decisions); each decision has an identified set of possible outcomes; and each outcome can be assessed for likely occurrence (probability %) and cash value (revenues and costs).

Fault tree analysis

3.18 **Fault tree analysis** is a similar approach, which maps combinations of possible occurrences within a system or process, which can result specifically in a **failure** or adverse outcome (for example: human error + hardware failure + software corruption) to calculate the probability of a given failure or risk occurring.

3.19 This is a form of **causal analysis**. For example, a fault tree may be used to analyse the probability that a crash will occur at a particular road junction (a real-life use of the technique by the Institute of Engineering and Technology). It tracks back to analyse what possible failures might have occurred to cause a crash: there may have been a car at the main junction; there may have been another car emerging from a side road and unable to stop; this in turn may have been caused by poor driving, or by poor road conditions. By assigning a probability to the full range of contributory factors in a crash, it is possible to estimate how many crashes might be expected to occur at the junction over a period.

3.20 You should be able to imagine how a similar technique could be used to map the possible causes (and therefore combined likelihoods) of supply disruption, quality failure or workplace accidents, for example.

Dependency modelling

3.21   Risks do not necessarily arise from a single failure. On the contrary, it is often a combination of factors (people, systems, circumstances) that give rise to risk. Dependency modelling is a software tool which analyses the links between interdependent variables which may combine to give rise to risk.

3.22   The model works from corporate goals down through a dependency network of all the variables required to achieve them. The outputs from the model are: an analysis of the risks faced by the organisation; the potential impact of those risks in financial and operational terms; and possible countermeasures at key points of leverage.

Value at Risk (VaR)

3.23   VaR is a measurement tool used to assess the extent of an organisation's risk exposure. It was developed in the banking and financial sector and at first applied primarily to organisations (such as banks and securities houses) with many different investments. However, the principles of VaR can equally be applied to non-financial organisations. For example, a large construction company may have many projects in progress at a given time, each of which can be regarded as a financial investment.

3.24   VaR assesses risk exposure by measuring the volatility of a firm's investment portfolio, in light of market conditions and the correlations between different investments (since a market development that impacts badly on Investment A may have a favourable impact on Investment B).

3.25   The Value at Risk is defined as the maximum amount of loss the organisation can expect (with a predetermined level of probability) to suffer on a given investment over a given time frame. For example, VaR may be estimated at a 97% probability that loss will not exceed $150,000 over the quarter.

3.26   There are four steps in a VaR calculation.

- Determine the time horizon over which the firm wishes to estimate a loss
- Select the degree of certainty required: is it sufficient to estimate our possible losses with 95% certainty, or is a higher level of certainty (say 99%) necessary?
- Create a probability distribution of likely returns for the investment(s), using historical market data combined with an assessment of market conditions in the period ahead.
- Calculate the VaR estimate.

Risk adjusted return on capital

3.27   Risk adjusted return on capital (RAROC) is a risk-based framework for measuring profitability, based on analysing risk-adjusted financial performance. In other words, it is based on recognising the trade-off between risk and return, allowing organisations to manage their investment exposure – as well as to better forecast their economic performance, maintain financial integrity and boost stakeholder confidence.

3.28   RAROC is defined as the ratio of **risk-adjusted return** (projected or actual risk-adjusted net revenue) to **economic capital** (projected risk). 'Economic capital' is the amount of money needed to secure the company's survival in a worst case scenario (similar to the concept of 'capital adequacy'): in other words, the amount of capital that will buffer the company against shocks in market values, and allow it to stay solvent. Economic capital is a function of market risk, credit risk and operational risk, and is often calculated using VaR. RAROC can therefore be expressed as:

RAROC = Expected return ÷ Value at risk (VaR)

3.29   RAROC can be used in investment appraisal, to determine whether a project is worth investing in. If RAROC is equal to or greater than the 'hurdle rate' (the minimum acceptable rate of return), the deal is worth doing – or was, in fact, successful. If projected net revenue from a deal is $15k and its VaR is $100k, RAROC

= 15%. If the hurdle rate is 20%, the return will not be worth the risk. The riskier a project or investment is, the higher the hurdle rate will be, as investors and managers will seek returns which compensate for risks.

4 Risk registers

4.1 A **risk profile** is a documented and prioritised overall assessment of the risks faced by the organisation.

4.2 A **risk register** is a concise, structured document listing all the identified risks for a business, project or contract, together with the result of the risk analysis (impact and likelihood), initial mitigation plans, and current status of each risk. It should be updated on a regular basis (at least monthly) in order to maintain an up-to-date risk profile.

Purpose and benefits of using a risk register

4.3 The purposes (and benefits) of using a risk register are as follows.

- To capture all analysis and decisions about identified risks in a co-ordinated, centralised (but accessible) data store
- To provide a template document, allowing risk information to be recorded systematically and in a standardised format – supporting analysis and use. The register can easily be computerised (eg using spreadsheet or tailored software packages) to support access, consolidation, analysis, modification, the triggering of risk alerts and mitigating action and so on.
- To develop risk visibility throughout the organisation, including immediate visibility of current risk status and exposure: relevant, accurate and up-to-date information for decision-making and problem-solving
- To identify accountabilities for monitoring and managing risks
- To provide a framework for risk monitoring, management and review activities. The format supports use at an operational level, for individual projects and units, but the data can also be consolidated for strategic risk management
- To provide a basis for allocating resources to risk monitoring, management and review, and for presenting a business case for risk management
- To encourage (and act as a tool for) communication about risk issues with key internal and external stakeholders: increasing risk-related learning, stakeholder involvement and input, and so on.
- To provide project sponsors, contract managers and other designated risk owners with a documented framework from which risk status can be reported.

Risk register template

4.4 A risk register will typically contain columns for the entry of data.

- A unique reference or code number identifying each risk
- Description of the type and nature of the risk
- The date on which the risk was first identified
- The risk owner: an identified individual (or role/position) with lead responsibility for monitoring and management of the risk.
- Probability of the risk event occurring: expressed as an appropriate rating, score, percentage or category. The organisation may have standard definitions for Low (L), Medium (M) and High (H); intermediate ratings such as M− or H+; and ranges such as L–M, where risk has not yet been fully or accurately assessed.
- Impact, cost or consequences if the risk event occurs (expressed as an appropriate cost value, score or rating, or described briefly)
- Identified possible responses or mitigation actions, to reduce probability or impact, or both. Where a risk is high-impact (regardless of probability), this should include contingency plans (or a link or cross-reference to the relevant contingency plan). It may also include recovery plans (planned actions to take once a risk event has occurred, in order to restore normal operations).

- The risk mitigation action chosen and its effect (if any)
- Regularly updated information on the current status of each risk (response actions put in place and whether they are effective) – with the date of the latest update.

4.5 A simple risk register for the procurement and supply function is shown in Figure 2.6. (Remember that this is only a generic example: the register will reflect the specific nature of risks, vulnerabilities and responsibilities in practice.)

Figure 2.6 *Template risk register*

ID	RISK	PROBABILITY RATING	IMPACT RATING	STRATEGY/ CONTROLS	ACTION TAKEN/ CURRENT STATUS	OWNER	REVIEW	UPDATED
1	Key supplier business failure	Low	High	*Treat:* Evaluate/select Multi-sourcing	Evaluation criteria developed Dual sourcing	Account managers	[date]	[date]
2	Quality failure	Low	Medium	*Treat:* Specification Quality assurance	Suppliers consulted	Quality manager		
3	Schedule variance (lead time extension)	Medium	Low	*Accept:* Monitor	Monitoring	Account managers		
4	Price/cost variances	High	Medium	*Treat/transfer:* Contract terms	Prices locked in	Account managers		
5	Non-availability of materials	Low	Low	*Accept:* Monitor	Monitoring	Materials manager		
6	Procurement fraud	Medium	High	*Treat:* Ethics codes Internal controls	Internal controls in place	Finance officer		
7	Reputation damage from supplier CSR failure	Medium	Medium	*Treat:* CSR policy monitoring	Suppliers consulted	Jones		
8	Loss/damage of goods in transit	High	Medium	*Transfer:* Insurance Contract terms	Insurance secured Incoterms used	Logistics manager		
9	Technology/system failure	Medium	Medium	*Treat:* Back-up systems	Computer bureau investigated	IT manager		

The traffic light system

4.6   One simple method of 'flagging' the level of risk in a risk register is the so-called 'traffic light system', where decisions (or items and categories within the procurement portfolio, say) are labelled as high risk (red), medium risk (amber) or low risk (green). Such a scheme is used in some computer systems, for example, as a tool to enable a quick visual assessment of risk. In a procurement risk register, the system may be used to label individual procurements or contracts for the following purposes.

- To promote risk-based communication and decision-making
- To encourage risk awareness and the more frequent monitoring and review of medium- and high-risk procurements or contracts
- To flag the need for additional approvals or authorisations of red-flagged decisions
- To allow procurement managers to analyse procurement decisions; evaluate the function's risk appetite; and evaluate whether procurement decisions are being made in line with the organisation's risk appetite.

Maintaining the risk register

4.7   The risk register should be reviewed and amended:

- As risk mitigation strategies are applied (changing the current status of risks)
- As new risks are identified, or existing risks escalate
- As required by a review and monitoring plan and timetable, which should be defined for each registered risk.

5   Involving stakeholders

5.1   So far in this Course Book, we have not explicitly addressed the issue of how risk management activity and responsibilities may be organised or allocated within an organisation. We have emphasised the extent to which risk management is a responsibility of *all* managers and members of an organisation. However, in practice there are a number of key stakeholders in risk management, who may have input to risk identification and assessment processes.

The board of directors

5.2   The senior management of the organisation (eg a board of directors or board of trustees) is charged with managing the organisation on behalf of shareholders or investors. Senior managers are therefore likely to be involved in:

- The assessment and management of strategic risk, as part of the process of strategic planning and management
- The expression of the organisation's risk appetite, as part of the organisation's core values and policies
- The formulation of risk management policies at a high level (which will cascade down to the formulation of risk management procedures and rules by functional managers and risk management officers)

5.3   Senior management also holds the ultimate responsibility to ensure that risk management procedures are being enforced in line with organisational objectives, policies and risk appetite. In the UK the Financial Reporting Council (FRC)'s UK Corporate Governance Code, which regulates the governance of listed companies, places responsibility on the board to conduct a review of and report on all material controls (including financial, operational and compliance controls) and risk management systems. The FRC guidance on risk management and internal controls identified the board's responsibility for:

- Considering what are the principal risks, and robustly assessing how effectively they have been identified, evaluated and managed

- Assessing the effectiveness of the internal control system in managing the principal risks, focusing particularly on any significant failings or weaknesses in internal control that were reported
- Considering whether necessary actions are being taken promptly to remedy any significant failings or weaknesses
- Considering whether the findings indicate a need for more extensive monitoring.

The risk management function

5.4   There may be a dedicated **risk officer or function** (depending on the size of the organisation), with defined responsibilities for formulating risk policies and procedures, assessing organisation-wide risks, and co-ordinating risk management planning and responses to risk events.

5.5   Designated risk officers may also be appointed at the functional level, to co-ordinate risk assessment, managing and reporting in regard to particular categories of risk. These may, for example, include: transport safety officers, health and safety officers, compliance officers and environmental protection officers.

Line management

5.6   Line managers and team leaders will have a responsibility at the functional level for risk identification, notification and management within their departments:

- Formulating and/or implementing the organisation's defined risk policies and procedures
- Enforcing adherence to risk mitigation rules and plans (eg through training, coaching, counselling and disciplinary or performance management interventions where required)
- Reinforcing a risk aware culture (through leadership style, communication, role modelling and acknowledging or rewarding responsible behaviours)
- Reporting on risk events (and/or ensuring that risk events are reported by witnesses, as required by relevant policies and regulations)
- Capturing information on hazards, vulnerabilities and risks from staff (eg initiating risk 'circles' or suggestion schemes, supporting whistle blowers, or encouraging upward reporting of concerns), other stakeholders (eg suppliers) and the wider environment (eg keeping up to date on risk knowledge in their occupation, profession or specialist area).

Risk owners

5.7   A designated risk owner should be allocated to all identified risks, and all parts of the risk process. Ownership should be allocated to individuals with the authority required to take action and mobilise resources. ISO 31000 defines a risk owner as a 'person or entity with the accountability and authority to manage a risk' – emphasising that:

- Ownership should be allocated to individuals with the authority required to take action and mobilise resources and
- Risk ownership must reside with management – not just with a 'risk manager'.

5.8   The roles and responsibilities of ownership should be well defined and communicated, particularly in relation to line managers and designated 'risk managers'. Risk managers will generally report on risk status and mitigation measures to the risk owner, whose task it is to maintain the relevant portion of the risk register.

External and internal audit functions

5.9   The role of internal and external auditors in risk management has increased with the introduction of the FRC UK Corporate Governance Code, its guidance on risk management and internal controls and the profile of corporate governance.

5.10 Specialist **external auditors** are engaged to carry out independent investigations into the corporate finances and internal controls of public companies. In the public sector, a similar role is carried out by the National Audit Office (NAO). The audit report will often include identification of areas of potential vulnerability and unmanaged risk. External audit is carried out only at intervals (usually annually) and with only limited objectives (usually, to report on the financial performance of the organisation). *In-house* auditors have an ongoing responsibility to ensure that internal controls are adequate and effectively applied, and will report to the board of directors (and audit committee, where applicable) on a regular basis.

5.11 The work of the **internal audit department** covers all aspects of the organisation's activities, not just the financial aspects: examining and testing all the internal controls in the organisation, and making recommendations for improvement. In the context of risk assessment, internal audit will work closely with other departments (such as procurement) to identify and assess potential risks specific to those departments. The internal audit function will report regularly to senior management and/or to the audit committee.

5.12 The primary responsibility for identifying risk lies with line managers, but the internal audit department has a major role in *managing* identified risks, through the systematic testing of internal controls and processes. In a procurement context, for example, auditors might test the adequacy of controls embedded in supplier appraisal, tendering procedures, contract development, contract management and so on. Internal auditors may also carry out project-related tasks. For example, if a large outsourcing contract tis being considered, auditors might contribute to a review of how the activity is currently carried out in-house.

Cross-functional risk management teams

5.13 Cross-functional teams will often be used in assessing, preventing and minimising risk. This approach has benefits in:

- Co-opting those involved with hazards on a day-to-day basis, in order to raise risk awareness, secure 'buy in' to risk management processes, and support a risk-managing culture
- Securing the input of people with the closest experience of hazards and work environments and processes, and people who network with valuable sources of risk information (such as suppliers), in order to gain multiple perspectives on risk
- Facilitating an integrated, process-oriented, cross-functional risk management approach and culture, rather than a piecemeal or 'silo'-based approach.

The procurement and supply function

5.14 The **procurement and supply function** may have a specific role in mitigating potential losses to the whole organisation, by (for example):

- Monitoring, identifying and assessing supply chain, supplier and supply market risks (through ongoing procurement research)
- Conducting supplier pre-qualification and appraisal to minimise supplier risk
- Developing contracts to minimise commercial and supply risk through the use of contractual terms
- Managing contracts, suppliers and supplier performance in such a way as to minimise financial, project, operational and reputational risk – particularly in regard to high-risk sourcing strategies such as international sourcing, single sourcing and outsourcing
- Supplying information and expertise for risk evaluation of strategic decisions (such as make/do or buy, investment and project appraisal, or supply chain structure)
- Supplying information and expertise to cross-functional project teams, to identify procurement, supplier relationship and supply chain risks of projects

- Managing commercial and financial risks of the organisation's external expenditure
- Managing the risks inherent in outsource contracts and other supply structures and relationships.

5.15 Applying rigorous risk management thinking, we might re-define the 'Five Rights' of procurement as delivery of the right quality of inputs, in the right quantity, to the right place, at the right time, at the right price – at the right (acceptable) level of risk.

Third party risk auditing and assessment services

5.16 Third party risk management consultants (or risk auditing services) may be given ongoing or project-based responsibility for the identification and assessment of defined areas of corporate risk. This is discussed in detail in Chapter 12.

Risk consultation processes

5.17 In the public sector, there is often a wider requirement for consultation and involvement of key stakeholders, including wider interest and participant groups. The Civil Contingencies Secretariat suggests the following approach to determining which stakeholders should be involved in risk assessment processes for any given issue or management decision.

- What are the potential issues?
- Who will be affected by the risk and consequences of any management decision?
- Which parties or individuals have knowledge and expertise that may be useful to inform any discussion?
- Which parties or individuals have expressed an interest in this particular, or a similar, risk problem?
- Which stakeholders will be prepared to listen to and respect different viewpoints, and might be prepared to negotiate?

Risk management roles in the public sector

5.18 Public sector bodies have traditionally led the way in governance and risk management, owing to the key public sector principles of accountability and transparency.

5.19 The activities of public sector bodies in the UK, for instance, are monitored and subject to policy leadership and best practice guidance, by a number of influential bodies.

- HM Treasury issues advice and guidance to public sector organisations on principles of sound governance and the effective governance of risk
- The National Audit Office (NAO) scrutinises public spending on behalf of Parliament, with a programme of regular reviews covering central government departments and a wide range of other public bodies. This role encompasses auditing risk management policies, procedures and effectiveness.
- The Public Accounts Committee (PAC) audits and scrutinises the probity of expenditure and value for money obtained: a powerful incentive for Accounting Officers to ensure that procedures are in place to avoid financial irregularities or lack of economy, efficiency and effectiveness in public procurement.
- The Crown Commercial Service (CCS) provides procurement, programme and project support across the public sector. It places risk management high on the agenda.

5.20 This level of accountability impacts strongly on public procurement. One key effect is an insistence on detailed procedures and record keeping: it may be difficult later to justify a course of action which breaches defined procedures or which is poorly documented. Reports of the Public Accounts Committee illustrate the kinds of behaviour which are required by public accountability, in areas such as: the need to record the reasons for all decisions; the need for procurement officers to declare any personal interests in procurement decisions; the need to avoid conflicts of interest; the need to secure proper authorisations; and the need generally to monitor and manage fraud risk.

5.21 However, it is often argued that the scrutiny and accountability regime also creates a 'risk avoidance' culture among public sector officials. The National Audit Office has stated that a lack of flexibility and innovation, in seeking to minimise risks, may itself cause failure to achieve value for money. Here are some examples.

- Rigid application of procedures and use of the same terms and conditions for all contracts regardless of the nature of the requirement, market conditions and relationship with potential suppliers
- Reluctance to involve procurement at an early stage in working with clients, technical experts and users in cross-functional teams
- Reluctance to use innovative approaches such as early dialogue with suppliers over market availability and specification, visits to or presentations by potential suppliers
- Reluctance (usually by Finance) to expand the use or coverage of purchasing cards

5.22 The NAO recommends a more flexible approach, which may be adopted by procurement staff, including:

- A proportional risk management approach ('control risk, not obviate it')
- Engaging external and internal auditors in dialogue about the cost and risk of over-control
- Applying directives and regulations creatively to meet customer needs.

> ## Chapter summary
>
> - Risk is often quantified using the formula: risk = likelihood x impact. A risk assessment grid may be used to map individual risks along these two dimensions.
> - A vulnerability assessment is a form of risk assessment specifically designed to identify weak spots in the risk profile.
> - The mathematical theory of probability may be used to quantify risks. Key tools are probability distributions (such as the binomial, Poisson, and normal distributions), decision tree analysis, and Value at Risk.
> - A risk register is a log of all identified risks allocating 'ownership' of each risk to a defined person or group.
> - Key stakeholders in risk management include the Board of Directors, the risk management function, line managers, the external and internal auditors, and the procurement and supply function.

 ## Self-test questions

Numbers in brackets refer to the paragraphs where you can check your answers.

1   Explain what is meant by (a) risk likelihood and (b) risk impact. (1.2)

2   List the stages in a vulnerability assessment. (1.6)

3   Explain the recommended approaches to risks in each segment of a risk assessment grid. (2.2)

4   Explain the steps involved in scenario planning. (2.10)

5   List sources of statistical data on risks. (3.5)

6   Give examples of applications of (a) the binomial distribution and (b) the Poisson distribution. (Table 2.2)

7   List the steps in a VaR calculation. (3.26)

8   List benefits of using a risk register. (4.3)

9   List responsibilities of line managers in relation to risk. (5.6)

10   List responsibilities of the procurement and supply function in risk management. (5.14)

CHAPTER 3

Risk Management Strategies

Assessment criteria and indicative content

4.3 Explain the development of a risk management culture and strategy to improve supply chains

- International standards for risk management such as ISO 31000 and ISO 28000
- The risk management process
- External reporting of risks in corporate accounts
- Resources required to achieve improved risk management in supply chains

4.4 Develop a strategy to mitigate risks in supply chains

- Developing risk management strategies to mitigate risks

Section headings

1 The risk management process
2 Risk management standards
3 Risk management strategy
4 Risk management culture
5 Resources for risk management

Introduction

In this chapter we complete our overview of the risk management process, as a foundation for an integrated approach to exploring the various risk categories and generic risk mitigation approaches discussed in the remainder of this Course Book.

We begin with an overview of the risk management process or risk management 'cycle' (recognising that the process is ongoing or continuous), which suggests a number of strategies or 'approaches' for dealing with identified and assessed risks.

We then examine two key international standards for risk management, which incorporate the risk management process. ISO 31000 is an integrative standard, linking general risk management principles, plus a framework for establishing and maintaining risk management, to a risk management process which can be used for specific risks.

In the remainder of the chapter we consider key aspects of risk strategy at an organisational and supply chain level: how risk strategies are developed; how an organisation can create a risk aware culture; and the resources required to promote and enable effective risk management in the organisation and supply chain.

1 The risk management process

The risk management process

1.1 The risk management process involves three key elements: risk identification, risk analysis and risk mitigation. ISO 31000 notes that: 'Organisations manage risk by anticipating, understanding and trying to control it. Through this process they communicate and consult with stakeholders and monitor and review the risk and the controls that are modifying the risk.'

1.2 The 'risk cycle' (or 'risk management cycle') is an expression of the continuous process of risk monitoring and management, portrayed as a cycle: Figure 3.1.

Figure 3.1 *The risk management cycle*

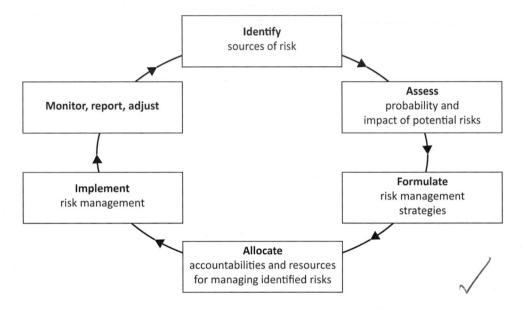

1.3 So far, the syllabus has mainly focused on:

- **Risk identification**: the process of seeking to identify potential problems or areas of uncertainty: in other words, asking 'what could go wrong?' (This was discussed in Chapter 1, where we focused on identifying different categories of risk.)
- **Risk assessment**: the appraisal of the probability and significance of identified potential risk events: in other words, asking 'how likely is it and how bad could it be?' This is often quantified using the basic formula: *Risk = Likelihood (probability) × Impact (adverse consequence).* (This was discussed in Chapter 2.)

1.4 Let's now complete the risk management process with an overview of its remaining elements.

Risk management and mitigation strategies

1.5 The phrase **risk mitigation** means lessening the adverse impact of a risk event. The objective of risk mitigation is to reduce inherent risk, to a level at which the assessed residual risk is acceptable to the organisation. (Remember that this will not necessarily be a matter of *eliminating* risk. Excessive levels of 'safety behaviour' may preclude flexibility, innovation, entrepreneurship or capitalising on opportunities.)

1.6 Identifying and quantifying vulnerability allows an organisation to prioritise planning and resources to meet the most severe risks, and to set defined risk thresholds at which management action on an issue will be triggered.

1.7   Risk management strategies ('what can we do about it?') are often classified as the Four Ts:

- **Tolerate** (or accept) the risk: if the assessed likelihood or impact of the risk is negligible (or there is no viable way to reduce the risk), no further action may, for the moment, be required, or justified (on a cost-benefit or business case basis). The risk may simply be acknowledged and registered – or it may be flagged for monitoring and periodic re-evaluation, in case the likelihood or impact of the risk escalates to the defined threshold for acceptable exposure. In either case, the rationale for risk acceptance should be clearly documented.

    Tolerance may be an adequate response for low-level risk, given competing demands for resources.

- **Transfer** (or spread) the risk: eg by taking out insurance cover, or not putting all supply eggs in one basket (in other words, avoiding dual or multi-sourcing) – or using contract terms to ensure that the costs of risk events will be borne by (or shared with) supply chain partners (eg by clarifying liability for risks at all stages of the contract, using liquidated damages clauses, insisting on supplier insurances, or sharing responsibility for risk monitoring as part of the contract management process).

    Risk transfer reduces the organisation's exposure – but at the cost of insurances, possible loss of economies of scale (from disaggregation), and possible damage to supply chain relationships.

- **Terminate** (or avoid) the risk: if the risk associated with a particular project or decision is too great, and cannot be reduced, the organisation may consider not investing or engaging in the activity or opportunity. So, for example, the decision to outsource a core function, or to enter a politically unstable foreign market (eg entering into joint ventures in a South American country which has recently nationalised foreign-owned energy companies) may simply be 'shelved' as too risky.

    Termination avoids unacceptable risk – but is not always possible. In addition, there may be a loss of opportunities and portfolio synergies.

- **Treat** (mitigate, minimise or control) the risk: take active steps to manage the risk in such a way as to reduce or minimise its likelihood or potential impact, or both. In relation to supply risk, this may involve measures such as: supplier monitoring and performance management; codes of conduct; supplier certification or pre-qualification; critical incident and/or variance reporting and analysis; contingency and recovery planning (eg alternative sources of supply); and so on.

    Risk mitigation is designed to create an acceptable level of residual risk – although it also incurs the costs of mitigation measures, and may raise the possibility of secondary risks (arising from risk mitigation measures).

1.8   Treating or mitigating risk is often explained in terms of the application of controls.

- **Preventative controls** are designed to limit the possibility of a negative outcome being realised. Examples could include separation of duties, supervision, the requirement for approvals and authorisations, or proactive 'issues management' in the field of reputation management.
- **Directive controls** are designed to ensure that a desired outcome is achieved. Examples could include health and safety regulations, supplier ethical policies and monitoring, staff training, the provision of protective equipment, the use of e-procurement procedures.
- **Detective controls** are designed to identify when an undesired risk event has occurred. They will usually be part of monitoring, project review, audit, or reporting processes, such as: vendor rating, project reviews, accident reporting, customer and supplier attitude surveys and so on.
- **Corrective controls** are designed to mitigate the effect of undesirable outcomes once they have occurred. Examples could include legal or contractual remedies for breach of contract, liquidated damages clauses, insurances, crisis management and disaster recovery plans and so on. Insurances and damages are basically deisgned to restore the organisation to the same financial position it would have been in had the loss not occurred.

1.9   Particular 'generic' risk mitigation approaches (such as project management, the use of contractual remedies and insurances) are highlighted by the syllabus, and discussed in later chapters of this Course Book. However, we will also suggest some approaches to risk treatment and mitigation as we explore various categories of risk, in Chapters 4–6.

1.10   All risk mitigation measures will – as our diagram of the risk cycle suggests – require the following steps.

- The allocation of accountabilities for managing the risk
- Identifying the resources required to mitigate the risk
- Developing action plans (including resource budgets and time scales)
- Obtaining management approval for the risk mitigation plan (where required)
- Obtaining stakeholder buy-in (and co-ordinated effort, where required) for the risk mitigation plan
- Implementing the approved risk mitigation plan (perhaps using a dedicated risk management or risk response team)
- Outlining the risk reporting requirements for ongoing risk monitoring.

1.11   In addition to implementing risk mitigation plans for high-probability risks, an organisation will need to develop **contingency plans** for low-probability but high-impact risks: alternative courses of action, alternative sources of supply, workarounds and fall-back positions ('What will we do if...?'). This important aspect of the risk cycle is discussed in Chapter 13.

Monitoring, reporting and review

1.12   As we have already suggested, a risk owner should be appointed for each identified risk, with a view to monitoring the risk situation, updating the risk register, and briefing the risk management team on a regular basis.

1.13   Monitoring, reporting and review ('What happened and what can we learn?') is an important part of risk management, in order to:

- Ascertain whether the organisation's risk profile or exposure is changing, and identify newly emerging or escalating contractual or relationship-related risks
- Give assurance that the organisation's risk management processes are effective, by demonstrating effective avoidance or mitigation of risks
- Indicate where contract risk management processes need improvement, or where lessons can be learned from critical incidents and contract problems.

1.14   The HM Treasury Orange Book states that review processes should:

- Ensure that all aspects of the risk management process are reviewed at least once a year
- Ensure that the risks themselves are subjected to review with appropriate frequency (with appropriate provision for management's own review of risks and for independent review or audit)
- Make provision for alerting the appropriate level of management to new risks or to changes in already identified risks, so that the change can be appropriately addressed.

1.15   The review can make use of a number of tools and techniques.

- The roles of individuals, work groups and project teams should include self-assessment on an ongoing basis and via regular reviews, audits and reports, including SWOT analysis, supplier appraisals, staff performance appraisals, quality assurance systems (eg statistical process control), environmental management systems, health and safety checks and so on.
- 'Risk self-assessment' (RSA) or 'control and risk self-assessment' (CRSA) are internal controls, through which each area of the organisation reviews its own activities using a documented framework or structured workshop approach. RSA allows risk owners to demonstrate and develop their involvement in the risk process, and their understanding of risk management issues.
- Departmental reporting or stewardship reporting requires that managers report upwards on the current status of risk in their areas and on the work they have done in keeping risk and control procedures up to date in their respective areas.
- HM Treasury produces a 'Risk Management Assessment Framework': a tool for evaluating the maturity of an organisation's risk management.
- The internal audit function provides an important, quasi-independent and objective report about

the adequacy of risk management. However, this is *not* a substitute for ownership of risk – or the embedding of risk management across organisations and supply chains.

External reporting of risks in corporate accounts

1.16   As we will see in Chapter 4, there has been increasing pressure to improve corporate governance and transparency. The demand for external disclosure of business risks has grown, as investors, financial analysts and other external stakeholders have become increasingly aware of the role of risk management. Pressure for external reporting may be supported by:

- Regulatory requirements
- The expectations of external stakeholders: investors, financial markets, customers, suppliers, business allies and other parties with an interest in the organisation's risk profile and exposure
- The organisation's own governance, CSR and risk management policies
- The reputational and other benefits of planned, *voluntary* disclosure (to both internal and external audiences): reduced regulatory scrutiny, enhanced reputation for transparency, reduced penalties for non-compliance and so on.

1.17   'Stakeholders want better information on the various risks organisations confront, and how to address them, and are interested in organisational risks far beyond the traditional scope of financial risks. They want concrete assurance that a sound system and process is in place to identify, assess and manage risks, so that they can better evaluate corporate performance and make more informed decisions. Increased measurement and reporting of this broader set of risks is necessary, not only to meet the new regulatory requirements, but also to improve managerial performance and stakeholder confidence.' (CIMA Global Management Accounting Guideline: *The Reporting of Organisational Risks for Internal and External Decision-Making*)

1.18   In the UK, the duty of directors to produce an annual report containing financial statements for shareholders is embodied in statute. It includes, for large companies:

- A **directors' report** with a business review explaining how the directors have fulfilled their duty to promote the success of the company with regard to the long-term interests of all stakeholders (including maintaining corporate reputation).
- A **strategic report** which:
  - provides context for the related financial statements
  - provides insight into the company's strategic management, including its business model and its main objectives and strategy
  - describes the company's internal and external business environment, including trends and key factors in its markets etc., the principal risks and uncertainties it faces, and how these might affect its future prospects.
  - provides an analysis of the company's past business performance and its current position.
- A **corporate governance report** to explain how the composition and organisation of the company's governance structure supports the achievement of it objectives.

1.19   For the business environment section of the strategic report, the full range of business risks, both financial and non-financial, should be considered. The principal risks and any change in them should be disclosed, irrespective of whether they result from strategic decisions, operations, organisation or behaviour, or from external factors over which the board might have little or no direct control. In particular, the assessment should include consideration of threats to solvency and liquidity. This section of the strategic report should also include information about:

- environmental matters (including the impact of the business of the entity on the environment)
- the entity's employees
- social, community and human rights issues.

1.20 For the business performance section of the strategic report, financial and non-financial key performance indicators (KPIs) should be included to help stakeholders: assess the company's progress against its objectives or strategy; monitor principal risks; and measure the development, performance or position of the company. Non-financial KPIs can be indicators of future financial prospects and progress in managing risks and opportunities including, for example, measures related to product quality and customer complaints.

1.21 Guidance on additional voluntary disclosure has been provided by various professional associations. ('Voluntary disclosure' means disclosures, often outside the financial statements, that are not explicitly required by generally accepted accounting principles or regulation.) In North America, for example, the COSO Enterprise Risk Management Integrated Framework proposes the inclusion of a section in financial reports devoted to describing the wider risk profile of the company.

1.22 Appropriate external disclosure of organisational risks and risk management initiatives (with due attention to information and compliance risk):

- Allows shareholders and financial analysts to more properly value company shares
- May enhance the corporate brand, supplier confidence and customer loyalty – where risk management is shown to be sound and responsible.

2 Risk management standards

ISO 31000: Risk management

2.1 ISO 31000: 2009 is a family of standards for the implementation of risk management, developed by the International Standards Organisation. It is intended to provide universal principles and generic guidelines applicable to 'any public, private or community enterprise, association, group or individual'. This is intended to provide a common, harmonising approach in support of a wide range of existing industry-, risk- or region-specific standards and methodologies.

2.2 ISO 31000 has replaced the previous main risk management standard, AS/NZS 4360, in the form of: AS/NZS ISO 31000: 2009. Whereas the original Standards Australia approach described a systematic process for managing risk, ISO 31000 also addresses the entire management system supporting that process. The standard 'recommends that organisations should have a framework that integrates the process for managing risk into the organisation's overall governance, strategy and planning, management, reporting processes, policies, values and culture.'

2.3 *ISO 31000: 2009 Principles and Guidelines on Implementation* provides: principles for managing risk; a framework for risk management; and a systematic risk management process. These are depicted in Figure 3.2.

Figure 3.2 *Summary of the ISO 31000 Principles; Framework; Process*

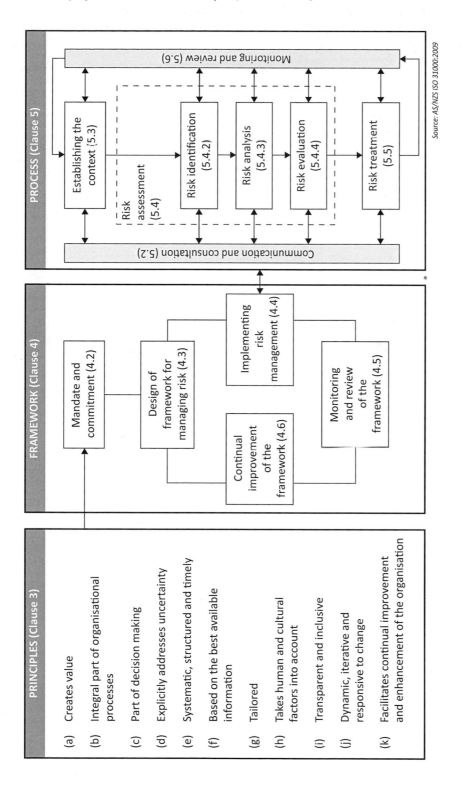

Source: AS/NZS ISO 31000:2009

2.4   The risk management **principles** are 'essential qualities' needed for risk management to be effective.

- *Risk management creates and protects value.* The Introduction to the Standard lists 18 benefits of managing risk, including increased likelihood of achieving objectives, improving stakeholder confidence and minimising losses.
- *Risk management is an integral part of organisational processes*: not separate from the activities and processes of the business, or the responsibility of a separate 'layer' of management.
- *Risk management is part of decision-making*: helping managers to make better decisions in all areas

- *Risk management explicitly addresses uncertainty*: seeking to mitigate the consequences of inherent uncertainty, and to establish resilience
- *Risk management is systematic, structured and timely*: it must be planned and controlled to ensure consistent results
- *Risk management is based on the best available information*: information is often limited, costly and imperfect, but risk management should take in information from valid and varied sources (observation, experience, forecasts, experts etc)
- *Risk management is tailored*: every organisation is unique, and risk management must 'fit' the organisation's context, risk profile, stakeholders and so on
- *Risk management takes human and cultural factors into account:* including the skills, capabilities, perceptions, motivation and awareness of people
- *Risk management is transparent and inclusive:* recognising the need to involve internal and external stakeholders in establishing context and determining risk criteria
- *Risk management is dynamic, iterative and responsive to change:* not a one-off activity, but an ongoing, dynamic, cyclical process
- *Risk management facilitates continual improvement and enhancement:* continually building resilience and capacity to maximise opportunities.

2.5   In relation to the **framework** component of the standard.

- *Mandate and commitment.* Risk management requires ongoing commitment: in order to be sustainable, it must be mandated from the board (or equivalent), implemented by senior managers and supported by all levels of management.
- *Design of framework to manage risk.* Effective implementation will be supported by a well-designed framework for: formulating risk management policy; embedding processes into practice; assigning resources; determining responsibilities; and planning for periodic communication and reporting to stakeholders.
- *Implementing risk management:* ensuring the risk management process is understood by risk owners (through communication and training); ensuring that risk management activities actually take place (through risk assessments, risk workshops, internal controls and so on); and ensuring that decisions and business processes factor in risk thinking.
- *Monitoring and review:* confirming that the various risk management elements are working in line with expectation; identifying, documenting and mitigating performance 'gaps'.
- *Continual improvement:* incrementally enhancing ('tweaking') the framework, as required, to improve current processes and to increase the maturity of the framework over time.

2.6   In relation to the risk management process:

- *Establishing context* means setting the parameters for risk appetite and risk management activities: STEEPLE analysis; alignment with internal factors (such as strategy, resources and capabilities); establishing risk management policy, processes, methodologies, plans, risk rating criteria, training and reporting processes etc.
- *Risk assessment* comprises the processes for identifying, analysing and evaluating risks. (ISO/IEC 31010: 2009 provides additional guidance on the selection and use of systematic risk assessment techniques.)
- *Risk treatment* comprises the strategies for risk avoidance, treating risk sources, modifying likelihood, changing consequences, or sharing risk – with a view to bringing the residual risk within the chosen risk appetite.
- *Monitoring and review:* keeping the process relevant to changing needs and risks. Monitoring will be undertaken by risk owners, management and the board (or equivalent), and an independent review may be undertaken periodically.
- *Communication and consultation* recognises the need to engage internal and external stakeholders throughout the risk management process. ISO 31000 promotes a 'consultative team approach' (involving communication between the risk management, risk owner and stakeholders) to secure stakeholder input and buy in.

2.7   The Standard summarises the five attributes of enhanced risk management (as a benchmark for organisations to measure their risk management maturity) as follows.

- Continual improvement (performance goals, measurements, reviews and refinements)
- Full accountability for risks (designated risk owners with authority to manage risk)
- Application of risk management in all decision making (documenting risk management thinking in all processes and activities, such as meetings)
- Continual communication (including reporting of significant risks and risk treatments)
- Full integration in the organisation's governance structure

ISO 28000: Supply chain security management systems

2.8   ISO 28000: 2007 *Specification for Security Management Systems for the Supply Chain* is the international standard for the development, implementation and maintenance of a Supply Chain Security Management System (SCSMS). Unlike ISO 31000, ISO 28000 is a certifiable standard, under which organisations can seek ISO accreditation (for enhanced credibility and brand recognition).

2.9   A security management system (SMS) is a network of elements intended to prevent, resist or withstand unauthorised acts designed to cause intentional harm or damage to a supply chain. In other words, it is a management system for the protection of people, property, information and infrastructure throughout supply chain operations. Security threats might include: piracy, terrorism or hijacking; theft of vehicles, goods or data; contamination or infiltration of goods (eg smuggling); sabotage; damage to goods in transit; unauthorised access to goods or data (eg industrial espionage); and so on.

2.10   ISO 28000 provides a systematic approach to the management of security programmes, aimed principally at improving international trade by ensuring that members of the supply chain are confirmed as 'secure traders'. This is based on establishing a protective security programme, based on the identification, prioritisation and control of risks. Like ISO 14001 (environmental management) and ISO 9001 (quality management), ISO 28000 uses a process-based approach based on the Plan-Do-Check-Act (PDCA) cycle, with the requirement for continual improvement.

2.11   This provides a best practice process framework for developing, documenting, implementing and maintaining an effective SMS including elements such as:

- Security management policy; objectives and targets; and programmes
- Security management structure (roles, responsibilities and authority)
- Security management competence (communication, awareness and training)
- Security planning: identifying and assessing risks; developing control measures
- Legal and regulatory requirements
- Documents, data and information systems and controls
- Operational control measures; emergency plans and procedures (dealing with incidents and breaches); and security response procedures (investigating security incidents and taking action)
- Monitoring and measuring security performance
- Auditing and evaluating the SMS, and seeking continuous improvement.

2.12   A Stanford University study (2006) found that: 'Where companies apply best practice security, they have demonstrated reductions in Customs inspections, increased the automated handling of imports, reduced transit times, improved on-time shipping to customers, reduced inventory theft, reduced excess inventory and reduced customer attrition rates'.

3   Risk management strategy

3.1   The phase 'risk management strategy' may be used in two different ways, to refer to:

- The formulation of a chosen 'approach' or 'plan' to deal with identified risks. In this sense, risk managers and teams at all levels will formulate risk management strategies, using the risk management cycle, and selecting the most appropriate of the various risk mitigation options (the 'Four Ts').
- The formulation of a corporate (organisation-wide), long-term, proactive strategic framework to manage risk in the organisation and supply chain, including accountabilities and governance structures; risk policies and tolerances; risk management processes and procedures; and plans to reinforce these arrangements through the creation of a risk-aware culture, in line with the organisation's desired risk appetite.

3.2   We have already laid out a broad framework for risk management strategy planning and implementation, in the first sense of the term. In the second sense of the term, however, an integrated, systematic and strategic-level approach to risk management involves the following elements.

- Integrated management of an organisation's full spectrum of risk
- Dealing with risk as a strategic issue, from a high-level corporate perspective
- Recognising that strategic success usually depends upon taking risks
- Engaging all fuctions and line management levels in the process
- Bridging the traditional 'silos' of risk disciplines (eg financial, strategic, supply, health and safety, technology, information and reputational risk).

3.3   The risk management strategy comprises the process that will be put in place to identify, assess, manage, review and report on organisational risk. However, the strategy should go further than the mechanics of risk management: it should aim to embed the principles and values of risk awareness and risk management throughout the organisation and organisational culture (an aspect discussed separately, later in the chapter).

3.4   A generic process for risk strategy is depicted in Figure 3.3.

Figure 3.3 *Risk strategy process*

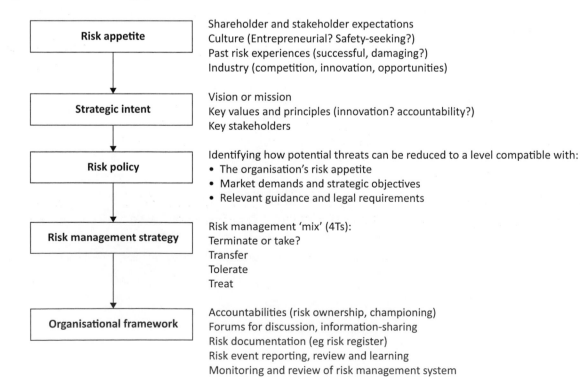

Framework for a strategic risk plan

3.5 The corporate risk strategy and supporting plan must acknowledge all major threats facing the organisation, and determine structures and reporting mechanisms for risk management. Publication of the strategy will normally be on an annual basis: because of the financial input and requirements for auditing and external reporting, it is common to publish it with the annual report and accounts.

3.6 A published risk management strategy might include six generic sections.

- **Section 1: Introduction and purpose**
  The risk strategy will usually define what risk is to the organisation, and give an overview of the organisation's strategic objectives and the role of risk management in ensuring that objectives will be met.
- **Section 2: Aim, principles and implementation**
  The aim (eg 'becoming one of the leading organisations in the management of risk and the innovative management of threats' or 'attaining a balance between risk and opportunity') sets the context.
  A principles statement will express the organisation's core values in regard to risk management (eg transparency, cross-functional and supply chain integration, stakeholder protection, entrepreneurship, corporate social responsibility and so on). The organisation's risk appetite should be identified and defined as far as possible.
  An implementation plan will set out roles and accountabilities for implementation of the strategy.
- **Section 3: Risk identification**
  The strategy will define and detail the main types of risk facing the organisation and state how the organisation will go about identifying emerging risks.
- **Section 4: Risk analysis and evaluation**
  Identified risks will be assessed in terms of their likelihood and impact, and risk owners nominated (with ongoing responsibility for reviewing the assessment and maintaining the risk register).
  Risk assessment methodologies, risk tolerances and escalation guidelines (when risks should be referred upwards) will be set out, ensuring that all risks are monitored and assessed at the appropriate organisational level, in a systematic and co-ordinated fashion. The organisation's risk register requirements should be clearly set out.
- **Section 5: Risk treatment**
  Guidelines may be given on the strategic options for addressing risks (tolerate, treat, transfer, terminate) and when each should be used.
  A statement may also be made in regard to the importance of contingency planning for particular levels or categories of risk, including the need for business continuity and disaster recovery plans.
- **Section 6: Risk review and reporting**
  The strategy must ensure that appropriate and effective review and reporting arrangements are in place, including stakeholder communication plans (the risk information requirements of identified stakeholder groups, and how communication with them will be conducted).

Example of risk strategy

3.7 To illustrate a systematic corporate strategy for risk management, we reproduce a published risk management strategy published by the Balfour Beatty Group: Figure 3.4.

Figure 3.4 *The Balfour Beatty group's risk management strategy*

The Board takes ultimate responsibility for the Group's systems of risk management and internal control and reviews their effectiveness. The Board has continued to assess the effectiveness of the risk management processes and internal controls during 2005, based on reports made to the Board, the Audit Committee and the Business Practices Committee; including:

- Results of internal audit's reviews of internal financial controls
- A Group-wide certification that effective internal controls had been maintained, or, where any significant non-compliance or breakdown had occurred with or without loss, the status of corrective action
- A paper prepared by management on the nature, extent and mitigation of significant risks and on the systems of internal controls

The Group's systems and controls are designed to ensure that the Group's exposure to significant risk is properly managed, but the Board recognises that any system of internal control is designed to manage rather than eliminate the risk of failure to achieve business objectives and can only provide reasonable and not absolute assurance against material misstatement or loss. In addition, not all the material joint ventures in which the Group is involved are treated, for these purposes, as part of the group. Where they are not, systems of internal control are applied as agreed between the parties to the venture.

Central to the Group's systems of internal control are the processes and framework for risk management. These accord with the Turnbull Guidance on internal controls and were in place throughout the year and up to the date of signing this report.

The Group's systems of internal controls operate through a number of different processes, some of which are interlinked. These include:

- The annual review of the strategy and plans of each operating company and of the Group as a whole in order to identify the risks to the Group's achievement of its overall objectives and, where appropriate, any relevant mitigating actions
- Monthly financial reporting against budgets and the review of results and forecasts by executive Directors and line management, including particular areas of business or project risk. This is used to update both management's understanding of the environment in which the group operates and the methods used to mitigate and control the risks identified
- Individual tender and project review procedures commencing at operating company level and progressing to Board Committee level if value or perceived exposure breaches certain thresholds
- Regular reporting, monitoring and review of health, safety and environmental matters
- The review and authorisation of proposed investment, divestment and capital expenditure through the Board's Committees and the Board itself
- The review of specific material areas of Group worldwide risk and the formulation and monitoring of risk mitigation actions
- The formulation and review of properly documented policies and procedures updated through the free and regular flow of information to address the changing risks of the business
- Specific policies set out in the Group Finance Manual, covering the financial management of the group, including arrangements with the Group's backers and bond providers, controls on foreign exchange dealings and management of currency and interest rate exposures, insurance, capital expenditure processes and application of accounting policies and financial controls
- A Group-wide risk management framework, which is applied to all functions in the Group, whether operational, financial or support. Under it, the key risks facing each part of the Group are regularly reviewed and assessed, together with the steps to avoid or mitigate those risks. The results of those reviews are placed on risk registers and, where necessary, specific actions are developed
- Reviews and tests by the internal audit team of critical business financial processes and controls and spot checks in areas of high business risk
- The Group's whistle-blowing policy.

Governance structure for risk management

3.8   Strategic leadership is crucial to effective risk management. In particular, there needs to be clear allocation of responsibility for risk management (expressed in a governance structure), in order to avoid exposure to the *further* risk of risks being unmanaged – causing damage or loss that could otherwise by avoided, anticipated or mitigated.

3.9   The development of a coherent risk management strategy, with the **board of directors** taking ultimate responsibility for governance structures and internal controls, ensures that strategic support will be maintained. The board has a fundamental role in the management of risk, including:

- Receipt of an annual opinion from the external auditors and/or internal audit committee, including a review of the process of risk management and internal control

- Consideration of risk issues as they affect strategy planning, policy-making and board-level decisions. (The 'top ten' risks to organisational viability, continuity and reputation should arguably be agreed, owned and addressed at board level.)
- Periodically reviewing risks as part of the monitoring of annual operating plans.

3.10 An accounting officer may be appointed by the board as the person ultimately responsible for the management of risk:

- Developing a clear and up-to-date awareness and understanding of risks which could prevent the delivery of corporate objectives
- Ensuring that the organisation has effective risk management processes and controls in place
- Seeking assurance that risk processes and controls are being effectively managed and implemented.

3.11 In larger organisations, the role may fall within the remit of a risk advisory group or risk management committee, led by senior executives or board members. The committee's remit will include the following activities.

- Consideration of risk management policy in respect of issues and activities that are organisation-wide, or above a nominated threshold of risk severity (for escalation upwards by line risk managers). ISO 31000 defines risk management policy as 'a statement of the overall intentions and direction of an organisation related to risk management'.
- Reviewing and agreeing the process of managing risk in the organisation, including risk awareness training
- Communicating emerging strategic and operational risks to the board, and lower level ('focal point') risks to line managers in relevant functions
- Reviewing and updating the risk register (eg through a nominated risk co-ordinator), and maintaining an overview of total risk to the organisation at any given time
- Championing risk management, and ensuring the sharing of best practice, across the organisation

3.12 As the risk management discipline is increasing in prominence, the role of a board-level chief risk officer (CRO) is being created in some companies. In smaller organisations, the finance director or chief executive will often add the role of risk management to his or her responsibilities.

3.13 Managers and staff throughout the organisation, however, should be aware of the relevance of risk to the achievement of their objectives. They need to be equipped with the relevant skills and tools to allow them to manage risk effectively.

4 Risk management culture

4.1 AS/NZS 4360 defines risk management as 'the *culture*, processes and structures that are directed towards realising potential opportunities whilst managing adverse consequences.' This definition highlights the need to embed risk awareness, and appropriate risk appetite, throughout an organisation: not just in terms of policies and procedures, but at the level of core values, attitudes and behavioural norms.

4.2 The Cranfield School of Management *(Supply Chain Vulnerability)* identifies four key variables that foster success in supply chain vulnerability management, continuity management and resilience.

- Risk awareness among top management
- Risk awareness as an integrated part of supply chain management
- An understanding by each employee of his or her role in risk awareness
- An understanding that changes in business strategies change supply chain risk profiles (and therefore that risk awareness must be constantly updated)

Organisational culture

4.3 Organisation culture has been defined as 'a pattern of beliefs and expectations shared by the organisation's members, and which produce norms which powerfully shape the behaviour of individuals and groups in the organisation' (H Schwartz and S Davis, 'Matching corporate culture and business strategy', in *Organisational Dynamics*). It has been summed up as 'the way we do things around here' (Edgar H Schein, *Organisational Culture and Leadership*).

4.4 Johnson, Scholes and Whittington *(Exploring Corporate Strategy)* use the 'cultural web' as a way of representing 'the taken-for-granted assumptions, or paradigm, of an organisation, and the behavioural manifestations of organisational culture': Figure 3.5.

Figure 3.5 *The cultural web*

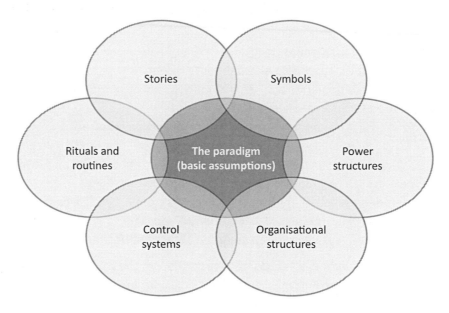

4.5 The elements of the web can be used as a framework to analyse and manage organisational culture in a wide range of settings. (Note that all the elements are interlinked: any one can influence the others to change the culture.)

- The **paradigm** may include core values and assumptions about risk and risk-taking, risk appetite, innovation, entrepreneurship – or, on the other end of the scale, duty of care, reliability, safety, stakeholder protection and so on.
- **Stories** form the 'mythology' of the organisation: tales of past successes or failures, disasters or rescues may shape the risk culture by typifying and reinforcing the perception that risk-taking behaviours bring dangers – or rewards.
- **Routines** include formal procedures for risk assessment and management, but also informal norms and 'short-cuts' developed in practice (which may by-pass risk management rules and safety procedures.) **Rituals** are more symbolic behaviours: an organisation may, for example, annually commemorate disasters, or include safety and risk warnings in weekly briefings or project team formations.
- **Control systems** refer to a wide range of ways in which behaviour is controlled in organisations. A risk-aware culture will be reinforced by relevant policies, procedures and rules; staff training, monitoring and supervision; rewards and sanctions; and mechanisms enforcing risk-managed behaviour (such as safety guards on machines, or built-in authorisation requirements for procurements).
- **Organisational structure** for risk management may include: allocated risk management roles and responsibilities; governance mechanisms such as division of duties, authorisation and approval requirements, and supervision; escalation routes (for referring risks upwards); communication channels for risk information sharing; and so on.

- **Power structures** refer to how power is distributed; whether it is based on formal authority, charismatic leadership or respect for expertise, say; and who the influential individuals and groups are. An organisation's risk culture will be created by informal 'influencers', not just the application of formal top-down authority. Such individuals and teams must be co-opted as risk champions to drive the organisation's desired risk values – otherwise, their influence may be used to undermine formal risk initiatives and messages.
- **Symbols** are any objects which take on symbolic value within the organisation. An organisation that has as its logo a pair of dice, for example, would be expressing a risk-enthusiastic culture, while an organisation whose employee awards represent a 'safe pair of hands' would be expressing a culture of risk awareness, safety and reliability.

4.6   An organisation's culture is partly shaped by its environment, as it will adopt elements of the other cultural spheres (nation, region and industry sector) in which it operates. It will also embrace some of the cultural values of influential individuals and groups within the organisation: the cultures of particular professional or occupational groups, social classes and so on. Charles Handy *(Understanding Organisations)* noted that: 'Organisations are as different and varied as nations and societies of the world. They have differing cultures … affected by events of the past and the climate of the present, by the technology of the type of work, by their aims and the type of people who work in them.'

Creating the desired risk culture

4.7   Cultures which are dysfunctionally risk-taking *or* dysfunctionally risk-averse (perhaps because the culture has failed to adapt to the changing risk profile of the organisation) can be changed. The key tools of cultural change include the following.

- Consistent expression and modelling of the new values by senior management (from the top down), leaders and influencers (who may need to be co-opted to the initiative by those in authority)
- Changing underlying values and beliefs, through communication, education and involvement of employees in discussing the need for new ideas and behaviours: spreading new values and beliefs, and encouraging employees to 'own' them (through incentives, co-opting people to teach others, getting employees involved in risk 'circles' and suggestion schemes, and so on); and reinforcing the change (through praise, recognition and rewards)
- Embedding desired attitudes and behaviours in policies, procedures, rules, systems, employee communications, management style and so on – so that they become 'business as usual', and are supported by all necessary information, resources and controls
- Using human resource management mechanisms to reinforce the changes: making the new values and behaviours criteria for recruitment and selection, employee appraisal and reward; including them in competency profiles and learning needs assessments for training and development planning; implementing education, training and coaching; applying disciplinary action, sanctions and penalties where required; and so on. These mechanisms are important because the organisation may need to bring in new people who will 'fit' the new culture – and squeeze out those who don't 'fit', if their attitudes and behaviour cannot be changed.

5   Resources for risk management

5.1   The resources allocated for risk management will reflect the business sector the organisation operates in, the nature of its vulnerabilities, and the extent of its exposure. Operations such as airlines, manufacturing, extraction and health care may have a high risk management budget, for example, because of the need to comply with health and safety regulations. Organisations which have invested time and money in establishing high-profile corporate brands will similarly allocate resources to the management of reputational risk. Organisations which are highly dependent on ICT and knowledge systems (such as social media and e-commerce organisations) will recognise the need to invest in information assurance. And so on.

5.2 Management will make strategic and tactical decisions to devote resources to risk management on a range of business case or cost/benefit factors, including:

- The intolerability of risk (eg the need for compliance) and the priority of vulnerabilities and exposure
- The availability and cost of management time (and the efficiency and prioritisation skills of risk managers)
- The availability of existing controls, infrastructure, systems (eg for quality assurance) and information sources
- The availability of systems for automatic identification and reporting of variances and threats
- Potential quantifiable and qualitative benefits of managed risk
- Costs of *not* implementing risk management systems (exposure)
- Costs of developing and maintaining risk management systems.

5.3 From a business case point of view, the cost of risk reduction and mitigation (prevention *and* appraisal) should be less than the potential loss incurred by risk events and/or lost opportunities. However, it is worth remembering that some investment in risk management should be regarded as a sunk or inevitable cost, regardless of quantifiable benefits: health and safety, for example, would come into this category.

Resourcing risk awareness and mitigation

5.4 A range of resource categories may be required to deliver effective risk management strategies.

- **Informational resources.** Risk judgements must be based on sound information – and this requires a robust internal and external management information system (MIS) that can supply appropriate and timely data in appropriate formats. Environmental scanning systems, supply chain and industry networking, benchmarking, stakeholder surveys and other risk identification processes may have to be set up. Risk databases and registers may have to be developed to start building up robust, accessible risk information and knowledge sharing. Informational resources include: internal records and databases; management information and decision-support systems (eg for scenario modelling and statistical risk measurement); bought-in environmental or market surveys, reports and risk assessments (or consultancy and advice); and risk-focused stakeholder communication strategies and programmes.
- **Human resources.** The implementation of risk management requires the allocation of managerial and staff time to risk identification, assessment and mitigation activities. This may simply be embedded in day-to-day workloads (eg team briefings, work planning, supervision, procedural compliance) – but it may also require additional responsibilities (eg for safety or risk officers), additional risk-focused activities (eg membership of risk committees, conducting risk audits and reviews) or added 'layers' of management (eg risk managers). People resources for risk management include: managerial input; trained and aware staff; and risk committees and audit teams.
- **Infrastructure development** may be required for new risk management initiatives, including the development of management and risk information systems, templates (eg risk registers), committees and governance structures.
- **Technology resources** to support risk management may include: risk management information systems, automated risk monitoring and reporting systems, and technology-based risk mitigation measures (such as safety equipment, machine-based alerts and alarms, the automation of dangerous tasks, transport 'black box' recorders for risk event analysis, computerised inventory management systems and so on).
- **Time resources** include the adequate allowance of managerial and staff time for risk management activities – and also effective scheduling and time management (as a tool for mitigating project risk).
- **Physical resources** include: safe and well-maintained premises, plant, machinery and vehicles; protective and safety equipment; safe and secure storage facilities for hazardous substances and general inventory; demand-managed inventory levels; and so on (depending largely on the type of hazard or vulnerability)

- **Financial resources** for risk management include adequate budgetary provision for costs of information, managerial and staff time, mitigation measures – and costs of pursuing opportunities (investments, innovation, product development and so on).

Promoting risk awareness

5.5   Risk awareness is a mindset which recognises the existence of threats and vulnerabilities, and takes (upside and downside) risk into account in decision-making and problem-solving.

5.6   The benefits of risk awareness for an organisation or supply chain include the following.

- Risk management principles are embedded in everyday work activity – not requiring separate mechanisms and costs to manage identified risks.
- All members of the organisation (and supply chain) can contribute to risk identification and response – maximising the leverage of 'front-line' (and supply market) knowledge and expertise, risk ownership and information sharing
- Risk awareness encourages greater environmental scanning, which may make a knock-on contribution to organisational learning, innovation and the identification of opportunities (as well as threats).
- Risk awareness enhances the organisation's ability to recognise and manage new, emerging and escalating risk factors and vulnerabilities, on an ongoing basis.

5.7   As an aspect of risk culture creation, the promotion of risk awareness involves processes such as the following.

- Communicating the vision: through risk policy statements, corporate image and stories, and modelling by top management
- Cascading down risk management objectives: through employee and stakeholder communication programmes, departmental and team briefings, incorporation of risk issues in staff intranet pages, procedures manuals, newsletters and so on
- Educating and training stakeholders: in risk awareness and hazard identification; relevant risk management procedures; and so on
- Sharing risk information: eg through the risk register; risk management manual (in print or on the corporate intranet); cross-functional risk teams and committees; and risk audits and reports
- Rewarding and valuing successful risk identification and minimisation (and/or resilience and recovery)
- Encouraging 'thinking outside the box', questions, challenges, divergent viewpoints and 'whistle blowing' on risk issues – to discourage 'groupthink': cosy, complacent, blinkered, forced-consensus thinking (Irving Janis).
- Monitoring and checking risk awareness: via internal and external audits, self-assessments and so on.

Communicating risks

5.8   Communication is a key element of risk management, but it is often a weak area in terms of both personal skills and organisational structures. A stakeholder risk information needs analysis can help to ensure that risk-focused communication is appropriately targeted and timely, and that it is disseminated using methods which maximise stakeholder access.

5.9   The organisation will need to:

- Identify all key risk stakeholders
- Determine the type and level of risk information they require, the purpose for which they require it, the required timing and frequency of delivery and the preferred medium or format for delivery.

5.10   A range of **outputs** should then be designed, with regard to:

- Content: a range of information formats can be produced at different levels of detail, cascading down from high-level executive summaries to more detailed operational risk descriptions and mitigation procedures

- Delivery method, as appropriate for the needs of each stakeholder group
- Responsibilities, with an owner responsible for the production, approval and updating of each output. A RACI chart (Responsible, Approver, Contributor, Informed) may be used to keep track of communications development and delivery
- Recipients. A circulation plan should be drawn up for different types and levels of risk information. Some stakeholders may only require a copy of the risk profile or risk register, or a relevant extract, summary report or narrative from it.

Involving suppliers

5.11   Suppliers can be involved in delivery of the risk management strategy through the following mechanisms.

- **Total involvement**: encouraging risk awareness at all point of contact with the supply network – buyers, contract managers, project teams, account managers, senior management contacts, professional networks and so on
- **Cross-functional collaboration:** developing an integrated, process-focused approach to risk identification and management across the internal and external value chain – avoiding 'silo' divisions of responsibility and barriers to risk-focused communication and problem-solving. Mechanisms for this may include the use of project and contract management teams and risk committees.
- **Supply chain collaboration and contribution**, through mechanisms such as:
  — Formally or informally gathering information from suppliers about risk factors in the supply market (and particular supplier vulnerabilities) – both at the market engagement and supplier appraisal and pre-qualification stage of particular projects, and on an ongoing basis
  — Gathering feedback from suppliers about risk factors arising from the buyer's systems and processes (eg failures of communication or demand management)
  — Collaboration to minimise risk through negotiated agreements, specifications and contract terms (eg equitable allocation and sharing of risks and liabilities; cost/price agreements; insurances; guarantees and indemnities and so on)
  — Early supplier involvement in new product and service development, or early contractor involvement in project definition: leveraging the supplier's knowledge for identifying risks, vulnerabilities and opportunities
  — Securing, motivating and rewarding the willingness of suppliers to share the risk (eg of partnership, joint investments, transport or storage risks and costs and so on)
  — Developing information flows across the supply chain (depending on trust) to increase risk visibility, and to support risk mitigation through improved demand forecasting, support for lean and agile supply, optimising costs (for economic sustainability for both buyer and supply base), and so on.
  — Securing, motivating and managing supplier compliance and diligence, in regard to quality, ethics and corporate responsibility issues: minimising the risk of buyer reputational damage, environmental damage, outsource quality issues and so on.

Chapter summary

- A systematic approach to risk can be modelled as a cycle of six stages: identification; assessment; strategy formulation; resource allocation; implementation; monitoring and reporting.
- Risk management strategies may be classified as the Four Ts: tolerate; transfer; terminate; or treat.
- Risk management principles are outlined in international standards, notably ISO 31000 and ISO 28000.
- Organisational culture has been described as a 'web' of elements. Risk management must be appropriately embedded in the cultural web.
- An effective risk management process requires resources: informational, human, infrastructure development, technology, time, physical and financial resources.

Self-test questions

Numbers in brackets refer to the paragraphs where you can check your answers.

1 Explain what is meant by each of the Four Ts. (1.7)

2 Describe tools that can be used in the 'monitoring and review' phase of risk management. (1.15)

3 What are the risk management principles laid down in ISO 31000? (2.4)

4 What is a security management system? (2.10)

5 Explain the stages in a systematic risk management strategy. (Figure 3.3)

6 List activities in the remit of a risk advisory group. (3.11)

7 According to the Cranfield School of Management, what are the four key variables that foster success in supply chain vulnerability management? (4.2)

8 Explain the seven elements in the 'cultural web' (J, S & W). (4.5)

9 Describe the categories of resources that are needed to deliver effective risk management strategies. (5.4)

10 Describe mechanisms to involve suppliers in delivery of a risk management strategy. (5.11)

CHAPTER 4

Fraud and Corruption Risks

Assessment criteria and indicative content

 Analyse the main methods for eliminating corruption and fraud in supply chains

- The nature of fraud in organisations and supply chains, why fraud takes place and different types of fraud
- The nature of bribery and corruption in organisations and supply chains
- The different types of corruption
- Legislation affecting bribery and corruption
- The use of ethical codes, including the CIPS Ethical Code
- Corporate governance including corporate accountability to stakeholders
- The Sarbanes-Oxley regulations

Section headings

1   Fraud
2   Bribery and corruption
3   Regulating ethical behaviour
4   Corporate governance

Introduction

In the first three chapters of this Course Book, we have outlined a framework for understanding risk and risk mitigation, broadly identified as the risk management process.

In Chapters 4–6 we explore several key risk categories affecting supply chains, as highlighted by the syllabus. In this chapter we look at the nature of fraud, bribery and corruption in supply chains, and at some of the main methods for eliminating such risks.

This embraces several key issues, including the internal controls applied by an organisation to prevent and detect fraud; the legislative framework, mainly applied to bribery and corruption; the broader framework of 'corporate governance' (the structure by which corporations are directed and controlled, in order to protect the interests of shareholders and other key stakeholders); and the still broader framework of 'corporate ethics' (the system of values by which corporations uphold what society considers to be 'appropriate' or 'right' conduct).

The concept of corporate social responsibility embraces corporate governance and ethics. However, this is considered separately in Chapter 6, together with the concept of sustainability (which explicitly raises aspects of environmental and social risk) and the key issue of reputational and brand risk.

Note that, unless otherwise specified, the law discussed in this chapter is that of England and Wales, as exemplar.

1   Fraud

The nature of fraud in organisations and supply chains

1.1   There is no precise legal definition of fraud, but a general definition is 'an act of deliberate deception, with the intention of gaining some benefit' *(Chambers Concise Dictionary)*, or, more specifically, 'deprivation by deceit': that is, taking something away from someone by an act of deception. This is a key area of risk management, as it raises financial, compliance and reputational risk.

1.2   In a corporate context, fraud generally falls into one of two main categories.

- The **removal of funds or assets** from an organisation. The most clear-cut example of this is outright theft of cash or other assets (such as stock, equipment or stationery). However, you should be able to recognise that this form of fraud also includes more complex and subtle methods such as the overstatement of expenses claims; the authorisation of salary payments to non-existent staff members; the creation and payment of false invoices purporting to be from suppliers (but actually benefiting the fraudster) – and so on.
- **Intentional misrepresentation** of the financial position of the business, in order to mislead shareholders, taxation authorities or regulatory authorities. This includes omissions or mis-recordings in the company's accounts, and falsification of data in financial statements: overstating (or understating) profits or stock valuations – and so on.

1.3   The removal of funds or assets obviously poses a threat to the organisation in several areas. Profits may be lower than anticipated, and the net asset position of the organisation weakened. Stock levels may be lower than anticipated, causing stockouts or urgent (higher-cost) replenishments. Morale may suffer owing to the climate of suspicion. The effects of a large-scale fraud are potentially very serious: a significant reduction in working capital, as a result of massive theft or misuse of funds, may make it difficult for the company to operate effectively – and may ultimately bring about a collapse (as in the case of Barings Bank, for example).

1.4   Intentional misrepresentation of a company's financial position likewise has potentially serious consequences. If profits are *overstated*, there may be unanticipated shortfalls in working capital, and poor decisions may be made, based on inaccurate resource information. Stakeholders such as suppliers may also be subjected to risk: eg extending credit facilities on the basis of false information. If profits are *understated*, access to loan finance may be restricted, and shareholders may be disillusioned, affecting the company's share price.

Why fraud occurs

1.5   Sadgrove argues that there are four main pre-conditions for fraud to be committed.

- The perpetrator must have a motive: a reason why he needs money or feels entitled to defraud the organisation.
- There must be assets worth stealing.
- There must be opportunity: to remove the assets, and to derive gain from them (eg by selling them on).
- There must be a failure of internal control or fraud risk management.

1.6   We might therefore say that fraud occurs for three main reasons.

- Because it represents an opportunity for (illegitimate) financial gain. A report by accountancy firm BDO Stoy Hayward (*Supply Management,* February 2009) suggested that the economic downturn has presented a significant fraud temptation, with the value of procurement fraud in the UK increasing 347% during 2008. 'The economic downturn has played a major role in encouraging both buyers and suppliers to try and secure money illegally.'

- Because individuals or groups have low morale and *esprit de corps,* or are actively hostile to the organisation, enabling them to justify activity to its detriment. The perpetrator of fraud may feel entitled to greater financial rewards, for example, or may bear a grudge against the employer for perceived injustice, or may simply be alienated by unsatisfying work and poor prospects of development or advancement.
- Because inadequate preventative and detective controls are in place to discourage, prevent and detect fraudulent behaviours. In other words, people commit fraud because the system allows them to – placing temptation in their way.

Different types of fraud

1.7 Organisations need to be aware of the range of activities that may be considered fraudulent – or present fraud risk – and there should be clearly articulated organisational policies, rules and expectations in this regard. We have already pinpointed the main categories of fraud. Table 4.1 suggests some examples in each category. Sadgrove gives an alternative classification of different 'types of fraud':

- **Online fraud:** involving fake or stolen credit cards used to buy merchandise from e-commerce businesses
- **Telephone fraud**: abuse of office telephones (eg to make expensive international calls) by employees and/or hackers
- **Being used for fraud**: the organisation being a 'vehicle' for employee fraud (eg money laundering or collusion)
- **Corporate identity theft**: 'phishing' – faking corporate identity in emails and websites to gain access to people's bank account details and passwords
- **Minor fraud**: eg employees using corporate facilities, equipment or staff for their own purposes; pilferage and so on
- **Competitor fraud**: competitors gaining unethical access to data or competitive intelligence (eg by bribing customers or staff).

Table 4.1 *Examples of fraud*

Removal of funds or assets	Theft of cash or stock. Employees with access to cash, stock, equipment or consumables may be tempted to steal.
	Payroll fraud: employees falsifying timesheets for overtime payments, for example, or payroll officers falsifying payroll lists.
	Procurement fraud: eg falsifying supplier invoices (and pocketing payments), or misusing corporate purchasing cards for personal use. Buyers may also defraud vendors on behalf of the organisation (rather than for personal gain), through tactics such as: falsely claiming that stock has been undelivered; temporarily withholding payment, on false excuses; and not settling invoices at all.
	Misuse of assets. For example: • Drawing on the corporate pension fund to use as collateral in obtaining loan finance, or for other purposes • Manipulating the book value of assets: eg over-depreciating assets in order to sell them at below-market value to colluding beneficiaries; or over-valuing assets transferred to the corporate pension fund to inflate its value.
	Collusion with customers to defraud the business: eg by discounting prices or despatching extra goods (in return for a share of the saving), or writing off debts in return for a financial inducement
	Collusion with suppliers to defraud the business: eg where suppliers issue invoices for larger quantities of goods than were actually delivered, splitting the additional payments between the perpetrators; or where buyers return goods already paid for as defective, allowing the supplier to re-sell them as new.

Continued . . .

Intentional misrepresentation	Over-stating profits, by: • Over-valuing and/or over-counting stock (eg by omitting to record stock outflows) • Inflating sales (eg by generating fictitious invoices, overcharging customers or manipulating sale-or-return arrangements) • Manipulating year-end accounting (eg by deliberately over-invoicing year-end sales, or delaying the recording of year-end purchases) • Failing to record expenditures and liabilities (or applying incorrect rates in order to understate depreciation) • Failing to write off bad debts
	Under-stating profits (in order to avoid tax liability), using the reverse of the above tactics.
	Misrepresentation to induce a contract. For example, a supplier may win a contract as a result of intentionally misleading a buyer about its financial resources, the terms of its offering, or the professional qualifications of its personnel. In legal terms, this is known as 'misrepresentation'. Contracts based on misrepresentation are 'voidable': they can effectively be cancelled by the aggrieved party. Additional damages may be payable, however, if the misrepresentation is fraudulent: that is, deliberately designed to mislead the buyer for the supplier's gain (and to the buyer's detriment).

1.8 The term **embezzlement** is used for the fraudulent appropriation of funds or property by a party to whom they have been entrusted, but which belong to someone else. For example, a lawyer or accountant could embezzle funds held in trust for clients – and an agent or employee of an organisation could embezzle funds or assets which he controls on behalf of the organisation. The key difference between embezzlement and theft is that the embezzler has been given the legitimate *right* to possess, use, and/or access the assets in question – but has then withdrawn, misappropriated and used them in a way that was *not* intended or sanctioned by the owners.

1.9 Embezzlement often occurs over long periods of time, with the trusted individual appropriating only a small fraction of the total he receives or controls in any one allocation or transaction, minimising the risk of detection. Examples of embezzlement would include removing funds or assets, and falsifying records to conceal the activity: for example, creating false vendor accounts and transactions. This is sometimes distinguished from fraudulent activity known as **skimming**: under-reporting income or revenue, and pocketing the difference between the recorded amount and the amount actually received.

Fraud prevention measures

1.10 An article in *Procurement Professional* (June/July 2007) suggested a number of general measures to prevent employee procurement fraud.

- Develop clarity around the definition and consequences of fraud, through a well-defined and widely communicated policy.
- Create a well-defined process for dealing with fraud, including the way in which evidence is managed.
- Remove as much expense as possible from reimbursements and petty cash, in favour of controlled and managed corporate or purchasing cards.
- Implement spend analysis techniques, for clear visibility, tracking and monitoring of expenditures.

1.11 We will look in more detail at internal controls, designed to prevent fraud, in Section 3 of this chapter.

2 Bribery and corruption

The nature of bribery and corruption

2.1 'Corruption' in essence means 'moral perversion' or a lack of integrity: it generally implies any kind of deliberate or intentional wrong-doing. For our present purposes, however, the most helpful definition may be that of the World Bank, which defines corruption as: 'the abuse of public office for private gain'. In other words, corruption covers a range of situations in which individuals or entities abuse a position of trust, authority or power to further their own interests – generally to the detriment of other stakeholders.

2.2   Focusing on the public sector, the World Bank briefing document *(Helping Countries Combat Corruption)* notes that: 'Public office is abused for private gain when an official accepts, solicits, or extorts a bribe. It is also abused when private agents actively offer bribes to circumvent public policies and processes, for competitive advantage and profit. Public office can also be abused for personal benefit even if no bribery occurs, through patronage and nepotism, the theft of state assets, or the diversion of state revenues.'

2.3   It should be obvious that similar processes can occur in the private sector, for example:

- Where buyers accept a bribe or other inducement to favour a particular supplier or contractor in a negotiation or contract award situation
- Where buyers award a contract or preferential terms to suppliers in which they – or people closely connected to them – have a personal or financial interest, creating a threat to their real or perceived objectivity
- Where a private sector firm offers a bribe or inducement to influential external stakeholders (including public officials) to support corporate plans or projects. (This is sometimes referred to as 'grease' money, because it 'oils the wheels' for industry...)

2.4   These issues have been re-ignited in recent years by high-profile exposés of bribery, and surveys showing that bribery and corruption are widespread in some overseas supply markets. The 2007 *Corruption Perceptions Index* (published by NGO Transparency International) revealed that more than 40% of 180 countries examined were perceived to have 'rampant corruption' in their public sector procurement *(Supply Management,* October 2007).

- A Munich court found German technology firm Siemens guilty of paying bribes to secure contracts in Nigeria, Libya and Russia in 77 cases between 2001 and 2004: the firm agreed to pay a fine of €201 million.
- Lambeth Council in London was reported for alleged procurement fraud involving purchases from firms in which a project manager had an interest. The authority's auditors reported 'inadequate reference checks and errors and omissions in relation to procurement, contract monitoring and the authorisation of payments' *(Supply Management,* 16 February 2006)
- US engineering firm Kellogg, Brown and Root (KBR) agreed to pay a fine of $402 million, as well as civil penalties, after admitting bribing officials to win a $6 billion contract in Nigeria. KBR also agreed to hire an independent auditor for a three-year period to design and monitor a programme to help make sure the company complied with anti-corruption laws. *(Supply Management,* 5 March 2009)

2.5   Corruption clearly represents a significant compliance and reputational risk for perpetrating organisations, or organisations employing perpetrators. On the other hand, it may also be seen as a necessary 'risk of doing business', in regions where operations may be actively constrained by *failure* to 'grease the wheels' with local officials, regulators and business partners.

Conflicts of interest

2.6   A key principle of business ethics is not offering or accepting gifts or inducements which may – or may be *perceived* to – influence the recipient's decision-making. A related principle is that individuals should not make decisions (or divulge confidential information) for personal gain. Such situations create a **conflict of interest**, because the best interests of the firm or internal client (eg contract award on the basis of best value) conflicts with the personal interests of the individual (eg personal gain). Another such situation would be if the buyer stood to gain from promoting a particular supplier because he had a financial or personal interest in the supplying firm: as a shareholder, perhaps, or as someone with a close relationship to the supplier's management.

Bribery, gifts and hospitality

2.7   The giving of gifts and offers of hospitality are among the common courtesies of business dealings. The problem for procurement professionals is to decide when such practices amount to an attempt to induce a favourable sourcing or contract award decision, information disclosure or other favourable treatment. There are obvious cases where buyer and seller collude to ensure that the seller wins a contract, the buyer in return receiving a reward. This is defined as bribery and corruption – and it is illegal in the UK (with strict legislation covering public bodies, in particular).

2.8   The more problematic cases are those where no explicit link is made between the gift and the award of business. A major difficulty may be the difference in perceptions between buyer and seller. To the seller, a gift may be merely a token of appreciation, of a kind that his organisation virtually expects him to bestow on most or all customers. To the buyer, however, the gift may become a material inducement to favour that supplier. (In international business dealings, this difference in perception may also be a cultural issue.)

2.9   Most organisations have clear rules on the receiving of gifts and hospitality, where this is perceived as an ethical issue. This is also the subject of codes of ethics in the procurement profession. As a general principle, any potential interest or conflict of interest should be *disclosed,* so that proceedings are transparent and open to control.

2.10   The CIPS Code of Conduct explicitly addresses these issues.

- Other than items of a very small intrinsic value, such as diaries or calendars, business gifts should not be accepted.
- The recipient should not allow himself to be influenced, or to be perceived by others to have been influenced, in making a business decision as a result of accepting hospitality. The frequency and scale of hospitality accepted should be managed openly and with care and should not be greater than the member's employer is able to reciprocate.

2.11   In practice, debate continually rages in the letters pages of *Supply Management*, around issues such as:

- What the 'reasonable' limit on the value of acceptable gifts should be
- Whether *any* gifts should be kept by individuals (or donated to charity, say)
- Whether gifts (of any value) should be formally logged (as the basis for taxation) and/or approved
- Whether there is flexibility for cultural differences in regard to gift-giving and hospitality.

Legislation on bribery and corruption

2.12   The UK **Bribery Act 2010** came into force in July 2011. It repealed all previous statutory provisions in relation to bribery (including the Public Bodies Corrupt Practices Act 1889 and Prevention of Corruption Acts 1906 and 1916), replacing them with the following crimes.

- **Bribery:** when a person offers, gives or promises to give a 'financial or other advantage' (eg non-monetary gifts, contracts or offers of employment) to another individual, in exchange for 'improperly' performing a 'relevant function or activity'.
  - The relevant function or activity is defined as: 'Any function of a public nature; any activity connected with a business, trade or profession; any activity performed in the course of a person's employment; or any activity performed by or on behalf of a body of persons' – *where* the person performing the function could be expected to be performing it in good faith or with impartiality, *or* where an element of trust attaches to that person's role.
  - The activity will be considered to be 'improperly' performed when the expectation of good faith or impartiality has been breached, *or* when the function has been performed in a way not expected of a person in a position of trust – having regard to what a reasonable person *in the UK* might expect of such a person in such a position.

Unlike the previous body of legislation, which applied primarily to public bodies, this applies to both private and public sectors, and to activities performed outside the UK.

- **Being bribed:** requesting, accepting or agreeing to accept such an advantage, in exchange for improperly performing such a function or activity.
- **Bribery of foreign public officials:** promising, offering or giving a financial or other advantage:
  — To a foreign public official (anyone carrying out a public function for a foreign country or its public agencies, or an official or agent of a public international organisation)
  — Either directly or through a third party (preventing the use of agents or 'go-betweens')
  — Where such an advantage is not legitimately due (meaning that if the law of the foreign country allows or requires the official to accept, then no crime is committed).
- **Failure of a commercial organisation to prevent bribery on its behalf.** This applies to all commercial organisations which have business in the UK. The organisation can be guilty of the offence if bribery is carried out by an employee, agent, subsidiary or third party (eg a supplier acting on the buyer's behalf). In its defence, the organisation must show that, while bribery did take place, it had in place 'adequate procedures designed to prevent persons associated with [it] from undertaking such conduct'. Guidance from the Secretary of State suggests that 'adequate procedures' might include provision for: proportionate procedures, top-level commitment, risk assessment, due diligence, communication (including training) and monitoring and review.

2.13　The penalties for committing one of these crimes, under the Act, include imprisonment, unlimited fines, the confiscation of property (under the Proceeds of Crime Act 2002) and the disqualification of directors (Company Directors Disqualification Act 1986).

Money laundering

2.14　Money laundering is a process by which criminals attempt to conceal the true origin and ownership of the proceeds of criminal activity. In UK law (Proceeds of Crime Act 2002, Money Laundering Regulations 2007), it is an offence to obtain, conceal or invest funds or property, if you know or suspect that they are the proceeds of criminal conduct or terrorist funding ('criminal property'). This includes the proceeds of tax evasion, benefits obtained through bribery and corruption, and benefits (eg saved costs) arising from a failure to comply with a regulatory requirement (such as health and safety provisions).

2.15　All businesses are required to adopt specific measures to identify and prevent money laundering and terrorist financing, including:

- Implementing due diligence (eg in customer acceptance), record-keeping and internal suspicion-reporting measures (including the appointment of a Money Laundering Reporting Officer)
- Not doing or disclosing anything that might prejudice an investigation into such activities (eg 'tipping off' the subjects of an investigation)
- Disclosing any knowledge or suspicion of money laundering activity (based on reasonable grounds) to the appropriate authorities (the National Crime Agency: NCA). This duty obtains, regardless of any confidentiality agreements or professional duties of confidentiality that may be in place.

Other ethical issues in procurement and supply chain management

2.16　A range of broader ethical issues may be raised by day-to-day procurement and supplier relationship management. Some of the key ethical issues typically provided for in codes of ethical conduct for procurement professionals include the following.

- The provision of fair, truthful and accurate (not false or misleading) information. This makes unethical, for example, the practice of deliberately inflating estimates of future order sizes in order to obtain a price that would not be offered if the true usage patterns were admitted.
- The confidentiality of information, where appropriate. Confidential information obtained in the course

of business should not be disclosed without proper and specific authority, or unless there is a legal duty to disclose it: for example, if there is suspicion of money laundering or terrorist activity.

- Fair dealing with supply chain partners. A temptation may be offered, for example, where a supplier makes an exploitable error in a quotation or invoice; where there is potential to delay or dispute an agreed payment; where quotations are sought from suppliers where there is no intention to purchase; or where some vendors are favoured over others in a tender situation. Deception or unfairness in such situations may be perceived as unethical and potentially damaging to ongoing trading relationships.

3 Regulating ethical behaviour

Internal controls

3.1 It may be argued that measures for the detection and prevention of fraud risk are particularly important in procurement and supply chain management, because individuals responsible for developing and managing commercial contracts and relationships:

- Operate in a 'stewardship' role, responsible for the custodianship of finance and assets which are owned by shareholders of the business
- Potentially control very large sums of organisational funds
- Are faced by many opportunities to commit financial fraud or to misuse systems, power or information for personal gain
- Are in a position of trust within a business
- Are responsible for the standing, credibility and reputation of the organisation in its dealings with supply chain partners and other stakeholders.

3.2 Mechanisms supportive of good **governance in procurement**, and specifically the prevention of fraud and corruption, include the following.

- A strong internal control environment designed to support business objectives and manage identified areas of risk: robust internal policies, checks and control mechanisms
- The development and application of codes of ethical conduct in procurement activities
- The effective budgeting, control and monitoring of procurement spend across the organisation
- Clearly defined roles, responsibilities, accountabilities and reporting structures for procurement
- Controls over the authority levels of individual buyers
- Clear requirements for approvals and authorisations of requisitions, procurements and payments
- Rigorous checking of purchasing card statements, invoices and other proofs of purchases, deliveries and payments
- The requirement of clear audit trails or 'paper trails' to enable the tracking of procurement decisions.
- The segregation or division of procurement duties (so that, for example, the same person is *not* responsible for authorising and making payments, which might enable falsification of transactions)
- Rotation of project buyers, to avoid any particular buyer becoming too 'cosy' with any particular supplier
- Mandatory use of holiday allowances (allowing time for fraud to come to light, in the employee's absence)
- Controls over preferred supplier lists and single-sourcing deals, to ensure that they are in the best interest of the organisation
- The use of e-procurement tools to minimise cash transactions; to minimise human potentially fraudulent intervention in procedures; and to automatically highlight discrepant (non-matching) data
- The use of physical security measures (such as safes, password protection and controlled access to facilities) to protect assets, cash and data
- The effective vetting, selection, supervision and development of staff in positions of responsibility (and suppliers)
- The use of standard terms and conditions of contract

- Internal audit of procurement processes, decisions and controls, including accounting checks and reconciliations, and periodic procurement audits.
- Encouraging suppliers and employees to report ethical breaches ('whistleblowing') without fear of reprisal
- Establishing an ethics forum or committee to discuss conflicts of interest and ethical issues arising in the course of work. Open communication is the cornerstone of an 'integrity based' approach to ethics management.

The use of ethical codes

3.3   A common first step in large business organisations is to prepare written standards of conduct to which staff are expected to adhere. These will apply not just to procurement staff, but to others in the business who may be subject to temptation or influence to behave unethically. Such written policies play an important role in raising and maintaining standards, and supporting fair disciplinary action where they are breached.

3.4   To ensure that the written policies are followed in practice, managers should ensure that they are published widely and reinforced through staff appraisal, development and training (including continuing professional development, where relevant). Performance should be monitored systematically: many buying organisations give their suppliers access to the standards, enlisting their help in identifying potential abuses. Above all, managers should foster (by example) an ethos where ethical behaviour is regarded as a positive, and key, organisational value, with zero tolerance for abuses – and open forums for discussing ethical issues of concern to staff.

3.5   National and international bodies representing procurement professionals have published ethical codes setting out (usually in fairly broad terms) what moral principles or values are used to steer conduct, and what activities are considered unethical.

3.6   The **CIPS Code of Conduct** is the ethical standard and disciplinary framework (the basis of best conduct) for procurement professionals in the area of procurement ethics. The code makes it clear that members' conduct will be judged against the code and any breach may lead to disciplinary action by CIPS.

3.7   The guidance emphasises the principle that members should maintain the highest standard of integrity in business relationships, and should not use a position of authority for financial gain. Equally, members have a responsibility to enhance and protect the standing (dignity and reputation) of the procurement profession and the Institute, by their conduct both inside and outside their employing organisations.

3.8   Specific guidance is also offered in the following areas.

- Members must disclose any personal interest which might affect their impartiality in decision-making, or which might appear to do so in the eyes of others.
- Members must never breach the confidentiality of information received in a professional capacity. The information they provide should be accurate and not misleading.
- Members should avoid any arrangements which might prevent genuine, fair and transparent competition.
- Except for nominal value items sanctioned by the employer, gifts should not be accepted.
- Members should not allow offers of hospitality to influence a business decision, or to appear to do so.

(You should download the CIPS Code of Conduct from the CIPS website, if you have not already done so as part of your studies or work.)

Whistle blowing

3.9   One of the most important tools for risk management is to support the reporting by employees and other stakeholders of illegal, unethical or hazardous practices which the perpetrators, or other vested interests, are deliberately attempting to ignore or conceal.

3.10   Social and organisation cultures are generally *not* supportive of disclosure (especially negative reporting on the behaviour of others) and there is a strong reluctance to be the bearer of negative reports (due to the common response of 'shooting the messenger'). However, recent legislation has been enacted to legitimise and mandate 'whistleblowing' in support of corporate governance, prevention of fraud and money laundering, and protection of health and safety, among other risk management issues.

3.11   In the UK, the Public Interest Disclosure Act 1998 protects employees from dismissal for disclosing otherwise confidential information internally, or to an appropriate regulator, if they do so in good faith and have reasonable grounds to believe:

- That a criminal offence has been committed, is being committed or is likely to be committed
- That the health or safety of any individual has been, is being or is likely to be endangered
- That the environment has been, is being or is likely to be damaged and/or
- That information on any of the above has been, is being or is likely to be deliberately concealed.

3.12   More generally, the corporate culture should support and reward transparency in regard to the disclosure and reporting of (a) newly identified risks, (b) escalating risks and/or (c) risk-taking behaviours which contravene the organisation's policies, procedures or defined risk appetite.

3.13   The importance of this was highlighted during investigations into an incident surrounding foreign exchange losses at a major Australian bank. It transpired that these losses had grown over a two-year period – to some $360,000 by the time they were announced in January 2004. According to the audit report, one of the reasons why these losses continued undetected for so long was that the issue was never escalated to the board and its committees: the bad news was suppressed by trading teams. Similar incidents have been widely reported in recent years.

4   Corporate governance

4.1   The term 'corporate governance' refers broadly to the rules, policies, processes and organisational structures by which organisations are operated, controlled and regulated, to ensure that they adhere to accepted ethical standards, good practices, law and regulation. The Cadbury Report defined it as 'the system by which organisations are directed and controlled' in the light of business ethics and responsibility to stakeholders.

4.2   The CIPS Practice Guide on CSR highlights the fact that: 'Good corporate governance – in essence, the integrity with which a company is managed – is a central component of a robust CSR management programme.'

4.3   Governance principles, structures and processes may be defined by the shareholders or constitution of the organisation (as, for example, in the Articles of Association by which a business is incorporated) or by the managers of the organisation (as, for example, in the policies, procedures and codes of conduct developed for various aspects of activity).

4.4   They may also be defined by external forces such as government policy, law and regulation; professional bodies (such as CIPS) which develop ethical codes and best practice frameworks; national or international standard-setting bodies (such as the International Standards Organisation); or membership of voluntary associations and initiatives (such as the Ethical Trading Initiative or International Labour Organisation).

4.5 In a more specific sense, 'corporate governance' refers to the system by which private sector organisations are directed and controlled in order to protect the interests of shareholders. Corporate governance issues came to public attention in the 1990s, with high profile corporate scandals and collapses including Polly Peck International, Enron, WorldCom and Barings Bank. In particular, concerns were expressed by investors about the power of directors, and the transparency and truthfulness of financial reporting: broadly, issues of **corporate accountability** to shareholders and other key stakeholders.

4.6 Various risks and problems were identified in organisational governance.

- Domination by a single senior executive, with weak oversight by the board of directors (failing to meet regularly, failing to monitor executive management, losing control over the company)
- Lack of adequate control functions, internal audit and/or technical knowledge in key roles (eg in the audit committee or senior compliance positions)
- Lack of independent scrutiny by external auditors
- Lack of internal controls such as supervision and segregation of key roles, enabling employees to create large losses through incompetence, negligence or fraud.
- Directors being out of touch with the views and interests of shareholders and other key stakeholders
- Directors' interests being out of alignment with the company's strategic objectives – with lack of accountability to stakeholders (eg in regard to directors' remuneration)
- Poor quality information from directors to stakeholders – including misleading information in financial statements.

The corporate governance framework

4.7 In the UK:

- The **Cadbury Report** made recommendations and created a Code of Best Practice, based on openness, integrity and accountability, in a number of areas, including: the role of the board of directors; division of responsibilities at the head of a company; the role of independent non-executive directors; and the remuneration of executive directors.
- The **Greenbury Report** considered the issue of rewarding executive directors, and made recommendations to improve transparency and performance, including: a remuneration committee of non-executive directors; reporting on the remuneration policy in the annual accounts; and performance-related incentive schemes which balance the interests of directors and shareholders.
- The **Hempel Report** reinforced the role of non-executive directors, the remuneration committee and the audit committee; recommended that companies communicate with institutional shareholders; and strengthened the voting rights of private shareholders at the annual general meeting.
- The recommendations of the three reports were merged into what was then called the **Combined Code** in 1998, with which companies listed on the London Stock Exchange were required to comply.
- The **Turnbull Report** (1999, revised 2005) focused on internal controls and risk management.

The UK Corporate Governance Code

4.8 In addition to detailed provisions on the role of directors, directors' remuneration and relations with shareholders, the Financial Reporting Council's UK Corporate Governance Code, updated in 2014, now contains the following principles for corporate accountability and audit.

- Financial reporting: the board of directors should present a fair, balanced and understandable assessment of the company's position and prospects in the annual accounts, and other reports (eg interim reports and reports to regulators)
- Risk management and internal control: the board must determine the nature and extent of the principal risks it is willing to take in achieving its strategic objectives. It should maintain sound risk management and internal control systems, and confirm this to shareholders in the annual report. It should also carry out a robust assessment of the principal risks facing the company, including

those that would threaten its business model, future performance, solvency or liquidity. As well as describing these risks, the directors should explain in the annual report how they are being managed or mitigated. The board should also report that it is monitoring the company's risk management and internal control systems and that it has, at least annually, conducted a review of the effectiveness of those systems.

- Audit: there should be formal and clear arrangements with the company's auditors, for applying the financial reporting and internal control principles. Companies should have an Audit Committee of non-executive directors, the majority of whom are independent, to review the audit and the independence and objectivity of the auditors.
- Compliance: companies must include in their accounts a statement of how they have applied the code's principles, enabling shareholders to assess how effectively they have been applied. Companies that did not comply fully, throughout the accounting period, must specify any provisions with which they did not comply, and give reasons for non-compliance.

FRC guidance on risk management

4.9   The Financial Reporting Council (FRC) publishes a document on risk management entitled *Guidance on risk management, internal control and related financial and business reporting* (formerly known as the *Turnbull Guidance*). It defines a risk management and internal control system as:

'A system encompassing the policies, culture, organisation, behaviours, processes, systems and other aspects of a company that, taken together:

- facilitate its effective and efficient operation by enabling it to: assess current and emerging risks; respond appropriately to risks and significant control failures; safeguard its assets
- help to reduce the likelihood and impact of: poor judgement in decision-making; risk-taking that exceeds the levels agreed by the board; human error; or control processes being deliberately circumvented
- help ensure the quality of internal and external reporting
- help ensure compliance with applicable laws and regulations, and with internal policies with respect to the conduct of business.'

4.10   The guidance makes clear that a sound internal control system aims to prevent the risks facing the business from actually occurring and causing the business harm. The company should therefore take a risk-based approach to determining whether the internal control system is sound, including considering:

- the nature and extent of risks facing the company
- the likelihood of the risks concerned materialising
- the company's ability to reduce the likelihood of the risks arising, and of the impact on the business of risks that do materialise.

4.11   The guidance also clarifies that, while managers are responsible for implementing internal controls and for day-to-day monitoring of the system, it is the board of directors as a whole which is responsible for:

- policy-making on an effective system of internal control in the company, covering financial, operational and compliance controls
- reviewing how effectively the internal control system addresses the risks that face the company
- reporting on the internal control system to shareholders each year.

The Sarbanes-Oxley Act

4.12   In the USA, a number of damaging corporate scandals (eg Enron and Worldcom) prompted legislation on financial and accounting disclosures, in the form of the Sarbanes-Oxley Act 2002 (SOX). The Act imposes provisions on all US public company boards, management and public accounting firms – but it also carries weight outside the USA as a model code in this area.

4.13 SOX contains extensive requirements aimed at preventing conflicts of interest, assuring the integrity of internal controls, and enhancing transparency in regard to corporate financial matters.

- Internal controls must assure that any information material to financial performance is made known to the CEO and CFO, who must in turn certify to investors that the controls meet statutory criteria and that the financial reports fairly represent the company's position. An independent auditor approved by an audit committee of independent directors must attest to these statements.
- The audit committee is also required to oversee controls, and establish financial risk management and assessment policies (including sustainability-related risks), in order to protect economic performance and sustainability.

4.14 The CIPS Knowledge Works document *Sarbanes-Oxley Act 2002* argues that SOX may affect procurement professionals dealing with US suppliers or subsidiaries, or seconded to US jurisdictions, or associated with non-US companies who are listed on US markets such as the New York Stock Exchange or NASDAQ. The document draws purchasers' attention to:

- Section 401 concerning periodic disclosure of all transactions, arrangements, obligations and relationships which may affect financial conditions, revenues or expenses
- Section 404, which requires annual reports to state the responsibility of management for establishing and maintaining an adequate internal control structure and procedures for financial reporting, and to contain an assessment of their effectiveness.

Chapter summary

- Fraud raises financial, compliance and reputational risks. It usually involves either the removal of funds or other assets, or intentional misrepresentation of the financial position of the business.
- Corruption implies any kind of intentional wrong-doing. Bribery is an attempt to induce corrupt behaviour by means of a financial benefit. In many countries this is illegal.
- Ethical behaviour may be promoted by internal controls and effective governance. In many countries, this is supported by legislative support for 'whistle blowers'.
- Effective corporate governance is strongly supported by CIPS guidelines. The framework for corporate governance in the UK is the UK Corporate Governance Code, applying to companies whose shares are listed on the London Stock Exchange.

Self-test questions

Numbers in brackets refer to the paragraphs where you can check your answers.

1   According to Sadgrove, what are the four pre-conditions for fraud to be committed? (1.5)

2   Distinguish between embezzlement and theft. (1.8)

3   What is meant by a conflict of interest? (2.6)

4   List areas typically covered by ethical codes for procurement and supply professionals. (2.16)

5   List mechanisms supportive of good governance in procurement. (3.2)

6   List areas covered by the CIPS Code of Conduct. (3.8)

7   What is meant by 'corporate governance'? (4.1)

8   Summarise the requirements of the Sarbanes-Oxley Act. (4.13)

CHAPTER 5

Operational Risks

Assessment criteria and indicative content

 Analyse the main operational risks in supply chains

- Contract failure
- Financial risks such as currency, supplier cashflow and insolvency
- Quality failure
- Security of supply
- Technology
- Logistics complexity
- Risks in outsourcing and offshoring

Section headings

1 Contract failure
2 Financial risks
3 Quality failure
4 Supply security
5 Outsourcing and offshoring risk
6 Technology and information risk

Introduction

In this chapter we continue our discussion of the main risk categories affecting supply chains.

'Operational risk' is a very broad category. Fortunately, the syllabus gives specific guidance, in its indicative content, as to what CIPS considers the 'main' operational risks in supply chains. We address each of the identified risk categories in turn.

Obviously, we aren't able to be exhaustive in identifying specific risks within each category, nor in discussing potential strategies for their mitigation. This is an area in which you will need to apply the *principles* and *processes* learned in Chapters 1–3 to any *specific risks* that may be featured in an exam question or case study. You should cultivate your awareness of supply chain risks, and mitigation measures used in practice by real organisations, through your further reading in *Supply Management* and the quality press.

One key risk category which, perhaps surprisingly, does not appear in the syllabus at this point, is **health and safety** risk. Issues of health and safety are covered, as the syllabus locates them, as part of project management, in Chapter 10.

1 Contract failure

1.1 Contract management is, essentially, a form of risk management. It is designed to minimise the risk of loss or damage to the organisation and its owners as a result of **contract non-performance** (or **contract failure**) – and the risk of the organisation having to curtail or cease its activities owing to supply failure or disruption, lack of resources or breakdown in supplier relationships.

Contract failure risk

1.2 Risks of contract failure arise from suppliers' reliability and performance – *and/or* from the buyer's contract, project and supplier management policies and practices. They refer to risks arising in the performance of a contract (or project) which:

- Jeopardise its successful performance (eg causing cost blow-outs, schedule delays or breaches of contract) or
- Create other risks for the organisation and supply chain (eg poor cost management, or buyer non-payment, leading to supplier failure; or poor ethical conduct by the supplier leading to reputational damage for the buyer).

1.3 Contract failure risks include factors such as:

- The capacity and capability of prospective suppliers and/or contracted vendors
- The percentage of supplier capacity utilised by the current contract and other customers (vulnerability to being over-stretched)
- The likelihood of unanticipated demand (over-stretching capacity)
- Supplier lead times for delivery and whether there is any 'slack time' or flexibility in the schedule
- Supply risks affecting the supply chain or individual suppliers, and the effectiveness of risk management and contingency planning
- The accuracy and clarity of specifications, contract terms and buyer expectations
- Vulnerabilities in supply chain quality assurance (especially if tolerances are tight)
- Accuracy of scheduling and forecasting
- The quality, reliability and transparency of data shared between contract participants and stakeholders (supporting risk-managed decision-making)
- Cost management; internal and external factors impacting on costs; and what price arrangements have been agreed (eg cost-plus or fixed-price contracts)
- Project and contract management effectiveness, to monitor and manage all these elements!

Legal risk

1.4 Legal, contract and related compliance risks may arise from factors such as the following.

- **Poor contract development and contracting processes**: ambiguous terms, lack of adequate protections for contractual risks (ensuring that remedies are available); unenforceable terms (eg unlawful or unreasonable limitation of liability; penalty clauses instead of valid liquidated damages clauses); lack of supporting documentation (eg specifications, KPIs or service level agreements) to specify performance expectations; lack of supplier incentives to promote committed performance; lack of provision for dispute resolution, contract termination, transfer and so on.
- **Unmanaged battle of the forms**, so that there is ambiguity about which set of standard terms (supplier's or buyer's) governs the contract, or the set of standard terms used unfairly disadvantages one party
- **Poor contract administration and change control**, eg: unauthorised or uncontrolled changes to contract; lack of version control; or lack of communication of contract changes to relevant stakeholders.
- **Lack of adequate protection of intellectual property**, assigning and protecting rights of ownership

(and licence for usage) of documents, drawings, computer software and work specifically prepared or developed in performance of the contract, or used in the performance of the contract. Protections may be secured within the contract (using IP clauses), as well as statutory provisions (such as registration of designs, patents, trademarks and copyright).

- **Issues of liability** for losses from problems such as injury, economic loss, damage to property or legal claims arising from performance of the contract – and whether these are effectively shared with, or assigned to, the supplier.
- **Costs and relational damage arising from commercial or contractual disputes** with suppliers. According to a research study *(reported in *Supply Management,* 18 October 2007)*, only 12% of risk management policies have detailed information on how to resolve conflict. Meanwhile, commercial disputes cost businesses £33 billion per year.

Negotiation risks

1.5 Negotiations with suppliers have traditionally been carried out by means of a competitive win-lose approach. There is an inherent risk that, even if the buyer is successful in 'winning' the negotiation (obtaining the immediate, task-based price or deal improvement objective), the process could damage the supplier's commitment, the buyer's status or reputation as a good customer, and the long-term buyer-supplier relationship – all of which could lead to damaging consequences at a later date.

1.6 Other risks which might be identified as inherent in the negotiation process can be summarised as follows.

- The risk of 'losing out' from the negotiation, if a zero-sum or 'win-lose' approach is used
- The risk that unacceptable or unfeasible concessions will be made, which will cause economic loss, conflict and other negative impacts if followed through
- The risk of reaching an impasse: not being able to reach a solution or agreement that is acceptable to both parties – and therefore wasting negotiation time and cost without ratifying or implementing an agreement
- Adversarial relations with the other party, if the negotiations have been win-lose in style: this may have critical secondary risks (eg if key suppliers or employees are alienated or resentful, and co-operation is damaged)
- Conflict or divergent tactics within a negotiating team undermining the bargaining position (and/or the acceptability of the result to internal stakeholders)
- Ethical and reputational risk: eg if negotiating power is used for personal gain, or there is breach of confidentiality during or following negotiations
- Compliance risk: eg if statutory procedures are not complied with.

1.7 The following are some measures to control and mitigate these risks.

- Detailed pre-negotiation research (eg supplier appraisal, price research)
- Careful position planning: establishing the 'range of negotiation' between best possible and worst acceptable outcomes, and having a prepared walk-away position (resistance point) and BATNA (best alternative to a negotiated agreement).
- Making provision for third party mediation or arbitration, where negotiation is insufficient to resolve a deadlock
- The segmentation of supply relationships, in order to select appropriate negotiating approaches and styles: for example, a more integrative, problem-solving approach for suppliers of strategic or critical items
- Rehearsals of negotiation tactics (especially by negotiating teams)
- Ethical policies and awareness programmes, supporting ethical negotiation
- Pre- and post-negotiation stakeholder communication, in order to minimise the risk of failure to accept and ratify the resulting agreement
- Evaluation, reporting and learning from negotiations, to improve performance next time.

Risks in particular types of contract

1.8 It should be obvious that particular types of contract carry their own particular risks. Fixed-price contracts, for example, may minimise the risk to the buyer of liability for cost blow-outs – but at the same time, they present secondary risks such as supplier corner-cutting (to absorb cost rises), supplier de-motivation, and supplier financial instability.

1.9 Be alert to the potential areas of risk in any contract type or structure you come across in your wider procurement studies – and in exam case studies. We will be discussing a range of contractual *remedies* for supply-related risks in Chapter 11.

1.10 We will also highlight the risks of particular contract arrangements – in the sense of supplier relationships such as outsourcing or single sourcing – a bit later in this chapter.

2   Financial risks

2.1 Financial risks may be *internal,* arising from the organisation's own financial structures and transactions. Here are some examples.

- Lack of price or cost analysis in setting or negotiating prices for a contract
- Lack of budgetary and cost control and management through the life of the contract, leading to cost blow-outs and lost profits
- Poorly designed or implemented financial controls and procurement or payment procedures, leading to the risk of financial fraud
- Financial penalties incurred as a result of poor contracting, or contract non-compliance (eg interest on late payments to suppliers)
- High capital investment in a contract or project, accompanied by inadequate investment appraisal, lack of whole-life costing, or high costs of loan finance
- Lack of liquidity: lack of provision (through cashflow and asset management) to have adequate cash (or assets such as stock and debtors which can be quickly converted to cash) available to cover short-term liabilities
- A poor credit rating, based on credit performance and financial strength, making it difficult or costly to obtain credit and/or loan finance.

2.2 Financial risks may also be *external,* resulting from factors such as:

- Macro-economic factors, such as: business cycles (eg economic recession, creating low demand, poor credit availability, supplier instability); fluctuating commodities prices; availability and costs of finance (interest rates); and fluctuating exchange rates (in international transactions)
- The financial strength, stability and general 'health' of suppliers: the risk of their suffering credit problems (limiting their access to short- or long-term finance to cover their liabilities or invest in development) or cashflow problems (affecting their ability to maintain operations and supply, by paying their own employees and suppliers); and – most critically – the risk of supplier insolvency and failure.

Currency and exchange risk

2.3 One of the key considerations in international sourcing is the need to manage risks arising from exchange rates: that is, the price of one currency (say, pounds sterling or euros) expressed in terms of another currency (say, US dollars). Exchange rates are important for firms in international supply markets. As an example, consider a UK company with extensive importing activities.

2.4 *Importers* want the value of their domestic currency to be as *high* as possible. If the value of sterling is strong or rising against a foreign currency, UK purchasers can acquire more of that currency to pay their foreign suppliers: imports will be cheaper in domestic terms. If sterling weakens, purchasers' ability to acquire overseas currency is reduced, and imports are more expensive in domestic terms. This is the major consideration for international purchasers.

2.5 It is worth noting that for *exporters*, the position is reversed. They want the value of their domestic currency to be as *low* as possible. If the value of sterling is low against a foreign currency, overseas purchasers will be able to buy more pounds to pay for UK goods: UK exports will be more affordable and attractive to overseas purchasers. If the value of sterling is high, UK goods will be more expensive to foreign buyers, and UK suppliers will find it harder to compete with other international suppliers (with weaker currencies).

2.6 Firms producing goods for the domestic market *in competition with foreign imports* similarly want the value of sterling to be *low*, as this makes imports more expensive in domestic terms, favouring domestic suppliers. If sterling rises, imports will be more competitive.

2.7 *Fluctuations in foreign exchange rates* therefore represent a source of financial risk for purchasing organisations. An overseas supplier will normally quote a price in its own currency, and the buyer will need to purchase currency in order to make payment. If sterling weakens between the time when the price is agreed and the purchase of the currency, the buyer will end up paying more. The risk is even greater if staged payments are to be made.

2.8 There are a number of ways of managing exchange rate risk.

- The purchaser might be able to transfer the risk to the suppliers, by getting them to quote prices in sterling. (This might be a tough negotiation, unless the purchaser has strong power in the relationship, or can offer concessions in exchange.)
- If fluctuations are not extreme, it may be possible to estimate the rate that will apply at the time of payment, and negotiate prices accordingly (perhaps with a contract proviso that prices will be *re*-negotiated if the exchange rate fluctuates by a stated percentage or reaches a stated rate).
- It may be possible to agree to pay for the goods at the time of contract (ie at today's known exchange rate), without waiting for later delivery. This is an example of a technique called 'leading' (making payment in advance of the due date to take advantage of a positive exchange rate): note, however, that it creates an additional risk for the buyer. A similar technique is 'lagging' (making a payment later than the due date, to take advantage of exchange rate improvements): again, note that this is at the expense of the supplier, and raises ethical, reputational and relationship risks.
- Another approach would be to use one of the available tools of currency management, such as a forward exchange contract, which enable the importer to 'hedge' the risk. Under this arrangement, the organisation contracts *now* to purchase the overseas currency at a *stated future date*, at a rate of exchange *agreed now*. For example, the importer might enter a forward exchange contract on Day 1, agreeing to purchase $1m on Day 60 in order to pay its US supplier. The cost of the US dollars will be fixed by the bank on Day 1, the rate being determined by market conditions and expectations of future exchange rate movements. There is a cost to doing this, but for the buyer, the uncertainty is removed: it knows on Day 1 exactly how much its purchase will cost.
- If exchange rate risks are severe, a purchaser may have to consider temporarily sourcing from the domestic market, from a single currency market such as the EU, or from other markets with less volatile currencies.

Credit risk

2.9 Credit risk is the risk that a customer will be unwilling or unable to pay amounts that it owes to a supplying organisation, disrupting the creditor's planned cashflow. This can be a high-impact risk if it concerns a major customer and/or a large amount, and if the supplying firm relies on the cashflow.

2.10   Here are some of the mitigating measures for credit risk.

- Due diligence: the process of gathering information prior to entering into a contract, in order to identify risks which would render it undesirable. In this case, due diligence might involve customer screening and the collection of credit reports or references prior to entering into agreements.
- Credit limits set and enforced (eg by the order processing and invoicing systems, and order authorisations)
- Credit control procedures: reporting on 'aged' and overdue debtors, chasing payment (debt collection) and applying contractual penalties (interest on late payment, withholding of further deliveries in pursuit of settlement and so on)

Supplier financial instability

2.11   The risks of a supplier encountering financial difficulty – particularly suppliers of critical items or strategic supply partners – is a major focus of contract and supplier management. A variety of tools is available for monitoring and assessing the financial stability and strength of prospective suppliers and existing vendors (in order to minimise the risk of their unexpectedly going bust and disrupting supply).

2.12   Financial information about suppliers can be obtained from various sources.

- Their published financial statements and accounts: balance sheet, profit and loss account and cashflow statements
- Secondary data on markets and suppliers: for example, analysis of financial statements and results in the business or trade press (and their websites); or published or bespoke financial reports by research agencies such as Dun & Bradstreet or DataMonitor
- Credit rating companies, which, for a fee, will provide information on the credit status of a supplier
- Networking with other buyers who use the same suppliers
- Inviting the supplier's financial director to make a presentation on its current and predicted financial position to procurement and finance managers. This may only be worth doing for major or strategic suppliers – and a prospective (or current) strategic supplier should not decline the invitation!

2.13   Examples of the kind of thing a sourcing or contract manager might be looking for, as part of due diligence in supplier appraisal, include signs that a supplier:

- Is not making much profit, is experiencing falling profit margins, or is making a loss, which suggests that it is operating inefficiently (revenue is too low or costs are too high) – and that it may run out of finance to continue or develop the business
- Is not managing its cashflow (the balance and timing of cash coming in and going out), or is experiencing a strong cash 'drain' from the business, making it difficult to meet its short-term debts and expenses
- Has more loan capital (borrowed from lenders) than share capital (invested by owners), incurring high finance costs (interest payments) and the obligation to repay the loan – a particular risk in periods of 'credit crunch'.

2.14   A number of models have been developed to assess the likelihood of supplier insolvency. Sadgrove *(Complete Guide to Business Risk Management)* cites as an example the Springate model. Gordon Springate identifies four important financial criteria.

A   The ratio of working capital to total assets. Ideally, this ratio should be high, meaning that a good proportion of the supplier's assets are in liquid form, rather than being tied up in the form of fixed assets (premises, machinery etc)

B   The ratio of net profit before interest and taxes to total assets. Ideally, this ratio should be high, meaning that the supplier makes a healthy profit from the assets it employs in the business

C   The ratio of net profit before taxes to current liabilities. Ideally, this ratio should be high, meaning that the supplier is making sufficient profits to enable payment of its creditors

D   The ratio of sales to total assets. Ideally, this ratio should be high, meaning that the supplier's assets are working hard to generate sales output.

2.15   Springate attaches weights to each of these ratios, and derives a Z-score (indicating financial strength and stability), using the following formula.

$$Z = 1.03A + 3.07B + 0.66C + 0.4D$$

A low Z-score indicates a risk of supplier insolvency. 'Where Z is less than 0.862, a firm is classified as failed' (Sadgrove). Dun & Bradstreet and similar credit agencies offer a financial appraisal service based on analysis of statistics such as these, as discussed in Chapter 12 of this Course Book.

2.16   An article in *Supply Management* (6 February, 2006) identified the following additional signs of supplier financial difficulty (other than poor financial ratios or posted losses), which a contract or supplier manager is well placed to pick up on.

- Rapid deterioration in delivery and quality performance
- Senior managers leaving the business within a short period of time
- Changes in the auditors and bankers of the firm
- Adverse press reports
- Very slow responses to requests for information
- Problems in the supply chain (and/or changes in subcontractors)
- Chasing payment before it is due

2.17   Mitigating measures against supplier financial difficulty (cashflow problems or the risk of insolvency) include:

- Due diligence in regard to supplier financial stability and performance prior to contract award
- Monitoring of financial ratios and indicators over the life of the contract
- Setting financial benchmarks, with a contractual requirement to trigger early notification by the supplier if benchmark criteria are not met
- Monitoring and notification requirements for key contingent factors (such as labour disputes, political unrest or commodity and input cost rises)
- Prompt or early payment of supplier invoices (especially for SME suppliers, for whom cashflow may be an acute issue) – and encouraging first-tier suppliers to do the same with lower-tier suppliers (who are often SMEs)
- Assisting key suppliers with loans of finance or assets, staged payments, financial management advice or other supplier development measures.

Investment risk

2.18   The detail of this topic should be beyond the scope of this syllabus, but you may be aware from your other CIPS studies of the need for proactive appraisal of investments and major capital projects, to ascertain risks arising from net cashflows, return on investment and payback periods. Relevant techniques include: the payback method, discounted cashflow (DCF) techniques and accounting rate of return (ARR) method.

3   Quality failure

3.1   For a buying organisation looking to buy materials, components or other supplies in a commercial setting – and for a marketing organisation looking to satisfy the quality expectations of customers and consumers – the most important definitions of 'right quality' (and the most clear-cut from a risk management point of view) are likely to be:

- *Fitness for purpose or use*: that is, the extent to which a product does what it is designed and expected to do; or, more generally, the extent to which it meets the customer's needs. The British Standards Institution definition of quality is: 'the totality of features and characteristics of a product or service that bear on its ability to satisfy a given need.'

- *Conformance to requirement or specification*: that is, the product matches the features, attributes, performance and standards set out in the specification. Conformance therefore also implies lack of defects, and therefore reflects on the quality of the producer's processes.
- *Comparative excellence*: how favourably a product is measured against competitive benchmarks (other products), best practice or standards of excellence – which adds an element of marketing, brand and reputational risk.

3.2   It should be fairly obvious that most organisations will seek to maintain the quality of their offerings to their customers, in order to:

- Differentiate their products advantageously in relation to their competitors. The ability to offer consistently high quality may be an important source of competitive advantage for the organisation: managing strategic and marketing risk.
- Position their brands in the market as 'quality' brands, enhancing corporate reputation and branding (and therefore building in resilience in the face of reputational risks)
- Develop customer retention and loyalty (again, building resilience in the face of reputational, economic and marketing risks) and manage the downside risks of poor quality (lost customers, negative 'word of mouth' about the brand etc)
- Comply with law and regulation (eg in regard to the safety and satisfactory quality of goods) – minimising legal and compliance risks
- Avoid the financial and reputational costs of product recalls, returns and customer compensation, as a result of poor quality.

3.3   By extension, it is important for an organisation to manage the quality of its specifications, suppliers and supply chains – and therefore of its materials, components and supplies – in order to maintain the quality of its offering to customers. The quality of the *inputs* to an organisation's goods and services will naturally affect the quality of its *outputs*.

Costs of quality

3.4   The cost of quality has been defined as: 'The cost of ensuring and assuring quality, as well as the loss incurred when quality is not achieved'. In other words, quality-related costs include *both*:

- The cost of appraisal and prevention activities, designed to minimise poor quality products entering the production process and/or reaching the customer (in other words, the cost of preventive risk management) – *and*
- The cost of 'failure': losses incurred because of poor quality products entering the production process and/or reaching the customer (in other words, the cost of risk events).

3.5   **Appraisal costs** are the costs incurred as part of the inspection process, in order to ensure that incoming materials – and outgoing finished products – are of the right quality. Examples include: the cost of physical or machine inspection; managing inspection processes; supplier performance appraisal (or vendor rating); and quality audits (checking that the quality system is performing as intended).

3.6   **Prevention costs** are those incurred in order to *reduce* appraisal costs, by proactively preventing or reducing the likelihood of defects or failures produced by operational processes. Examples include: the time and cost of building quality into product and service designs and specifications; developing 'quality circles' (quality problem-solving groups) and other mechanisms for involving staff (and suppliers) in quality issues and improvements; setting up processes, systems, technology and training for quality assurance (defect prevention); and the costs of preparing for auditing and accreditation under international quality management standards such as ISO 9000.

3.7   These costs are obviously substantial. Would it not be more cost effective to spend less on preventive measures, and simply deal with a few defects now and then? Or will there not come a time when the benefits of improving quality (or reducing quality risk) 'that little bit more' will be outweighed by the costs of doing so? The answer generally given these days is: no. The costs of getting quality wrong may well be higher than the costs of getting it right – and the law of diminishing returns may not apply, because there will always be some benefit to improvement.

Costs of quality failure

3.8   The costs of quality failure can be divided into two categories: internal and external failure costs.

3.9   **Internal failure costs** are those that arise from quality failure, where the problem is identified and corrected *before* the finished product or service reaches the customer. Here are some examples.

- Loss or reworking of faulty items discovered during the production or inspection process
- Scrapping of defective products that cannot be repaired, used or sold
- Re-inspection of products that have been reworked or corrected
- 'Downgrading' of products (to lower quality grades) at lower prices, resulting in lost sales income
- Waste incurred in holding contingency stocks (to allow for scrapped work and delays), providing additional storage and duplicating work
- Time and cost of activities required to establish the causes of the failure (failure analysis)

3.10   **External failure costs** are those that arise from quality failure identified and corrected *after* the finished product or service reaches the customer. Here are some examples.

- Costs of 'reverse logistics' to collect and/or handle returned products
- Costs of repairing or replacing defective products (which may be returned by the customer, or require servicing at the customer's location), or re-doing of inadequate services
- The cost of customer claims for compensation under guarantees or warranties, or where the company is liable for negligence (if the customer has been injured or subjected to loss arising from defective goods or services). Quality is a key source of compliance risk, since consumer protection legislation (eg the UK's Consumer Protection Act 1987) imposes strict liability on manufacturers whose defective products cause damage or loss to consumers (regardless of whether negligence is involved).
- The administration costs of handling complaints, processing refunds and so on
- The cost of lost customer loyalty and future sales
- Reputational damage arising from word-of-mouth by dissatisfied customers, poor product reviews and/or publicity (eg about product recalls)

3.11   Since the costs of 'getting it wrong' are generally perceived as being higher (and further-reaching) than the costs of 'getting it right', there has generally been an increased emphasis on quality management, with the aim of 'getting it right first time'.

Approaches to managing quality failure risk

3.12   Techniques for managing quality risk generally fall into two basic categories or approaches: quality control (QC) and quality assurance (QA).

3.13   Systems for the detection and correction of defects are known as **quality control**. This is an essentially reactive approach, focusing on:

- Establishing specifications, standards and tolerances (parameters within which items can vary and still be considered acceptable) for work inputs and outputs
- Inspecting delivered goods and monitoring production processes, often on a 'sampling' basis (although '100% inspection' may be used on critical features, or where zero defects are required).
- Identifying items that are defective or do not meet specification
- Scrapping or re-working items that do not pass inspection – and passing acceptable items on to the next stage of the process.

3.14   You may already be able to see that a quality control approach, based on inspection, has certain limitations for risk management.

- A very large number of items must be inspected to prevent defective items from reaching production processes or end customers. W Edwards Deming argued that this ties up resources – and does not add value (or indeed 'improve' quality).
- Defective items may slip through without being spotted or even inspected, in unacceptable numbers, owing to budget and schedule pressures (especially if the buyer is operating a strategy of just in time supply).
- The process aims to identify and reject defective items once they have already been made. By this time, however, they may already have incurred significant – wasted – costs (of design, raw materials, processing, overheads and so on). You are 'locking the door after the horse has bolted'.
- Inspection activity tends to be duplicated at each stage of the supply process – magnifying the inefficiencies and wastes.

3.15   Systems for the proactive *prevention* of defects are known as **quality assurance**. This is a more proactive and integrated approach to quality risk management, building quality into every stage of the process from concept and specification onwards. It includes the full range of systematic activities used within a quality management system to 'assure' or give the organisation adequate confidence that items and processes will fulfil its quality requirements. In other words, quality assurance is a matter of 'building in quality' – not 'weeding out defects'.

3.16   From a procurement and supply chain management point of view, you are seeking to ensure that your buying processes, and your supply chain's quality management processes, work together to prevent defective products or materials ever being delivered. Quality assurance programmes may build quality measures and controls into:

- Product designs
- The drawing up of materials specifications and contracts
- The evaluation, selection, approval and certification of suppliers
- Communication with suppliers, feedback mechanisms and quality record-keeping
- Supplier training and development (where required to integrate the two organisations' quality standards and systems)
- Education, training, motivation and management of employees and suppliers to maintain required levels of performance.

All this would normally be in addition to inspection, sampling, testing and other quality-control techniques.

Quality management

3.17   The term quality management is given to the various processes used to ensure that quality inputs and outputs are secured: that products and services are fit for purpose and conform to specification; and that continuous quality improvements are obtained over time. Quality management thus includes both quality control and quality assurance.

3.18   A **quality management system** (QMS) can be defined as: 'A set of co-ordinated activities to direct and control an organisation in order to continually improve the effectiveness and efficiency of its performance'. The main purpose of a QMS is to define and manage processes for systematic quality assurance.

3.19   A QMS is designed to ensure that:

- An organisation's customers can have confidence in its ability reliably to deliver products and services which meet their needs and expectations
- The organisation's quality objectives are consistently and efficiently achieved, through improved process control and reduced wastage

- Staff competence, training and morale are enhanced, through clear expectations and process requirements
- Quality gains, once achieved, are maintained over time: learning and good practices do not 'slip' for lack of documentation, adoption and consistency.

3.20 There are several international standards for measuring and certifying quality management systems of various types, including the ISO 9000 standard. Organisations can use the framework to plan or evaluate their own QMS, or can seek third party assessment and accreditation.

Total quality management

3.21 The term total quality management (TQM) is used to refer to a radical approach to quality management, as a business philosophy. TQM is an orientation to quality in which quality values and aspirations are applied to the management of all resources and relationships within the firm – and throughout the supply chain – in order to seek continuous improvement and excellence in all aspects of performance.

3.22 Laurie Mullins (*Management and Organisational Behaviour*) synthesises various definitions of TQM as expressing: 'a way of life for an organisation as a whole, committed to total customer satisfaction through a continuous process of improvement, and the contribution and involvement of people'. From a supply chain management point of view, the provision of quality-risk-managed inputs is only one part of a total quality picture, which also embraces excellent supply chains; continuous collaborative improvement; cross-functional co-operation on quality; and so on.

Service quality risk

3.23 The management of service quality risk is recognised as a more complex process, owing to the intangibility and variability of service provision, and the subjective element of customer expectations and perceptions. Zeithaml, Parasuraman & Berry argue that the quality of a given service is the outcome of an evaluation process by which buyers compare what they expected to receive with what they perceive that they have actually received. The SERVQUAL model suggests that there are five distinct areas which might help buyers and suppliers to understand apparent *quality gaps* between expectation and delivery, which represent points of risk for quality management: Table 5.1.

Table 5.1 *SERVQUAL model of 'service gaps'*

GAP	EXPLANATION	RISK MITIGATION MEASURES
Gap between buyer and supplier perceptions of quality	The supplier's definition of quality may not be the same as the buyer's.	Buyer and supplier will need to work together to develop mutual understanding of the requirement, using service specifications and service level agreements.
Gap between concept and specification	Resource constraints or poor specification skills may mean that the buyer's needs or the supplier's service concept are not translated fully or accurately into service specifications.	Buyers will need to co-operate with users and suppliers to develop service specifications which accurately reflect their needs and expectations and the supplier's best capabilities.
Gap between specification and performance	Specifications and service level agreements do not translate into actual service levels (eg because of operational failures).	The buyer will have to pre-evaluate the supplier's capability and capacity to deliver (eg getting references from other customers; using 'pilot' programmes prior to contract etc.)
Gap between communication and performance	The supplier's communications may create inaccurate quality expectations.	Buyers will need to verify information provided by service providers.
Gap between buyer expectations and perceived service	What buyers or users perceive they have received may fall short of what they expected.	Buyers will need to manage user expectations and perceptions; and specify service performance against objective measures, where possible.

4 Supply security

Supply risk and security of supply

4.1 'Supply risk' is the risk associated with an organisation's suppliers being unable to supply, or supplying goods of inadequate quality. Securing supply is a basic function of the procurement and supply chain management function.

4.2 Supply risk may arise from a number of factors, including risk from supplier-side reliability and performance *and* risk from procurement-side policy and practice.

- Inadequate buyer-side processes for supplier evaluation, appraisal and selection processes (eg pre-qualification of suppliers for tender)
- Inadequate buyer-side and supplier-side processes for contract and performance management (eg poorly developed contract terms, KPIs, contract performance monitoring, supplier motivation and incentives, problem-solving and so on)
- Unanticipated levels of demand, exacerbated by poor demand forecasting and management, lack of data sharing and communication, lack of capacity assessment in supplier selection and so on
- Unanticipated materials shortages or price fluctuations due to environmental factors
- Unmanaged performance issues (such as quality problems or delivery delays)
- Excessively 'lean' supply chains, with little provision for buffer or safety stock to enable the supply chain to absorb disruptions or extra demands
- Inadequate provisions for the physical security of supplies and stocks (both in transit and in storage), leaving them open to the risk of piracy, hijacking, theft or pilferage; tampering, contamination or sabotage; damage and deterioration.
- Natural or human-caused disasters, such as flood, fire or explosion, affecting supplier plant or logistics services
- Market risks, such as industrial action, financial instability (eg cashflow problems) or business failures among suppliers
- Commodity risk, such as the impact of political instability on the price of oil or gas, or the growth in competing demand for commodities from emerging economies
- Transportation risk, including delays, disruption of transport routes due to weather, congestion or political instability
- Lack of lesson-learning and continuous improvement, as risks are identified.

4.3 Key supply risk factors therefore include: the capability, capacity and financial stability of current suppliers; lead times for delivery; the complexity and criticality of the procured item; supply market competition; the length and complexity of the supply chain; the length of product lifecycles (putting pressure on innovation); technological developments in the supply market; and physical security measures for goods in transit and in storage.

4.4 The workbook *Understanding Supply Chain Risk* (Cranfield School of Management/Department of Transport) identifies a series of generic questions that should be considered when looking at market-based supply risk.

- Is the supply chain dependent on dominant or specialist suppliers, where failure to supply could disrupt output?
- Are any suppliers, particularly critical suppliers, in potential financial difficulties that could interrupt output?
- Do any suppliers have extended lead times that potentially impact on inventory or customer service?
- Is there a record of poor quality from any suppliers, and are there risks that could arise as a result?
- Are there any suppliers who have poor schedule compliance, and if so, are they among the suppliers on whom we depend?

- What is the state of the supply market? Is our company taking a large slice of the supply? Are there any tight spots in the supply market that might disrupt output?
- Are there measures of performance in place with suppliers, providing a platform for a risk management and performance improvement programme?
- Do suppliers in the market have the capacity and capabilities to plan and fulfil demand? Are they using systematic, good-practice methods or working hand to mouth?

Logistics complexity

4.5 Supply chain networks continue to increase in complexity, as a result of factors such as globalisation, outsourcing and reliance on ICT infrastructures. The particular risks of international sourcing are covered in Chapter 11.

4.6 Global supply networks are increasingly complex and lengthy. The Cranfield School of Management (*Creating Resilient Supply Chains*) emphasises that 'supply chains are not simply linear chains or processes: they are complex networks'. The interdependence between organisations and their supply chains presents mutual risks: the buying organisation being at risk from failure within its supply chain; and the supply chain being at risk from a business or operational failure.

4.7 Moves to **lean thinking** in supply chain management have reduced wastes – but at the same time, reduced security by removing buffer or 'safety' stocks, rationalising supply chains and narrowing the margin of error (by creating the expectation of zero defects and reduced lead times). The optimisation of each part of the supply chain can result in sub-optimal performance by the end-to-end supply chain, because of potential for dis-integration and lack of flexibility (or 'agility') and resilience. As supply chains get leaner, with less buffer stock, and more inventory being held overseas or 'on the water', there is less ability for the supply chain to soak up and respond to any shocks that occur.

4.8 The effective delivery of supply chain management is increasingly dependent on the **ICT infrastructure** that underpins it. The management of knowledge and information is a key driver for supply chains, and an integrated approach is increasingly essential for supply chain visibility, supply tracking, demand management and just in time supply. The ICT-driven supply chain places a high degree of reliance on the integrity and consistency of data, and dependency breeds risk. If systems crash or data connections fail, the organisation may find itself in a vulnerable position (as discussed in Section 6 of this chapter). Contingency plans will need to be developed to ensure that information can still flow in the face of technology failure.

Resource scarcity

4.9 Resource scarcity was identified as one of the key present risks for global supply chains and business prospects, by the Control Risk Group's *RiskMap* report. 'The year 2008 saw huge volatility in the availability and price of many resources, ranging from food to power to shipping capacity, and CRG's thesis is that global demand will exceed supply from now on, creating inherent instability and risk... There are mounting concerns over water availability, infrastructure capacity and institutional integrity.'

4.10 According to Amon Cohen ('Global Warning'; *Supply Management):*

- Buying firms need to build up greater reserves. 'Just-in-time principles create many efficiencies, but from now on businesses will need to store more raw materials to anticipate disruptions to supply. This will lead to changes not only in strategies for procurement but also to management and logistics – not the least of which will be creating additional storage space.'
- There is an even greater need for business continuity planning, to mitigate the impact of supply disruption.
- In the longer term (and at a more strategic risk management level), scarcity could lead to a slowing or

reversal of the trend towards international sourcing. 'Local supply sources will be more reliable – or, at least, more verifiable – and far less prone to disruption.'

Security risks

4.11   In any business or supply chain, there are likely to be significant security risks to supplies and stocks (whether in storage or in transit), arising from factors such as: unauthorised access; tampering, sabotage or vandalism; theft, shoplifting (in retail settings) and pilferage; robberies, hold-ups and hijackings; and industrial espionage.

4.12   In addition, businesses are increasingly faced with security risks to personnel, especially in developing countries and politically unstable markets. These include robbery and hijacking, kidnap and ransom, politically-motivated kidnapping and murder, and the risk of personnel being caught up in civil or political unrest, war and terrorist activity. An identification and assessment template for security risks, suggested by Sadgrove, is shown in Figure 5.1.

Figure 5.1 *Identification and assessment template for security risks*

Risk	*Question*	✓
Buildings	Does the business have manufacturing or warehousing premises? Are the company's premises easily accessible to the public, or visited by many people?	☐ ☐
Information	Could your paperwork or computer data have commercial value to a competitor?	☐
Espionage	Does the business operate in markets subject to fashion or technological advance?	☐
Intellectual property	Does it have inventions, trade marks or well-known brand names?	☐
Attacks on premises	Does it employ large numbers of people?	☐
Tampering	Does the company sell fast-moving consumer goods (FMCG)?	☐
International	Do your executives travel to unstable developing countries? Does the company have assets in unstable developing countries?	☐ ☐
Review	Has the company failed to carry out a security review?	☐

Total points [score one point for each box ticked]:

[Score: 0–3 points: low risk. 4–6 points: moderate risk. 7–10 points: high risk.]

4.13   A range of security measures will be required: some on an ongoing basis, and some only occasionally (which presents an argument for outsourcing or contracting to third party service providers, as discussed in Chapter 12). You should be able to identify a range of basic security measures, including deterrent measures, observation and monitoring, physical barriers and warning systems or alarms. These may include:

*   Clear signage warning of security measures in place
*   Security fences, grilles, doors, locked storage areas, clear (and well lit) perimeter zones and so on – and protocols for ensuring that they are effectively utilised
*   The use of security guards stationed at (or patrolling) vulnerable areas
*   Identification cards, security codes and passes, reception security, sign-in protocols and other methods of ensuring that access is limited to authorised personnel
*   Security protocols supported by staff information and training (eg end-of-day procedures, pairing of staff when transporting cash, varying of cash transport routes, confidentiality policies) and technology (eg use of EPOS, CCTV monitoring, unauthorised entry alarms)
*   Protections against natural threats to premises (eg fire and flooding): prevention protocols and provisions (eg fire doors, alarms, sprinklers), warning systems, tested emergency response procedures
*   Reporting, recording and reviewing all security breaches and incidents, to assess ongoing vulnerabilities.

Supply chain relationship risks

4.14　A further key category of business and supply risk is the nature, structure and management of relationships with suppliers. Different risks attach to different types of relationship, sourcing approaches and supply chain configuration decisions. Here are some situations giving rise to particular risks.

- **Sole sourcing arrangements** (where there is only one supplier available in the supply market) and **single sourcing arrangements** (where the organisation chooses to use only one supplier for a given requirement) – because of the extent of the buyer's dependency on one supplier, and vulnerability to risks of supplier (and possibly therefore supply chain) failure, complacency or leverage.
- **Outsourcing arrangements** – because the organisation is effectively replacing its own assets, resources, knowledge and competencies with those of an external contractor, and perhaps rendering itself vulnerable to reputational, performance and marketing risk by having the contractor deliver services to customers on its behalf. There may also be risks related to loss of control, intellectual property and confidential data sharing. We will discuss this in more detail below.
- **Long-term partnership relations** – because the organisation is effectively 'locked in' to a long-term collaborative relationship with a partner who may turn out to be under-performing, incompatible, strategically divergent and/or complacent (in the absence of competition, or continuous improvement agreements). The potential value of partnership may not be realised – or may be lost as internal and external changes erode its rationale. Collaboration may itself pose risks to confidential data and/or intellectual property.
- **Supplier tiering** (an approach to structuring the supply chain whereby the buying organisation develops partnership relations with a few lead providers or 'first tier' suppliers, who take responsibility for managing the lower levels or tiers of the supply chain) – because of the 'distance' this causes between the buyer and lower tiers, in terms of performance and CSR monitoring and management. There may be insufficient supply chain transparency to enable the buyer to 'drill down' to lower levels – and it may not be able to rely on the supply chain management and quality or CSR assurance of the lead provider.
- **Supplier switching** or opportunistic buying. There may be a range of reasons for changing or switching suppliers, but doing so causes upheaval and cost (identified as 'switching costs') – especially where strong relationships have been established, and relationship-specific plans and investments made. Risks include: the new supplier failing to perform; process or systems incompatibility (eg if relationship-specific integration was made with the old supplier); cultural or inter-personal incompatibility (where patterns of understanding and behaviour developed in the old relationship); loss of knowledge (where collaborative processes with the old supplier were undocumented); learning curve and teething problems of the new supplier; exposure to new or unfamiliar supply risks; exposure of intellectual property and confidential data (without trust yet having been built up); and problems of adversarial handover from the old supplier to the new (accessing designs, documents, assets, work in progress and so on).

4.15　We will look in more detail at the risk of supply partnerships and outsourcing strategies, in the following section of this chapter.

General supply chain risk management

4.16　Supply chain risk management is 'the identification and management of risks within the supply chain, and risks external to it, through a co-ordinated approach among supply chain members to reduce supply chain vulnerability as a whole' (Cranfield University School of Management, *Supply Chain Vulnerability*). The ability to see from one end of the supply chain network to the other is important in this approach: **supply chain visibility** implies a clear view of upstream and downstream demand and supply, inventory, logistics and production issues that may impact the ability of the supply chain to deliver (and or to recover from risk events).

4.17 Supply chain risk management is ideally a proactive process, with managers assessing supply chain maps and market models on an ongoing basis. A proactive approach is directed toward three main goals.

- Constantly monitoring the supply chain for signals that predict problems
- Ensuring timely and precise decision making when problems arise
- Modelling what may happen, and making contingency plans for negative outcomes

4.18 Supply risk mitigation approaches include the following.

- **Supplier evaluation and selection**: careful supplier evaluation, pre-qualification and selection (in regard to technical capability, capacity, compatibility and so on); and ratio analysis and financial monitoring of suppliers (to ensure financial stability)
- **Supply chain management**: multiple or back-up sourcing; supplier monitoring, performance management (against defined KPIs) and contract management; supply chain information flows, risk visibility and collaborative demand management; contingency planning for supplier failure (and other supply risks); the application of technology for exception reporting (on schedule, cost and quality deviations); the development of agile (responsive) and resilient supply chains; and so on.
- **Demand and inventory management**: eg appropriate levels of buffer or safety stock to cover supply delays or disruptions
- **Logistics management**: eg transport risk assessment, insurances and contingency or back-up plans; appropriate packaging, storage, transport mode planning and other measures to ensure the security and integrity of supplies in transit
- **Contract development and management**: using contractual terms to transfer or share risk and liability with the supplier; the use of *force majeure* clauses to mitigate liability for events beyond either party's control; the use of intellectual property protection and confidentiality clauses; monitoring and management of contract performance; and so on.
- **Insurances** for a range of insurable risks

5 Outsourcing and offshoring risk

5.1 Outsourcing may be defined as the process whereby an organisation delegates major non-core activities or functions, under contract, to specialist external service providers, potentially on a long-term relational basis. Lisa Ellram & Arnold Maltz *(Outsourcing Supply Management)* define it as: 'the transfer of responsibility to a third party of activities which used to be performed internally'.

5.2 Organisations now routinely contract with specialist external suppliers to provide services such as cleaning, catering, security, facilities management, IT management, recruitment and training, accounting, legal, transport and distribution – and procurement.

5.3 Outsourcing has developed in part as a response to business risk. In the 1970s and early 1980s, companies looked to spread their business risk by diversifying into a number of different business areas through mergers and acquisitions. In very many cases, these diversification strategies were unsuccessful, as the acquiring organisations basically lacked the skills and knowledge to be effective in unfamiliar business areas. Many organisations subsequently reviewed their strategic focus and decided to concentrate on core activities – or 'stick to the knitting' (Peters & Waterman, *In Search of Excellence)*.

5.4 A parallel development has been the growing emphasis on outsourcing public service delivery in the public sector: the 'commissioning' or 'externalisation' by local authorities of services previously provided to the public by local authorities themselves (such as housing and roads construction, garbage removal, leisure and arts services, children's and youth services, health and aged care services, and so on), where external partners – especially in the private sector – have better resources or capabilities to meet community needs, and to bear financial risk.

Risks of outsourcing

5.5 Broadly speaking, some of the potential upside and downside risks of strategic outsourcing can be summarised as follows: Table 5.2.

Table 5.2 *Upside and downside risks of outsourcing*

ADVANTAGES/OPPORTUNITIES	DISADVANTAGES/RISKS
Supports organisational rationalisation and downsizing: reduction in the costs of staffing, space and facilities	Potentially higher cost of services (including contractor profit margin), contracting and management: need to compare with costs of in-house provision, and consider potential loss of cost control
Allows focused investment of managerial, staff and other resources on the organisation's core activities and competencies (those which are distinctive, value-adding and hard to imitate, and thus give competitive advantage)	Difficulty of ensuring service quality and consistency and corporate social responsibility (environmental and employment practices): difficulties and costs of monitoring (especially overseas)
Accesses and leverages the specialist expertise, technology and resources of contractors: adding more value than the organisation could achieve itself, for non-core activities	Potential loss of in-house expertise, knowledge, contacts or technologies in the service area, which may be required in future (eg if the service is in-housed again).
Access to economies of scale (and smoothing of demand fluctuations) since contractors may serve many customers	Potential loss of control over key areas of performance and risk (eg to reputation, if service or ethical issues arise): over-dependence on suppliers
Adds competitive performance incentives, where internal service providers may be complacent	Added distance from the customer or end-user, by having an intermediary service provider: may weaken external or internal customer communication and relationships, and weaken market knowledge
Leverages collaborative supply relationships, and can support synergies (2 + 2 = 5) from collaboration or partnership	Risks of 'lock in' to an incompatible or under-performing relationship: cultural or ethical incompatibility; relationship management difficulties; contractor inflexibility, conflict of interest, complacency or loss of client focus.
Cost certainty (negotiated contract price) for activities where demand and costs are uncertain or fluctuating: shared financial risks	Risks of loss of control over confidential data and intellectual property
	Ethical and employee relations issues of transfer or cessation of activities
	Potential risks, costs and difficulties of in-sourcing if the outsource arrangement fails

Outsource failure risk

5.6 Numerous surveys, together with anecdotal evidence, suggest that outsourcing projects often fail to deliver the expected benefits. Some of the possible reasons for this are listed below.

- The organisation fails to distinguish correctly between core and non-core activities.
- The organisation fails to identify and select a suitable supplier, leading to poor performance of the outsourced activity, or in the worst cases to supplier failure.
- The organisation has unrealistic expectations of the outsource provider, owing to exaggerated promises or claims in negotiation, or underestimation of the risks of costs (and potential for cost escalation).
- The outsourcing contract contains inadequate or inappropriate terms and conditions.
- The contract does not contain well defined key performance indicators or service levels, which means that it is difficult to establish where things are going wrong.
- The organisation lacks management skills to control supplier performance and relationships.
- The organisation gradually surrenders control of performance to the contractor, which is then able opportunistically to take advantage of the organisation's dependency.

5.7   Much of this can be avoided if the outsourcing exercise is carefully planned within a defined strategic framework.

Managing outsource risks

5.8   Effective contract negotiation and management is an essential part of ensuring outsourcing success. Measurement against key performance indicators, regular meetings and defined contacts are vital. From a risk perspective, outsource deals require careful and ongoing monitoring with concerns logged in the risk register.

5.9   Here are some key elements in a risk mitigation strategy for outsourcing.

- The need for the outsource decision to be based on clear objectives and measurable benefits, with a rigorous cost-benefit analysis
- The need for rigorous supplier selection, given the long-term partnership nature of the outsource relationship to which the organisation will be 'locked in'. In such circumstances, selection should not only involve cost comparisons but considerations such as quality, reliability, willingness to collaborate, and ethics and corporate social responsibility (since the performance of the contractor reflects on the reputation of the outsourcing organisation).
- Rigorous supplier contracting, so that risks, costs and liabilities are equitably and clearly allocated, and expected service levels clearly defined
- Clear and agreed service levels, standards and key performance indicators, with appropriate incentives and penalties to motivate compliance and conformance
- Consistent and rigorous monitoring of service delivery and quality, against service level agreements and key performance indicators
- Ongoing contract and supplier management, to ensure contract compliance, the development of the relationship (with the aim of continuous collaborative cost and performance improvement), and the constructive handling of disputes. This is essential if the organisation is not to gradually surrender control of performance (and therefore reputation) to the contractor.
- Contract review, deriving lessons from the performance of the contract, in order to evaluate whether the contract should be renewed, amended (to incorporate improvements) or terminated in favour of another supplier (or bringing the service provision back in-house).

Offshoring

5.10   The term 'offshoring' refers to the relocation of business processes to a lower cost location, usually overseas. This practice is in essence a form of outsourcing, but the overseas element gives rise to *additional* risk management considerations.

- Protection of patents, designs and copyright, in countries where intellectual property law is weak
- Additional transport and logistics risk from long, potentially complex supply chains to domestic markets
- Risks arising from political instability, corruption and other risks in particular markets
- Operational risks arising from difficulties in monitoring and controlling quality, ethical and sustainability standards of the outsource provider, owing to distance
- Operational, reputational and compliance risks arising from cultural, legal and linguistic differences (eg lower quality or health and safety standards)

5.11   From the buyer's point of view, there may be particular concerns that the quality of the service provided may decline. Many large companies have met with hostility from customers who have received poor customer service and technical support from overseas centres. Often the complaints have focused on an inadequate level of skill in spoken English, together with the resentment that some people feel at the general principle of 'exporting jobs overseas'.

5.12   A further reputational risk of offshoring is that workers in less developed countries may be subject to exploitation. Some critics even go so far as to say that the very reason why companies are adopting this approach is so that they can avoid the higher standards of employment and health and safety protection that prevail in the West.

5.13   Offshoring may be argued to increase the overall level of risk in the supply chain, since it is more difficult for a buyer to exercise control over a service provider who is geographically distant (eg in terms of quality, environmental and ethical monitoring). Reputational problems have been faced by Apple, for example, owing to the exposure of poor employment conditions at several of the companies in China to which assembly of its products has been outsourced, allegedly resulting in the suicide of several workers.

Managing risks of long-term supply relationships

5.14   The benefits and risks of long-term strategic partnership relations, regardless of supplier location, are summarised in Table 5.3

Table 5.3 *Upside and downside risks of long-term supply relationships*

BENEFITS FOR THE BUYER	RISKS FOR THE BUYER
Established track record creates trust	Complacent performance by the supplier
Supplier knowledge of requirements allows better service, collaborative improvement	Dependence on supplier may erode bargaining power
Sharing of data and plans allows forward planning, joint product and service development	Dependence increases vulnerability to supplier failure or supply disruption (eg strike, disaster)
Quality problems ironed out over time: pooled expertise enhances quality	Vulnerability to reputational damage by association (eg re supplier ethical failure)
Reduced supplier evaluation and selection, contracting, transaction and dispute costs	Investment in integration raises cost of supplier switching
Supplier may give preferential treatment in event of materials shortages, crisis demand etc	Collaboration increases risk of loss of control over confidential data, intellectual property etc.
Suppliers are motivated to invest in R&D, low-cost solutions, quality improvements	Investment in collaboration may not be warranted by priority or frequency of purchases
Suppliers are motivated to dependable performance	Investment may be wasted if supplier turns out to be unsuitable or incompatible
Systems can be progressively integrated for greater efficiency	

5.15   In order to mitigate the risks, it may be necessary for either or both organisations to:

- Analyse the most appropriate relationship type for the situation (eg using procurement positioning and supplier preferencing tools)
- Engage in careful partner evaluation, selection, contracting and relationship management processes
- Put in place multiple or back-up sourcing arrangements (buyer) or diversified customer base (supplier)
- Establish joint (or mutual) performance measures and continuous improvement targets and incentives
- Use legal means to protect intellectual property rights and confidentiality
- Share information for accurate demand forecasting
- Engage in joint contingency and continuity planning
- Prepare exit strategies for managing relationship termination.

5.16   One of the key elements of partner evaluation and selection will be to appraise the operational and strategic compatibility of any prospective partner: in other words, to ensure that both organisations' processes, objectives and cultures are compatible. This is sometimes referred to as 'cross-organisational goal and process alignment', which may also be reflected in 'KPI alignment': ensuring that both parties clarify their expectations and understand each other's expectations.

5.17 Identification and comparison of potential differences (misalignments) can support pre-contract clarification and negotiation – to avoid conflict (and resulting risk) as the contract or relationship progesses. Misalignments may come in the form of conflicting or diverging KPIs (desired outcomes) and/or 'gaps' between the level of importance given to a particular KPI: for example, if one party considers CSR or innovation crucial, while the other considers it unimportant.

6 Technology and information risk

6.1 The effective application of information and communications technology (ICT) lies at the heart of organisational management and operations. Increasingly, organisations are reliant on their ICT systems and infrastructure to manage knowledge and information; mediate organisational communication (including 'virtual' teamworking and global business); support managerial decision-making; facilitate supply chain relationships and processes (such as e-sourcing and e-procurement); and support process efficiency, quality and safety by automating tasks (eg in operations and stores).

6.2 Technological vulnerability and risk is higher where there is an exclusive or excessive reliance on technology, and where vital data or materials are stored and retrieved via ICT systems – especially when combined with the particular vulnerability of technology and systems. We will survey some of the main categories of technology risk briefly here.

Hardware and software theft

6.3 Computers and telecommunications devices are an increasingly attractive proposition to a thief, as (a) they are increasingly portable and (b) there is a ready market for the stolen goods. Organisations should:

- Ensure that general security measures are in place to prevent unauthorised access to premises and areas where hardware is kept
- Utilise security mechanisms to prevent theft of hardware (eg marking, securing or alarming devices)
- Make provisions to prevent loss and theft of *data* associated with theft of IT hardware: data backups (eg using cloud computing services), password protections, automatic locking or destruction of data on notification of hardware theft; and so on.

Cyber attack and data theft

6.4 Various forms of deliberate cyber attack and cyber crime have come to prominence with the increasing storage of organisational and personal data on networked systems.

- **Hacking** is unauthorised access to a data system, often by circumventing systems security. Hackers often have a malicious intent, such as industrial espionage, data destruction (eg by virus infection), system 'hijacking' (eg co-opting computers to a 'botnet' for mass SPAM or distributed denial of service (DDOS) attacks), the public exposure of confidential data, or the theft of data to support other criminal activities (such as credit or identity fraud). DDOS attacks are incidents in which multiple (often hijacked) computers are used to bombard a corporate website with web requests, crashing the system.
- **Viruses** and other forms of **malware** (malicious programmes designed to exploit systems vulnerabilities and misuse data) are increasingly common. A virus is a self-replicating programme, usually intended to cause damage to a computer system. Variants include 'worms', which sit in a computer's memory reproducing themselves, 'logic bombs' that lie dormant waiting for a specified date and then 'explode' to destroy files, and 'Trojan horses' that start infecting only after the user has interacted with them. 'Spyware' captures information about the user's internet activities, financial details input to e-commerce transactions and so on.
- **Phishing** is a fraudulent attempt to acquire information (such as usernames, passwords and financial details) by masquerading as a trustworthy entity (eg an IT administrator, e-commerce entity or bank) often in an email.

6.5 Various technology-based tools are available to protect systems against cyber attack.

- Firewalls enable the restriction of access to selected systems and data through a single gateway, enabling password protected access to authorised users.
- Internal and external access to sensitive data should be password protected with passwords changed regularly.
- Anti-virus and anti-malware software will particularly focus on the interface with email and the internet. Viruses often enter a system when employees download programs from the internet or utilise their own external media (DVD, flash drive etc): organisational policy and training should discourage this.

6.6 The user component of the system must also be addressed. There should be clear organisational policies, rules and protocols for data security: backing up data; changing passwords; running anti-virus software; avoiding the use of external media; not sharing access codes; and so on. All relevant staff should be trained or coached in data security awareness, protocols and techniques.

Technology failure

6.7 Technology failure in any area can significantly disrupt operations, especially if the organisation has a high degree of reliance on operational machinery or ICT systems. Here are some technology failure risks.

- 'Teething problems' following the introduction of new machinery or systems
- Performance problems, failure or damage caused by incorrect use (exacerbated by poor user training and instruction) – which may additionally cause health and safety risks (eg from the by-passing of safety protocols or settings)
- Compatibility problems, where one technological system is unable to interface or integrate successfully with another (in a related process within the same organisation, or with customer, supplier or third party systems). This may happen owing to lack of integration in system design and development; lack of compatibility with systems used by external supply chain partners; or technological obsolescence (where one organisation's system is 'left behind' others).
- System or technology breakdown (due to hardware or software problems, poor maintenance, age and deterioration, power failure – or interference, such as sabotage or computer virus infection).

6.8 Organisations that have a high reliance on real-time data processing (such as e-commerce businesses or airlines and other booking agencies) or computerised operations (such as automotive manufacturers) are at serious risk in terms of lost business and reputational damage. Other impacts of lost production and lost data from technology failure could include: resulting cashflow problems, inability to pay staff, backlog of work and service and quality reduction issues.

6.9 The risk management process will assess likely causes and impacts of technology failure, and will generally seek to develop contingency plans (and disaster recovery plans) to mitigate the impact of failure.

Implementation of new technology

6.10 CIPS guidance suggests a checklist of issues to be considered ahead of new technology or systems implementation, which highlights the key risks involved.

- Objectives – was there a good set of reasons for change, and a business case?
- Personnel – do we have staff members and an organisational culture that will respond well to change?
- Relationships – can we cope with the changes in relationships that will arise when the new system is implemented?
- Technology – do we have sufficient expertise in-house, or sufficient knowledge to source from outside?
- Finance – has the project been appraised in financial terms?
- Power – will the new system shift power from one department or individual to another?

6.11   The guidance further suggests that there are four key elements in a successful implementation of new technology.

- Adoption of a lifecycle perspective, giving systematic attention to the issues that may arise at all stages of the system's life: design; development; testing; commissioning and installation; user training and support; maintenance and repair; upgrading; and disposal
- Taking a participative approach: involving designers, users, potential users and other network stakeholders (such as suppliers and customers with whose systems the new technology will have to be integrated and/or compatible) in design and development, risk assessment, testing and implementation. This both enhances the quality and diversity of inputs *and* helps to secure 'buy-in' by users.
- Accepting that changes will emerge as the project develops: building in the flexibility for emerging challenges and constraints, identifiied risks and opportunities, innovations and stakeholder responses.
- Taking account of the politics: recognising the interests and influence of stakeholder groups, some of which may actively or passively resist the change agent, the change or the particular technology.

Information risks

6.12   As information and knowledge become increasingly systemised and transparent, so they become more vulnerable. A number of risks may arise from knowledge and information systems, including the gathering of information in supplier databases; the sharing of intellectual property and confidential data with suppliers in the course of collaboration; and the management of relationships via a corporate extranet.

6.13   Here are some of the information-related risks which might arise for a business, particularly in supply chain management.

- Risks to the organisation's intellectual capital from unauthorised access to intellectual property (eg patents, designs or prototypes) and sensitive commercial data (eg on competitive plans or risk assessments) – perhaps as a result of industrial espionage, hacking, phishing or data theft
- Risks to the organisation's intellectual capital and commercial advantage from misuse of data by parties with whom it was shared (eg a supplier's breach of confidentiality, or the sharing of data with competitors) – and corresponding risks of liability if the buying organisation breaches the confidentiality, or misuses the intellectual property of a supplier
- Risks to the integrity and security of data, through a range of factors including software corruption; computer viruses; input or transcription errors; and deliberate fraud – exacerbated by poor house-keeping and internal controls
- Systems failure, and associated data loss (hence the need for all data to be 'backed up' to external hard-drives or servers, and the rise in the use of 'cloud' computing using external servers)
- Compliance risk in regard to law and contractual provisions on issues such as data protection (secure storage and relevant use of personal data by corporations), intellectual property (protecting the rights of owners of designs, patents and copyrights) and confidentiality (preventing the unauthorised disclosure of commercially or personally sensitive data)
- Risks to the integrity and value of data through lack of effective change control protocols (resulting in multiple conflicting versions)
- Risks and inefficiencies in the design and implementation of management information systems, extranets, contract databases and other relevant systems: eg inefficient storage and retrieval protocols; lack of integration and compatibility with supplier systems; teething problems; and systems breakdown
- Turnover of key personnel and loss of their intellectual property (where relevant) and/or knowledge of the organisation's procurement needs, contract histories and supplier relationships
- Loss of organisational knowledge, information and capabilities through the outsourcing of functions to external suppliers.

6.14 A range of risk mitigation measures may therefore be put in place in the following areas.

- Risk identification and assessment at the system design stage (including stakeholder involvement in system design and implementation)
- System testing and change-over arrangements for new systems (eg parallel running or phased implementation)
- Preventive maintenance, repair, updating and replacement of hardware, software and peripherals (along with other plant and equipment)
- Ensuring that all buyer-side and supplier-side information systems are subject to robust access controls (eg passwords, user IDs and firewalls) – and that 'human mediated' information exchanges, such as negotiations, are subject to appropriate confidentiality guarantees
- Rules and protocols for the effective and secure use of information systems (eg the use of firewalls and anti-virus software, and the training of staff in correct systems use and security awareness)
- Protocols for the backing-up of stored data, to prevent loss due to systems failure or data corruption (eg use of 'cloud' computing, regular back-ups to external servers or hard drives and so on)
- Systems maintenance, contingency planning and back-up systems, to minimise loss in the event of systems breakdown, hardware theft or power failure. There should also be business continuity and disaster recovery plans in place for catastrophic failure
- Database management, ensuring that useful information and knowledge is captured and maintained, and obsolete information is deleted or archived
- Protocols and controls over contract changes, variations, versions and updating (with authorised individuals having controlled rights to make amendments and administer versions)
- Internal controls, checks and balances to prevent misuse of data or funds, and fraud: examples include authorisations and sign-offs; reconciliation of contracts, delivery notes and invoices; and separation of duties (eg the same person does not authorise ordering and payment)
- Intellectual property protection, through the use of registered design rights, patents and copyrights; and appropriate contractual clauses to control access to intellectual property (eg via exclusive or non-exclusive licences) and to protection ownership rights (eg who will own IP generated in the course of the contract?)
- Confidentiality of commercially sensitive data exchanged in the course of the contract (eg using confidentiality and non-disclosure clauses in contracts, training staff in confidentiality, and publishing and enforcing ethical codes)
- Training staff in the requirements of relevant legislation (including intellectual property law, data protection and freedom of information)
- Documentation of best practice, supplier relationship histories, learning from contracts – and other value-adding knowledge and information – to support organisational learning and prevent loss of data through personnel departure or outsourcing.

The role of information assurance

6.15 Information assurance (IA) is the practice of managing risks related to the use, processing, storage, and transmission of information or data and the systems and processes used for those purposes. It is related to the field of 'information security' (a branch of computer science aimed at the protection of information systems and their contents, mainly by applying security controls and defences against malicious attacks). However, information assurance embraces a wider range of issues, including:

- Corporate governance: regulatory standards compliance, internal controls and auditing in regard to data protection, IT systems and fraud prevention
- Contingency, business continuity and disaster recovery planning in relation to key systems risks (data loss, security breaches, systems breakdown)
- Strategic development and management of IT systems to fulfil the current and future needs of the organisation (and supply chain), while minimising risk, through areas such as systems integration, compatibility, flexibility and security.

6.16 A typical IA project will involve the following steps.

- **Systematic risk assessment:** identification of information assets to be protected; identification of vulnerabilities in information assets and systems; identification of threats capable of exploiting or damaging the information assets; probability and impact analysis of identified risks
- **Risk management planning:** proposing counter-measures to 'treat' identified risks, including prevention, detection and response to threats. These may include technical tools; employee training in data security awareness; or the resourcing of specialist IT security departments or incident response teams. Proposed plans are tested for feasibility and analysed in terms of costs and benefits.
- The **agreement, implementation, testing and evaluation** of the risk management plan, often by means of systematic audit. Performance data is gathered and reviewed on an ongoing basis, so that the risk management plan can be continually revised in the light of performance gaps or emerging risks, as required.

BS 7799 (ISO 17799)

6.17 BS 7799 (ISO 17799) is an information systems management standard, designed to:

- Enable organisations to identify the risks facing their information and introduce controls to counter them
- Ensure that personal information is kept secure in line with data protection law
- Reassure trading partners that the organisation protects and controls its own information and that of its partners.

6.18 The BS 7799 (ISO 17799) 'information system security best practice' list provides a thorough and rigorous checklist covering: security policy; security organisation; asset classification and control; personnel security; physical and environmental security; computer and network management; systems access controls; systems development and maintenance; business continuity and disaster recovery; and compliance.

6.19 BS 7799 (ISO 17799) involves putting in place the following actions designed to minimise the impact of IT risk issues.

- Define the organisation's information security policy.
- Define the scope of the system.
- Assess the risk; identify the threats and vulnerabilities and assess the impacts on the organisation.
- Identify the risk management areas.
- Select and put in place the controls that will be used.
- Document the selected controls.

Chapter summary

- Risks of contract failure arise from suppliers' reliability and performance and/or from the buyer's contract, project and supplier management policies and practices.
- Financial risks may be internal (eg lack of cost control) or external (eg weakness in the financial position of suppliers).
- The costs of quality failure are both internal (arising before the product reaches the customer) and external (after the product reaches the customer). Modern approaches to this issue are based on quality assurance rather than quality control.
- Supply risk is the chance that suppliers may not be able to supply inputs of adequate quality. This may arise from supplier failure, resource scarcity, security failures or poor relationship management.
- Outsourcing is an increasing trend in modern business but carries serious risks. Effective contract negotiation and management are essential for success.
- Technology and information risks arise from theft of hardware and software, cyber attack, failure of hardware or software, and theft or corruption of information.

 ## Self-test questions

Numbers in brackets refer to the paragraphs where you can check your answers.

1   List possible risks in negotiating with suppliers. (1.6)

2   List possible financial risks arising from within the organisation. (2.1)

3   List possible measures for mitigating credit risk. (2.10)

4   In relation to costs of quality, explain what is meant by (a) appraisal costs and (b) prevention costs. (3.5, 3.6)

5   Describe limitations to a quality control approach based on inspection. (3.14)

6   List possible sources of supply risk. (4.2)

7   List situations giving rise to particular risks in relation to supply chain relationships. (4.14)

8   List possible reasons for failure of outsourcing agreements. (5.6)

9   What additional risks arise in an overseas offshoring arrangement? (5.10)

10   List issues to be considered ahead of new technology implementation. (6.10)

CHAPTER 6

CSR and Sustainability Risks

Assessment criteria and indicative content

 Evaluate the main risks in supply chains that can impact on organisational corporate social responsibility and sustainability standards

- Defining corporate social responsibility and sustainability
- Assessing corporate risks and risks associated with brands
- Standards for sustainable procurement (including the UN, ILO and ETI standards)

Section headings

1 Corporate social responsibility and ethics
2 Sustainability
3 The regulatory framework on sustainability
4 Reputational and brand risk

Introduction

In this chapter we continue our discussion of particular risk categories highlighted by the syllabus: in this case, risks in supply chains which impact on an organisation's corporate social responsibility and sustainability performance – *and* the risk of CSR and sustainability failures to corporate reputation and branding.

We start by exploring the issues of corporate responsibility and ethics – building on our discussion of corporate governance and ethics in Chapter 4. We then go on to look at the closely related area of 'sustainability' and sustainable procurement, which explicitly raises issues of corporate responsibility in relation to the environment ('planet') and society ('people').

We examine a range of risks and mitigating measures in the areas of environmental risk (eg the risk of environmental damage) and social risk (eg the downside risk of poor labour standards in supply chains, and the upside risk of using small and medium enterprise suppliers).

A key source of risk related to CSR and sustainability comes from increasing public awareness (creating reputational risk) and regulatory pressures (creating compliance risk) around sustainable procurement issues. We therefore examine some of the main standards and frameworks set up for regulation, and voluntary self-regulation, in these areas.

Finally, we explore the important concepts of corporate reputation and corporate branding, as high-value intangible assets which can – all too easily – be put at risk by CSR and sustainability failure. We consider the sources of reputational risk, and some of the mitigating measures that can be put in place. The discussion of issues and crisis management – branches of public relations management with a specific focus on reputational defence – will also be highly relevant to our later consideration (in Chapter 13) of disaster recovery, since reputational crisis is one form of potentially business-damaging 'disaster'.

1 Corporate social responsibility and ethics

1.1 In Chapter 4, we discussed ethics, and ethical codes, as an element in preventing fraud and corruption. Looking at the bigger picture, however, ethical issues may affect businesses and public sector organisations on a number of levels.

- At the wider macro level, there are issues concerning the role of business and capitalism in society, and the need for sustainable development: the impact of globalisation, the impact of industrialisation on the environment, and so on.
- At the corporate level, there are issues that face individual organisations as they formulate strategies and policies about how they interact with their various stakeholders. The sphere generally referred to as 'corporate social responsibility' (CSR) covers policies that the organisation adopts for the good and wellbeing of stakeholders, including issues of corporate governance.
- At the individual level, there are issues that face individuals as they act and interact within the organisation and supply chain: whether to accept gifts or hospitality which might be perceived as an attempt to influence supplier selection, as an example. This is the sphere that is often covered in professional Codes of Ethics, as discussed in Chapter 4.

1.2 CSR is defined by CIPS as 'an approach by which a company recognises that its activities have a wider impact on the society in which it operates; and that developments in society in turn impact on its ability to pursue business successfully.'

Ethical sourcing and supply chain management

1.3 Ethical sourcing and supply chain management at the level of corporate social responsibility may cover a range of matters, depending on the ethical risks and issues raised by the organisation's activities and markets. Here are some examples.

- The promotion of fair, open and transparent competition in sourcing (and the avoidance of unfair, fraudulent, manipulative or coercive sourcing practices)
- The use of sourcing policies to promote positive socio-economic goals such as equality and diversity in the supply chain; support for local and small-business suppliers; and minimisation of transport miles (to reduce environmental impacts and carbon emissions)
- The specification and sourcing of ethically produced inputs (eg certified as not tested on animals; drawn from sustainably managed or renewable sources; or manufactured under safe working conditions)
- The selection, management and development of suppliers in such a way as to promote ethical trading, environmental responsibility and labour standards at all tiers of the supply chain (eg by pre-qualifying suppliers on CSR policies, ethical codes, environmental management systems, reverse logistics and recycling capabilities, and supply chain management; and incentivising, monitoring and developing supplier ethical performance)
- A commitment to supporting the improvement of working terms and conditions (labour standards) throughout the supply chain, and particularly in low-cost labour countries with comparatively lax regulatory regimes
- A commitment to supporting sustainable profit-taking by suppliers (eg not squeezing supplier profit margins unfairly) and to ensuring that fair prices are paid to suppliers back through the supply chain, particularly where buyers are in a dominant position (eg in developing and low-cost supply markets)
- Adherence to the ethical frameworks and codes of conduct of relevant bodies such as the International Labour Organisation (ILO), Fair Trade Association or Ethical Trading Initiative, the International Standards Organisation guidelines on Corporate Social Responsibility (ISO 26000: 2010), or the Codes of Ethics of relevant professional bodies (such as CIPS)
- A commitment to compliance with all relevant laws and regulations for consumer, supplier and worker protection.

Why should organisations be socially responsible?

1.4 Economist Milton Friedman took the view that 'the social responsibility of business is profit maximisation': to give a return on shareholders' investment. Spending funds on objectives *not* related to shareholder expectations is irresponsible. Regard for shareholder wealth is a healthy discipline for management, providing accountability for decisions. The public interest is already served by profit maximisation, because the State levies taxes.

1.5 'Consequently,' argued Friedman, 'the only justification for social responsibility is *enlightened self interest*' (or ethical egoism) on the part of a business organisation. So how does CSR serve the interest (and manage the risk) of a firm?

- Law, regulation and Codes of Practice impose certain social responsibilities on organisations (eg in relation to health and safety, employment protection, consumer rights and environmental care). There are financial and operational penalties for failure to comply (eg 'polluter pays' taxes).
- Voluntary measures (which may in any case only pre-empt legal and regulatory requirements) may enhance corporate image and build a positive brand. A commonly quoted example is the environmental and sustainability strategy adopted by The Body Shop.
- Above-statutory provisions for employees and suppliers may be necessary to attract, retain and motivate them to provide quality service and commitment – particularly in competition with other employers and purchasers.
- Increasing consumer awareness of social responsibility issues creates a market demand for CSR (and the threat of boycott for irresponsible firms).

1.6 Strategy guru Henry Mintzberg notes that a business's relationship with society is in any case not purely economic: a business is an open social system which makes a variety of non-economic exchanges with the society in which it operates (people, information, image), and creates a variety of non-economic impacts. Social responsibility helps to create a social climate and infrastructure in which the business can prosper in the long term.

1.7 In the same way, ethical sourcing and supply chain management helps to create a climate in which mutually-beneficial long-term trading relationships can be preserved. Exploitation, abuse and disappointed expectations will inevitably lead to broken relationships or reciprocal 'corner cutting' by suppliers.

1.8 Ethical sourcing, trading and supplier management are therefore important to the management of compliance, reputational and performance-based risk, for a number of reasons.

- Unethical conduct leads to poor relationships with stakeholders who have been badly treated – which in turn may result in poor customer status with suppliers, poor supplier motivation and performance, and increased risk of conflict and disputes. Exploitation, abuse and disappointed expectations will inevitably lead to broken relationships or reciprocal 'corner cutting' by suppliers.
- Poor stakeholder relationships, as a result of unethical conduct, also represent loss of the opportunities, value and profits that might arise from positive relationships, in terms of committed performance, innovation, collaboration and synergy and so on. Lack of capability to seize such opportunities is a source of long-term business and competitive risk.
- Poor treatment of employees and suppliers may make it difficult to attract, retain and motivate them to provide quality service and commitment – particularly in competition with other employers and buyers in the market.
- Unethical conduct may lead to increased regulatory, media and pressure group scrutiny – increasing reputational and compliance risk.
- Exposure of unethical conduct may result in reputational damage, damage to the organisation's product or employer brand, loss of goodwill (from customers, employees and supply chain partners), lost sales – and perhaps even consumer boycott.
- Illegal behaviours create additional compliance and legal risk – including penalties and sanctions for

non-compliance (financial penalties, rectification orders, costs of litigation and damages, reputational damage through 'name and shame' schemes and so on).

1.9 There may be costs and challenges involved in ethical sourcing and supplier management. For example, major organisations such as Nike, Vodafone and Marks & Spencer have taken on the responsibility of educating, monitoring and managing overseas suppliers, to ensure that they treat their workers fairly and observe environmental standards.

1.10 However, *failure* to do this is now regarded as a major business risk, with significant potential costs. One high-profile example was the reputational damage suffered by social charity Oxfam, when it became known that overseas suppliers of its 'Make Poverty History' wristbands were in fact themselves exploiting their workers. Another recent example is the public pressure applied to the popular Apple brand, following the exposure of exploitative working conditions in the factories of some of its major Chinese assemblers.

1.11 A range of CSR and ethical risks, and examples of control and mitigation measures, are summarised in Table 6.1.

Table 6.1 *Overview of CSR and ethical risk*

CSR AND ETHICAL RISKS	EXAMPLE MITIGATION STRATEGIES
Financial and operational penalties of irresponsible behaviour (eg 'polluter pays' taxes, litigation costs, clean-up costs)	Formulate and enforce CSR objectives, policies and codes of practice
Social, political or economic instability arising from inequity, protest, loss of 'operating licence'	Encourage CSR practices through the supply chain (eg via supplier selection, vendor rating, approved status, contract KPIs and penalties)
Unsustainable use of resources, leading to scarcity or rising prices	Education, training and development of staff and supply chains
Reputational and brand impacts of CSR issues: lost customer loyalty, brand equity and reputational capital	CSR and ethical monitoring and reporting (especially in areas of vulnerability eg overseas suppliers)
Loss of sales, profits, shareholder value and credit rating as a result of public exposure	Sharing best practice eg benchmarking CSR leaders
Loss of preferred employer or trading partner status: damage to credibility, relationships, resources	CSR and ethics forums and task forces to encourage CSR-focused communication

2 Sustainability

2.1 Sustainability has become an extremely important aspect of procurement policy in both the public and private sectors in recent years. The term 'sustainability' is often used interchangeably with 'corporate social responsibility' and/or environmental responsibility. More specifically, however, it describes strategies designed to balance economic viability with considerations of environmental and social responsibility (Profit, Planet and People – sometimes referred to as the 'Triple Bottom Line').

2.2 CIPS has adopted the definition of sustainable procurement used by the UK's Sustainable Procurement Task Force (SPTF) in its influential report, *Procuring the Future*.

'[Sustainable procurement is] a process whereby organisations meet their needs for goods, services, works and utilities in a way that achieves value for money on a whole-life basis in terms of generating benefits not only to the organisation, but also to society and the economy, whilst minimising damage to the environment.'

2.3 The 'Triple Bottom Line' concept argues that businesses should measure their performance not just on the basis of profitability, but on the basis of:

- **Economic sustainability (Profit):** profitability, sustainable economic performance – and its beneficial effects on society (such as employment, access to goods and services, payment of taxes, community investment and so on)
- **Environmental sustainability (Planet):** sustainable environmental practices, which either benefit the natural environment or minimise harmful impacts upon it
- **Social sustainability (People):** fair and beneficial business practices towards labour, suppliers and the society in which the business operates.

2.4 A strong business case can be made for environmentally and socially sustainable supply, on the basis of factors such as the following.

- Ensuring that the organisation retains its 'licence to operate' from stakeholders
- Contributing to the reputational capital and revenue-earning potential of the business, by creating a positive sustainable brand (which increasingly appeals to consumers)
- Minimising the risk (and associated costs) of reputational damage as a result of unethical or irresponsible conduct (or association with the unethical or irresponsible conduct of suppliers)
- Preserving scarce and non-renewable resources for the future
- Reaping value for money and cost benefits (eg through recycling, and minimising resource wastage, packaging and energy use)
- Minimising failure costs (eg 'polluter pays' taxes, penalties for non-compliance with law and regulation, rectification orders, lost sales, product recalls and so on)

Environmental risk management

2.5 The environment is defined in the UK's Environmental Protection Act 1990 as 'consisting of all, or any, of the following media: namely the air, water and land.'

2.6 Sadgrove identifies eight key ways in which a business may damage or degrade the environment (or behave in an environmentally unsustainable way) – which may be regarded as environmental threats.

- Emissions to the air (including air pollution; the emission of carbon dioxide and other greenhouse gas emissions; and possibly also noise pollution)
- Discharges to water (including water pollution and effluent)
- Solid waste (including waste to landfill)
- Owning (or acquiring) environmentally damaged assets such as land
- Producing, using and/or transporting toxic or hazardous materials
- Consuming fossil fuels or energy derived from them (non-renewable energy)
- Consuming scarce or non-renewable resources, or consuming renewable resources at a rate faster than the rate of renewal
- Damage to nature (eg by construction, change of land usage, deforestation – and resulting threats to habitats, eco-systems and biodiversity).

2.7 Sadgrove identifies all the above as broadly 'polluting' behaviours, and points out that such behaviours put the organisation at risk of social and financial penalties.

- Costs of compliance: meeting regulatory requirements for scrutiny, reporting and operational measures (such as developing low-polluting processes, recycling and reverse logistics, safe disposal of end-of-life assets)
- Costs of non-compliance: fines, litigation costs, reclamation and clean-up costs, and reputational damage
- Increased vulnerability to scrutiny and increased regulatory burden: failure by industry to demonstrate voluntary responsibility risks more stringent legislation
- Difficulties getting finance (investment funding) and insurance (especially at competitive rates), due to a poor environmental track record and repeated liability for environmental fines
- Damaged employer brand, making it harder to attract and retain quality staff

- Damaged brand image and reputation, through the impact of adverse media coverage, and the subsequent loss of 'green' customers and consumers
- Loss of competitive advantage and market share, in the face of more environmentally responsible competitors

2.8 A range of control and mitigation measures for environmental risks include the following.

- Environmental auditing (discussed in more detail below)
- The formulation of environmental objectives and policies (as part of a wider sustainability or CSR policy)
- The development of environmental management systems, which may be modelled on – or accredited under – ISO 14000 (discussed in the following section of this chapter)
- The appointment of sustainability champions, cross-functional sustainability committees and other mechanisms for stimulating communication and environmental risk awareness, and securing stakeholder 'buy-in' to sustainability measures
- The commissioning of environmental impact studies as part of project planning (eg for construction projects)
- Lifecycle assessment of asset and product portfolios: assessment of environmental risks and impacts throughout the life of products and assets, including sourcing and production issues (such as energy and raw materials use); waste products (pollution, emissions, waste to landfill); consumer usage issues (eg energy consumption and recycling); and end-of-life issues such as disposal, reverse logistics and so on.
- The formulation of environmental criteria and templates for product and service designs and specifications; supplier pre-qualification, appraisal and contract award; contract KPIs, monitoring and performance management; and performance evaluation (vendor rating)
- Education, training, involvement and development programmes for key stakeholders (including suppliers)
- The adoption of environmental performance measures for the organisation as a whole (perhaps as part of a Triple Bottom Line approach), and the inclusion of environmental targets and progress measurements in corporate reporting
- The planning, implementation and control of measures to address identified environmental issues: reduced emissions, resource and energy usage and wastes to landfill; efficient transport planning; product re-design; sourcing of 'green' materials (initially, on a 'quick win' basis); upgrading of polluting plant and machinery; and so on.

Environmental and sustainability audit

2.9 An environmental audit is the inspection of a company to assess the environmental impact of its activities, or of a particular product or process, as the basis for managerial decision-making and risk management. For example, the audit of a manufactured product may look at the impact of production (including energy use and the extraction of raw materials used in manufacture), usage (which may cause pollution and other hazards), and disposal (potential for recycling, and whether waste causes pollution).

2.10 An environmental review would normally start with the identification of areas of a site to be assessed: external areas (such as vehicle access, waste storage and drainage areas) and internal areas (offices, process areas). A checklist of environmental issues (wastes, emissions, hazardous substances, energy consumption) can then be assessed for each area, using observation, interviews and review of relevant documentation and records. An assessment report will be communicated to key stakeholders, and a register of risks and impacts drawn up, as the focus for problem-solving, risk assessment and management, and ongoing improvement planning.

2.11 The Envirowise agency, a government-funded business consultancy focusing on environmental sustainability, recommends audit tools similar to those used in supplier audits: an audit checklist (to structure the audit and ensure completeness); self-administered questionnaires (to cover matters of fact); interviews (to test staff awareness of issues and policies); discussion (for briefing, consultation and clarification); and reporting on findings, highlighting areas for decision-making and action.

2.12   Environmental audits may be general (eg in the case of supplier appraisal or vendor rating), or as a first step in developing an environmental management system – or in gaining accreditation for such a system, under standards such as ISO 14001 and EMAS (discussed below). Alternatively, they may focus on particular areas, such as waste production and handling, or water usage and pollution.

Social risk management

2.13   Issues in social sustainability, for the purposes of risk management in supply chains, broadly centre on two main issues.

- **Human and labour rights**: the eradication of child labour and slavery; workers' rights to association and representation; the improvement of labour conditions (working hours and health and safety); the payment of fair wages; and so on.
- **Access to contracts** for small (SME), local and diverse (women-owned or ethnic minority-owned) suppliers, which would otherwise be disadvantaged by factors such as: lack of competitive pricing (due to lack of economies of scale); lack of capacity and capability (especially to take on large aggregated or framework contracts); lack of access to information about contracts; and lack of resources to tackle the complexity and costs of large tender processes.

2.14   The main risks for businesses in regard to unethical labour practices in their supply chains have already been discussed in relation to corporate social responsibility – and will be discussed further, as a source of reputational and brand risk, in Section 4 of this chapter.

2.15   The main risk for business in regard to supply chain diversity is, arguably, lost opportunity. There will be a key sourcing trade-off between:

- The economic advantages of dealing with large suppliers (the ability to aggregate requirements for reduced transaction costs and bulk discounts, and more competitive pricing due to economies of scale) *and*
- The potential for 'better value' arising from dealing with SME suppliers:
  — Access to a wider supply market, potentially enhancing competition
  — Competitive pricing due to lower administrative and management overheads
  — Greater responsiveness and flexibility
  — Innovation capability and diversity of business solutions
  — Willingness and ability to produce small-order, niche, bespoke and customised items
  — Higher commitment and levels of service (due to the value of the business).

2.16   On the other hand, sourcing from SMEs carries its own risks. The buyer will need to take into account issues such as: the supplier's limited capacity to handle large-volume and aggregated contracts; the supplier's potential financial instability (due to cashflow issues and difficulties securing credit); and the ethical and business risk of a small supplier becoming overly dependent on a large customer.

The sustainability agenda and macro-economic crisis

2.17   The difficult economic conditions following the Global Financial Crisis of 2008–2009 pose particular challenges for the sustainability agenda in business organisations, as social and environmental sustainability objectives are often the first to go when economic sustainability (or profitability) becomes a priority in times of economic recession and loss of business confidence.

2.18 A survey for *Supply Management* (27 August 2009) found that 64% of purchasers are not getting 'significant' financial benefit from sustainable procurement. 'There may be opportunities to benefit from implementing facets of CSR, but at the present time this is quite low on the agenda.'

- Recessionary pressures may reduce demand for sustainable products, services and commodities.
- Budgetary and funding restrictions (and/or cost reduction targets) may make extra expenditure on sustainability impossible – or difficult to justify.

2.19 In short, the focus is on economic survival – and although this can be seen as a legitimate sustainability issue in its own right, it may create a barrier to other social and environmental sustainability measures.

3 The regulatory framework on sustainability

3.1 Legislation enacted at the national and transnational (eg EU) level covers a range of areas relevant to sustainability and corporate social responsibility, including: human rights law; employment law (including equality, health and safety, employment rights); corporate, finance and tax law; anti-corruption law; competition law; data protection and freedom of information law; and environmental law.

3.2 In addition to legislation or statute, various international and governmental agencies, NGOs and commercial organisations have developed a range of voluntary regulatory codes of practice, and benchmark standards, in areas such as:

- *General sustainability:* eg the UN Global Compact and the Earth Charter
- *Environment:* eg the ISO 14001 Environmental Management System Standard; the European Eco-Management and Audit Scheme (EMAS)
- *Human rights, labour standards and fair trading:* eg the Ethical Trading Initiative base code; and the International Labour Organisation standards on human rights.

Environmental regulation

3.3 The Environment Agency in the UK has the responsibility of regulating business and industry: implementing EU directives, issuing permits, monitoring compliance and carrying out risk assessments. There are five basic approaches to regulation.

- Direct regulation: enforcing legislation, and issuing permits, which typically set limits and targets, and require operators to carry out management processes
- Environmental (or 'polluter pays') taxes, such as the Landfill Tax or Climate Change Levy
- Offset or trading schemes, such as the EU Emissions Trading Scheme (for greenhouse gases) and the Landfill Allowances Trading Scheme.
- Voluntary or negotiated agreements, jointly agreed by businesses (usually to avoid the threat of legislation or compulsory regulation). The motor industry, for example, has a voluntary agreement with the EU on emission reduction targets.
- Education and advice: the promotion of regulatory requirements, risk assessment consultancy, and showcasing emerging issues and successful initiatives.

ISO 14001: the environmental management system standard

3.4 Launched in 1996, ISO 14000 is a series of international standards on the design, implementation and control of environmental management systems (EMS). An EMS gives an organisation a systematic approach for assessing and managing its impact on the environment: that is, the environmental consequences of its operations. The standard is designed to provide a framework for developing such a system, as well as a supporting audit and review programme.

3.5 The major requirements for an EMS under ISO 14001 include the following.

- An environmental policy statement which includes commitments to: prevention of pollution; continual improvement of the EMS leading to improvements in overall environmental performance; and compliance with all relevant legal and regulatory requirements
- Identification of all aspects of the organisation's activities, products and services that could have a significant impact on the environment (whether or not regulated): focusing on environmental aspects that are within the organisation's control or ability to influence
- Establishing performance objectives and targets for the EMS, taking into account legal requirements and organisational policy commitments and information about significant environmental protection issues
- Implementing an EMS to meet these objectives and targets, including: training of employees, establishing work instructions and practices, establishing performance metrics and so on
- Establishing a programme for periodic auditing and review of environmental performance against the environmental policy and legal and regulatory framework
- Taking corrective and preventive actions when deviations from the EMS are identified
- Undertaking periodic reviews of the EMS by top management to ensure its continuing performance and adequacy in the face of changing environmental information

3.6 An organisation can make a self-assessment and self-declaration, or be audited and certified by a third party, if desired, to demonstrate compliance to customers, clients and regulatory bodies. Here are some of the benefits claimed for an EMS based on ISO 14001 by various Environmental Protection Agencies.

- Improvements in compliance and reduced costs of non-compliance; improvements in overall environmental performance
- Enhanced predictability and consistency in managing environmental obligations
- Increased efficiency and potential cost savings when managing environmental obligations
- Enhanced reputation and relationship with internal and external stakeholders

The European Eco-Management and Audit Scheme

3.7 The European Eco-Management and Audit Scheme (EMAS) is a voluntary EMS certification process created under European Community regulations. Certification under EMAS can be obtained by an organisation or site which has an ISO 14001 certification and, in addition:

- Issues a public, externally verified report on its environmental performance
- Has a verified environmental audit programme in place
- Has no apparent failures of regulatory compliance.

The United Nations (UN) Global Compact

3.8 The Global Compact was launched in 2000, setting out ten principles for business, derived from the Universal Declaration of Human Rights; the International Labour Organisation (ILO) Declaration on Fundamental Principles and Rights to Work; and the Rio Declaration on Environment and Development.

3.9 The ten principles include: support for human rights (freedom of association and collective bargaining, and elimination of forced and child labour); labour rights (elimination of labour discrimination); environmental responsibility (embracing a precautionary approach, and developing and sharing environmentally friendly technologies); and anti-corruption measures (working against bribery and extortion).

3.10 This is said to be the largest and most prestigious of all global sustainability codes: adopted by thousands of corporations and dozens of international NGOs and labour federations. However, criticisms focus on the lack of a system for transparent assessment and reporting on what endorsing companies have actually done to implement the principles.

International Labour Organisation (ILO) standards

3.11 The ILO is the UN's specialised agency promoting human, civil and labour rights. It develops consensus documents (Conventions), and less formal codes of conduct, resolutions and declarations (Recommendations). These have included the *Declaration of Principles Concerning Multinational Enterprises and Social Policy* ('The MNE Declaration'), on the contribution of multinational enterprises to economic and social progress, and how to minimise and resolve problems arising from their actions. The ILO has also issued *Guidelines on Occupational Health and Safety Management Systems*, among other matters.

3.12 The MNE declaration makes recommendations for: general sustainable development and compliance policies; employment (increasing employment opportunities and standards, building links with local supply chains, and promoting equality, employment security and fair treatment); training (encouraging skill development); work/life conditions (providing equitable and competitive remuneration, benefits and conditions, recognising the need for work/life balance, respecting minimum employment ages, and maintaining high standards of health and safety); and industrial relations (respecting freedom of association, collective bargaining and representation, and allowing for consultation and fair grievance and dispute procedures).

3.13 The general aims and objectives of the ILO illustrate their sustainability concerns: Table 6.2.

Table 6.2 *Objectives of the ILO*

OBJECTIVE	COMMENT
Decent work for all	Considering the aspirations of people in their working lives: for opportunity and income; rights, voice and recognition; family stability and personal development; and fairness and gender equality
Employment creation	Policies that help create and maintain decent work and income
Fair globalisation	Seeking ways of ensuring that the benefits of globalisation and economic development reach more people
Rights at work	Freedom of association; elimination of forced labour; elimination of discrimination; and elimination of child labour
Social dialogue	All types of negotiation, consultation and exchange of information between, or among, representatives of governments, employers and workers on issues of common interest
Social protection	Access to an adequate level of social protection in the form of medical cover, social security payments
Working out of poverty	Opportunities for people to improve their situation, in terms of income, respect, dignity and communication – supporting economic, social and political empowerment.

The Ethical Trading Initiative (ETI)

3.14 The ETI is an alliance of companies, NGOs and trade union organisations committed to working together to identify and promote internationally agreed principles of ethical trade and employment, and to monitor and independently verify the observance of ethics code provisions.

3.15 The ETI publishes a code of labour practice (the 'base code') giving guidance on fundamental principles of ethical labour practices, based on international standards. These principles should by now be familiar.

1 Employment is freely chosen
2 Freedom of association and the right to collective bargaining are respected
3 Working conditions are safe and hygienic
4 Child labour shall not be used

5   Living wages are paid

6   Working hours are not excessive

7   No discrimination is practised

8   Regular employment is provided

9   No harsh or inhumane treatment is allowed.

3.16   CIPS affirms that 'ethical supply chain management is one of the greatest challenges facing organisations. It is becoming unacceptable for organisations to be unaware of how the workers involved in making their products or supplying their services are treated. The global nature of trade often leads to complexity within the supply chain; this alone can make ethical trading a daunting task in itself' (Practice Guide on CSR).

ISO 26000 Social Responsibility

3.17   ISO 26000: 2010, *Guidance for Social Responsibility,* was launched in November 2010. The Standard provides voluntary guidelines: it is *not* a management system standard, and is not intended to be used for certification purposes (like ISO 90001 or 14001) or regulatory or contractual use.

3.18   The core subjects and issues identified by the standard are listed in Table 6.3.

Table 6.3 *ISO 26000: 2010 core issues in CSR*

CORE SUBJECT	ISSUES
Corporate governance	
Human rights	Due diligence; human rights risk situations; avoidance of complicity; resolving grievances; discrimination and vulnerable groups; civil and political rights; economic, social and cultural rights; fundamental principles and rights at work
Labour practices	Employment and employment relationships; conditions of work and social protection; social dialogue; health and safety at work; human development and training in the workplace
The environment	Prevention of pollution; sustainable resource use; climate change mitigation and adaptation; protection of the environment, biodiversity and restoration of natural habitats
Fair operating practices	Anti-corruption; responsible political involvement; fair competition; promoting social responsibility in the value chain; respect for property rights
Consumer issues	Fair marketing, factual and unbiased information and fair contractual practices; protecting consumers' health and safety; sustainable consumption; consumer service, support and complaint resolution; consumer data protection and privacy; access to essential services; education and awareness
Community involvement and development	Community involvement; education and culture; employment creation and skills development; technology development and access; wealth and income creation; health; social investment

4   Reputational and brand risk

4.1   The emerging recognition of reputational risk is one of the driving factors behind the growth in profile and importance of risk management as a business discipline.

4.2   During the 1950s and 1960s, the main focus of risk management was the management and protection of physical assets (eg plant and equipment). However, subsequent decades saw the face of business changing: world markets became more mature, and marketing (and particularly branding) techniques developed; and intangible assets such as knowledge, branding and service became increasingly valuable.

Corporate reputation

4.3   Corporate reputation is defined *(*Charles J Fombrun, *Reputation: Realising Value from the Corporate Brand*) as 'the overall estimation in which a company is held by its constituents. A corporate reputation represents the "net" affective or emotional reaction – good-bad, weak or strong – of customers, investors, employees and general public to a company's name'. In other words, corporate reputation describes the *aggregate* effects of corporate identity (or corporate brand) and image on stakeholders' *overall evaluation* of the organisation: as a good employer, a trustworthy service provider, a socially responsible and ethical operator, a worthwhile investment – or not.

4.4   John Doorley & HF Garcia *(Reputation Management: The Key to Successful Public Relations and Corporate Communications)* summarise the concept of corporate reputation as follows:

Reputation = Sum of images = (Performance + Behaviour) + Communication

In other words, reputation is not simply an artefact of 'spin', public relations, corporate communications or image management: it is built up, over time, by the *experience* of stakeholders with the organisation. It is thus crucially related to issues such as quality and customer service, ethics, corporate responsibility and sustainability.

4.5   A **positive reputation** is potentially a key source of:

*   Distinctiveness, which can help differentiate the organisation from its competitors
*   Support for and trust in the organisation and its products (protecting or enhancing its market share, and potentially allowing premium pricing)
*   Stability and resilience in the face of change, crisis and issues (such as product recalls or environmental disasters) because of stakeholder trust
*   Positive stakeholder-generated word-of-mouth promotion and public relations (often trusted more than marketing messages)
*   A positive brand in labour and supply markets, enabling the organisation to attract and retain quality staff, supply partners, business partners and allies ('competitive architecture')
*   A positive brand in the financial markets, enabling the organisation to attract new sources of financial capital
*   Relationships of influence within the business environment (eg with local and national governments, pressure groups and interest groups, the media and so on)
*   Reduction of risk arising from all the above areas.

4.6   A key case study in this area is Johnson & Johnson's prompt recall of top-selling pain-relief drug Tylenol, when some capsules were found to have been contaminated with cyanide (as part of an extortion attempt). 'Market research showed a high level of confidence in both the Johnson & Johnson name and the Tylenol brand, and this trust was used as the basis to re-launch the drug after the packing had been redesigned to make it tamper-proof. The company's speed of response and highly effective communications throughout the crisis process... has become the management template for ethically prompt product withdrawal and transparency. Jim Burke [chairman of J & J at the time] said: 'The reputation of the corporation, which has been carefully built over 90 years, provided a reservoir of goodwill among the public, the people in the regulatory agencies, and the media, which was of incalculable value in helping to restore the brand' (Grahame R Dowling, *Corporate Reputations).*

4.7   Conversely, a **negative reputation, or reputational damage**, is a source of risk. It can:

- Erode support and trust for the organisation and its products and brands
- Create negative expectations (which make it more likely that people will have negative perceptions of their encounters with the organisation)
- Attract burdensome or hostile scrutiny from pressure groups, regulators and the media
- Damage the organisation's relationships with its key stakeholders – with negative effects on productivity, employee relations, sales and profitability, share price, supply chain relationships and so on.

Corporate brands and brand equity

4.8   A 'brand' is defined by marketing guru Philip Kotler as 'a name, term, sign, symbol or design, or combination of them, intended to *identify* the goods or services of one seller or group of sellers, and to *differentiate* them from those of competitors [in the perceptions of customers]'.

4.9   The term 'corporate brand' is used to describe the way an organisation as a whole (as distinct from its particular products or product families and ranges) projects itself: creating a distinctive name, visual identity and set of associations, as an expression of core corporate values and attributes. Virgin, Unilever, Diageo and Johnson & Johnson are examples of strong corporate brands – which also embrace families of strong product brands.

4.10   According to CBM Van Riel & Charles J Fombrun *(Essentials of Corporate Communication):* 'the purpose of a corporate brand is to personalise the company as a whole in order to create value from the company's strategic position, institutional activities, organisation, employees and portfolio of products and services. The corporate brand is increasingly being used to cast a favourable halo over everything the organisation does or says – and capitalise on its reputation.'

4.11   Fombrun further argues that 'Better-regarded companies build their reputations by developing practices which integrate social and economic considerations into their competitive strategies. They not only do things right – they do the right things. In doing so, they act like good citizens. They initiate policies that reflect their core values; that consider the joint welfare of investors, customers and employers, that invoke concern for the development of local communities; and that ensure the quality and environmental soundness of their technologies, products and services.'

Reputations and brands as corporate assets

4.12   Reputation and brands have increasingly been recognised as significant **intangible assets** of an organisation – which can be measured, valued and systematically managed. It has been estimated that the total value of organisations (their market value or capitalisation) could exceed the total value of their physical assets (book value or liquidation value) by a factor of 10 or more, based on the potential long-term earning potenital of their brands and reputation. 'The reputation component of market capitalisation – reputational capital – is a concept closely related to 'goodwill' and it is worth many billions of dollars in many large corporations. It has a value in not-for-profits, government and universities as well. For instance, a good reputation helps a university attract students and donors' (Doorley & Garcia).

4.13   The concept of 'brand equity' recognises the role that brands play in consumer purchase decisions, and measures the proportion of business value that can be attributed directly to branding. Various commercial tools are available to measure brand equity and value, using different variables, such as: brand strength (differentiation, relevance, differentiation), growth potential, value (enterprise value *minus* balance sheet assets), contribution to business earnings and so on.

Reputational and brand risk

4.14   As valuable assets, reputations and brands have also been recognised as highly vulnerable to risk. It is often said that reputations are hard won – and easily lost. Michael Regester & Judy Larkin (*Risk Issues and Crisis Management in Public Relations)* note that: 'Threats to reputation – whether real or perceived – can destroy, literally in hours or days, an image or brand developed and invested in over deacdes. These threats need to be anticipated, understood and planned for.'

4.15   A survey on risk management by the Economic Intelligence Unit places reputational risk (52%) above regulatory risk (41%) and human capital risk (41%) as the priority of corporate risk management activity.

4.16   Risks to reputation or corporate brands may arise from internal and external sources.

- Poor financial performance: falling profitability (or losses); collapse in share price; downward revision of profits and dividends and so on
- Crises of corporate governance and management, such as allegations of fraud or mismanagement
- Product or service quality failure, leading to gradual erosion of quality and reliability reputation and brand identity – or crisis (such as product safety recalls)
- Poor ethical, environmental or social responsibility performance (in general or in crisis) by the organisation or its supply chain
- Poor corporate or individual behaviour, arising from problems in the corporate culture or employee relations
- Failure to comply with legislation and regulation (ie compliance risk)
- Poor management of crises (lack of transparency or accountability, lack of ethical response, poor service recovery)
- Unmanaged negative communications (media coverage, internet discussion, rumours and so on)
- Association with other parties (including supply chain partners) or entities (eg country of origin or industry) whose reputations are damaged by any of the above.

Reputation and brand risk management

4.17   Reputational and brand risk management therefore requires a clear focus on a wide range of issues.

- The formulation and expression of clear core values and principles: what the organisation and brand 'stands for' and is willing to be responsible for – as a guide to reputation-consistent conduct
- Ensuring that corporate social responsibility and ethical values and policies are clearly communicated and managed within the organisation and across the supply chain
- The monitoring and measurement of reputational and brand strength, using methods such as: brand equity valuation; third party brand tracking tools (such as the Brand Asset Valuator, Brand Power, BrandZ or RepTrak); communications audits; media coverage monitoring; and third party measurement systems (eg *Fortune's* 'Most Admired Companies')
- A robust risk assessment and management system, with continuous monitoring and evaluation of reputational threats, and early warning of emerging and developing issues. Reputational exposure is often the consequence of *other* risk events (such as fraud, human error, supply disruption, technology failure, quality failure or health and safety incidents), so the identification, assessment and mitigation of *all* categories of risk will support reputation and brand defence.
- Sound risk management practices, with consistent enforcement of controls on governance and legal compliance (eg internal controls, accountabilities and reporting structures, codes of ethics and conduct, supplier codes, disciplinary frameworks)
- Proactive communication with stakeholder groups to understand their expectations, perceptions and sensitivities to particular issues (issues management).
- Establishing and regularly updating crisis management plans, defining specific decision-making and communication responsibilities within a nominated crisis management team

- Prompt, considered and effective communication with internal and external stakeholders, when crises (significant risk events) begin to develop. This should be supported by an open, trust-based communication climate, facilitating the flow of risk and problem information to decision-makers, minimising the risk of potentially damaging 'cover-ups' and supporting organisational learning.

Issues management

4.18　'Issues management' is a proactive process of identifying and analysing emerging controversies and issues which could potentially impact on reputation, and initiating action to manage stakeholder perceptions about them. It endeavours not just to fight public perception problems as they arise, but to: proactively initiate dialogue with stakeholders to identify potential sensitivities and issues of concern; educate stakeholders in the organisation's position on issues; and establish networks of goodwill and support.

4.19　Issues management may be the responsibility of the corporate communication department or risk management function. It consists of seven main phases (Regester & Larkin).

- Monitoring: establishing an early warning system by scanning research findings, media coverage and 'what is being said' by stakeholders and influencers
- Issue identification: identifying trends and stakeholder cues signalling issues that could potentially damage reputation or brands
- Issue prioritisation, on the basis of risk/impact and immediacy assessment (how likely, how costly, how urgent?)
- Issue analysis and preparation: determining how the issue is likely to develop; auditing the company's present position on the issue; appointing 'issue champions' (individuals who will develop authoritative, up-to-date knowledge of the issue); building influential relationships with supportive stakeholders; and setting up an issue task force to define and manage issue response strategies
- Response strategy formulation: deciding what the organisation's response to the issue should be
- Action programming and implementation: formulating policy and co-ordinating resources to support the response strategy
- Evaluation: assessing the success of response policies and programmes; capturing learning from failures and successes to inform future issues management.

Crisis management

4.20　'Crisis management' is the management of corporate response to a crisis, aimed at minimising or countering the potential reputational or brand damage. A crisis may be defined as any event that has the potential to cause significant reputational, operational or financial harm: interfering with operations; attracting negative scrutiny; damaging reputation; or impacting on profitability or shareholder value.

4.21　Examples of crises might therefore include: an ecological disaster (such as an oil spill); revelations of unethical behaviour by the organisation or its suppliers; a product recall due to safety problems; the discovery of fraud or mismanagement; consumer boycotts; major industrial accidents; product tampering or contamination (sabotage or extortion); and so on.

4.22　You should be able to think of your own examples: from suicides at the factories of Apple manufacturers in China; to the mass recall of Toyota cars (due to safety problems) or Mattel toys (due to the illegal use of lead paint) or Cadbury confectionery products (due to traces of salmonella); the grounding of Tiger Air (due to safety concerns) and Qantas (due to industrial action); the financial scandal at Enron; the Costa Concordia maritime disaster; the contamination of Perrier water by benzene; the recall of Dell computers due to fire hazards reported in their Sony battery packs; revelation of unethical labour practices by the suppliers of Oxfam's 'Make Poverty History' wristbands...

4.23　Doorley & Garcia argue that: 'Whether a company survives a crisis with its reputation, operations and financial condition intact is determined less by the severity of the crisis – the underlying event – than by the timeliness and quality of its response to the crisis... Effective crisis response – including both what a company does and what it says – provides companies with a competitive advantage and can even enhance reputation. Ineffective crisis response can cause significant harm to a company's operations, reputation and competitive position.'

4.24   Norman R Augustine ('Managing the crisis you tried to prevent', *Harvard Business Review)* proposes a six-stage model of the crisis management process.

- **Avoid the crisis**, using robust risk analysis and preventive measures
- **Prepare to manage the crisis**, with contingency planning (eg action plans, communication plans, back-up systems and suppliers), crisis simulation (eg fire and evacuation drills), and the establishment of a crisis-response team and resources
- **Recognise the crisis** when the risk event occurs. Monitor criticisms, concerns and questions and seek outside assessment: ignoring the first signs of crisis allows escalation. Understand how others will perceive the issue: address concerns and acknowledge the emotional aspects of the crisis
- **Contain the crisis:** take tough decisions fast and decisively to minimise harm; have a dedicated crisis management teamworking on the crisis; appoint a spokesperson for all public comment; keep stakeholders informed; control the agenda and messages.
- **Resolve the crisis:** take the facts direct to the public (backed by independent corroborators or champions if possible); demonstrate responsibility, willingness and transparency in investigation and resolving the problem; promote all resolutions and improvements made; offer incentives (if required) to win back stakeholders.
- **Profit from the crisis:** reap the benefits of enhanced stakeholder trust; learn from mistakes for enhanced risk management in future.

Chapter summary

- Organisations have increasingly accepted a responsibility to be good corporate citizens. This is the concept of corporate social responsibility.
- Businesses are increasingly ready to measure performance in light of the 'Triple Bottom Line': economic sustainability (profit); environmental sustainability (planet); and social sustainability (people).
- The importance of sustainability in business operations is now recognised in number of national and international standards (eg ISO 14001).
- Consumer pressure has caused organisations to guard against reputational and brand risk. Positive reputational image is regarded as a source of competitive advantage; negative image is a source of risk.

 ## Self-test questions

Numbers in brackets refer to the paragraphs where you can check your answers.

1   List measures that organisations can take to promote ethical sourcing. (1.3)

2   List reasons why ethical sourcing is increasingly pursued by organisations. (1.8)

3   What is meant by the 'Triple Bottom Line'? (2.3)

4   List control and mitigation measures that an organisation can adopt in relation to environmental risks. (2.8)

5   List the requirements for an EMS laid down by ISO 14001. (3.5)

6   List the objectives of the ILO in relation to sustainability. (Table 6.2)

7   List the general principles of the ETI. (3.15)

8   Define corporate reputation. (4.3)

9   List advantages of a positive corporate reputation. (4.5)

10 List sources of risk to reputation or corporate brands. (4.16)

CHAPTER 7

Project Risks

Assessment criteria and indicative content

2.1 Analyse the main risks in supply chain projects that are addressed by effective project management

- Definitions of a project and project management
- Achieving a balance between cost, quality and time
- The causes of risks in projects
- Relationships with contractors and allocating risk in projects and in the outsourcing of work or services

Section headings

1 Projects
2 Project management
3 Project variables and outcomes
4 Project-related risks
5 Allocating project risks

Introduction

In this chapter we shift focus from generic risk management to the specific contexts of projects. Although the syllabus refers to 'supply chain projects', it is clear from the indicative content that this does not imply purely procurement and supply projects such as supply base rationalisation, procurement research, cost reduction, supplier development or the development of e-procurement platforms. You are invited to consider the risks inherent in the complexities of project working, and in major projects such as IT, construction and engineering, in which procurement and supplier or contractor management will play a crucial role.

In this chapter we give an overview of the nature of project working and project management, and focus on identifying the main risks in projects – which the disciplines of project management are intended to address. Remember that, in this unit, the focus is on project management *as a way of mitigating supply chain risk:* in other words, how does managing activity as a *project* help to manage risk? It also addresses *project risk* (the vulnerability of projects to failure, cost and schedule overruns, health and safety issues, stakeholder conflict issues and so on) – and how effective project management can reduce those risks.

In Chapter 8 we will go on to look at the process of project management in more detail, using the 'lifecycle' model of project stages. And in Chapters 9–10, we will explore tools and techniques of project management in more detail.

1   Projects

What is a project?

1.1   The US Project Management Institute (PMI) defines a project as 'a temporary endeavour undertaken to create a unique product or service.' The UK Association for Project Management (APM) similarly defines projects as 'unique, transient endeavours, undertaken to achieve a desired outcome'.

- A 'temporary' or 'transient' nature distinguishes project work from the day-to-day operational tasks that are carried out in an organisation. A project, by contrast, has a defined start and end point, after which its activities and structures are disbanded.
- 'Uniqueness' highlights the fact that each project is effectively a 'one-off', designed to achieve a particular specified objective, desired outcome or outputs. Many construction projects, for example, require similar inputs and processes – but the output of one construction project (eg London's Wembley Stadium) is different from that of another (Heathrow Terminal 5).

1.2   Meredith and Mantel (*Project Management: a Managerial Approach*) suggest seven key characteristics of projects.

- *Importance:* the task must be important enough to justify the setting up of a special unit and activity outside the routine structure and processes of the organisation.
- *Performance:* all project activity is aimed towards a well defined set of desired outcomes, end results or deliverables. Problems can often occur when changes are made to the specification during the project that can cause delays and subsequent additional costs.
- *Lifecycle with a finite due date:* projects progress from a defined starting point to a defined termination point. They are not 'open ended'.
- *Interdependencies:* projects are complex exercises, in which activities must be carefully scheduled so that dependent activities can begin on time.
- *Uniqueness:* projects are 'one-off' activities. Even in the case of a 'repeat' project (such as building the same model of a house) there will still be differences in the time taken, resources used, personnel involved, etc.
- *Resources:* projects are carried out within the parameters of defined resource budgets.
- *Conflict:* projects are subject to the conflicting goals of stakeholder groups, and conflicting objectives (time, quality, cost). They also often compete for resources with 'business as usual' functions and functional departments.

1.3   Two other definitions, incorporating some of these key characteristics, are as follows.

- 'A unique set of co-ordinated activities, with definite starting and finishing points, undertaken by an individual or team to meet specific objectives within defined time, cost and quality parameters' (Office of Government Commerce)
- 'An activity, or usually a number of related activities, carried out according to a plan in order to achieve a definite objective within a certain period of time and which will cease when the objective is achieved.' (Lysons)

Examples of projects

1.4   In practice, projects take many forms, and are undertaken in many areas of business: 'from road building to databases, from new products to overseas factories, and from corporate acquisition to drug research' (Sadgrove). You can no doubt think of your own examples, from the building of London's Wembley Stadium to the management of the London 2012 Olympics; marketing research projects; new product or service development, re-design or launch; the design, development and installation of IT systems; or a business process re-engineering (BPR) exercise.

1.5   Lysons distinguishes four different types of project.

- **Manufacturing projects**: such as prototyping a new product, development work or any discrete application of machinery or equipment to attain a defined end goal.
- **Construction projects**: characterised by being based off-site from a headquarters or central location.
- **Management projects**: activities, often utilising cross-functional teams, that have a defined purpose, eg office relocation, simultaneous engineering teams etc.
- **Research projects**: aimed at the expansion of knowledge or the acquisition of new data or information.

1.6   Examples of projects in procurement and supply chain management might include: procurement research; supply base rationalisation or single sourcing; outsourcing; standardisation or variety reduction; warehouse relocation or re-design of the distribution system; the development and roll-out of a sustainable procurement policy; the implementation of quality management initiatives; or the development and implementation of an e-procurement system.

1.7   Many businesses are wholly project-based: examples might include management consultants, events management agencies, construction engineers and architects, and film and recording studios. Whatever the main work of the organisation, however, all firms must react to environmental change – and a project approach is often used to drive and manage change: in systems and processes, structures, products, supply chains and so on.

Project stakeholders

1.8   Project stakeholders are the individuals and groups in an organisation or supply chain who have an interest or 'stake' in the project, either by virtue of participation, or of interest in the outcome. *Process* stakeholders have an interest in how the project process is conducted (eg the project manager and participants, and groups such as users who want their views heard in relation to the project). *Outcome* stakeholders have an interest in the outcomes, outputs or deliverables of the project (eg users of a new system, or suppliers affected by supply chain change programmes).

1.9   Here are some identified stakeholder roles in a typical, formally structured project.

- The *project owner*: the person or group for whom the project is being carried out (eg an external or internal client or senior manager) – with a primary interest in outcomes
- The *project sponsor*: the person or group which provides, and is accountable for, resources invested in the project, and which is responsible for achievement of the project's business objectives and deliverables
- The *project champion:* representing the project to the rest of the organisation, promoting its business case, and securing 'buy in' and resources where required
- The *project board or steering committee*: a body representing the interests of the owner and sponsor, with responsibility for oversight of the project
- The *project manager*: the person responsible for planning, organising, co-ordinating and controlling the project, and managing the project team; reporting to the project board
- Specialist managers, such as a *risk manager* and/or *quality manager* to control these aspects of large projects, and *technical specialists* (such as engineering, legal, HR or procurement specialists)
- The *project team(s) and team leader(s):* the people responsible for carrying out the project work, reporting to the project manager. There may additionally be a *project support team* who contribute to the project (eg supplying information or services) but do not report directly to the project manager.
- Customers, beneficiaries, users, contractors and other stakeholders (including the wider community) who are either participants in the project or affected by its activities or outcomes.

1.10   Stakeholders may be a source of product risk, owing to multiple – potentially divergent or conflicting – stakeholder interests. This creates a critical need for:

- Analysis of stakeholder influence, viewpoints and interests (for example, using the Mendelow matrix or other stakeholder mapping and analysis techniques) in order proactively to manage potential conflicts and issues, and establish communication and issue-handling processes (such as grievance or dispute mechanisms)
- Managed communication with stakeholders throughout the project, to ensure the alignment of objectives and the co-ordination of activity – as well as making sure that direct participants have the information flows they need to fulfil their roles
- Managed expectations and perceptions: avoiding over-promising, providing regular progress reports and so on
- The establishment of grievance or dispute mechanisms to manage stakeholder conflicts. These may include consultation and negotiation mechanisms, or provision for mediation (facilitated negotiation) or arbitration (third party adjudication). On major projects, a Disputes Review Board (DRB) may be formed, with the responsibility of making immediate decisions on disputes, so that project work can proceed, subject to review and escalation if required.

2   Project management

2.1   The APM defines 'project management' as 'the process by which projects are defined, planned, monitored, controlled and delivered such that the agreed benefits are realised... Projects bring about change and project management is recognised as the most efficient way of managing such change'.

2.2   The Official Terminology of the Chartered Institute of Management Accountants (CIMA) defines project management as 'Integration of all aspects of a project, ensuring that the proper knowledge and resources are available when and where needed, and above all to ensure that the expected outcome is produced in a timely, cost-effective manner. The primary function of a project manager is to manage the trade-offs between performance, timeliness and cost.'

2.3   Maylor summarises the main differences between general management and project management: see Table 7.1

Table 7.1 *General management and project management*

GENERAL MANAGEMENT	PROJECT MANAGEMENT
Responsible for managing the status quo	Responsible for overseeing change
Authority defined by management structure	Lines of authority 'fuzzy'
Consistent set of tasks	Ever-changing set of tasks
Responsibility limited to own function	Responsibility for cross-functional activities
Works in 'permanent' organisational structures	Operates within structures that exist only for the life of the project
Tasks described as 'maintenance'	Mainly concerned with innovation
Main task is optimisation	Main task is resolution of conflict
Success determined by achievement of interim targets	Success determined by achievement of stated end goals
Limited set of variables	Contains intrinsic uncertainties

2.4   One of the key roles of project management is to monitor, reduce and manage risk. Effective project management puts in place a governance structure where lines of accountability are short and the responsibilities of individuals are clearly defined. Its processes are clearly documented and repeatable, so that those involved in the project can learn from the experiences of others.

Disciplines of project management

2.5   The PMI models the process of project management as embracing nine key disciplines or knowledge areas.

- *Project integration management*: project plan development and execution, and integrated change control
- *Project cost management*: resource planning, cost estimating and budgeting, and cost control
- *Project communications management*: communications planning, information, performance reporting and administrative closure
- *Project scope management*: project initiation, scope planning and definition, and scope change control
- *Project quality management*: quality planning, assurance and control
- *Project risk management*: risk management planning, risk identification, qualitative and quantitative risk analysis, risk response planning, and risk monitoring and control
- *Project time management*: activity definition and sequencing, activity duration estimating, schedule development and schedule control
- *Project HR management*: organisation, staff acquisition and team development
- *Project procurement management*: procurement planning, market engagement, source selection, contract administration and contract closure.

2.6   These knowledge areas support five project management **process areas**: initiation, planning, implementation, control and closure. We will discuss these processes in detail, as part of our exploration of the project lifecycle, in the following chapters.

The project management context

2.7   Maylor (*Project Management*) illustrates the context within which project management occurs by highlighting the nature of a project as a conversion process. This process depends on appropriate inputs; a carefully managed mechanism for working on the inputs; within a range of internal and external constraints; in order to produce pre-determined outputs: Figure 7.1. This is known as the ICOM (inputs, constraints, outputs, mechanisms) model.

Figure 7.1 *Project management as a conversion process*

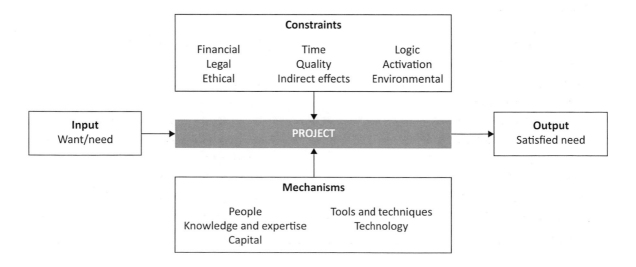

Project management software tools

2.8   Dennis Lock *(Project Management)* points out that for many projects it is quite feasible to draw up basic project schedules and resource plans (such as a critical path analysis or Gantt chart) by hand. Indeed, in the case of very simple projects this will actually be quicker than entering all the data on to a computerised system.

2.9   In practice, however, a project manager will invariably make use of available software tools, especially the industry standard Microsoft *Project*, and web-based applications which can be accessed by multiple users, regardless of location. One reason for this is the increasing *complexity* of modern projects and programmes, which can often be beyond the scope of manual techniques. Another reason is that *change* occurs very frequently over the life of a project: initial assumptions often have to be re-thought as the work progresses. Using a manual system, a project planner would have to re-compute all schedules and costings with each change.

2.10   The advantages of using software are numerous.

- The computer processes large volumes of data quickly and accurately.
- Where change is necessary, the computer re-calculates times and resources in a fraction of the time it would take manually.
- Software allows rapid production and communication (and flexible formatting) of management information.
- Recipients of the management information can interrogate the system or work interactively with it.
- A computer makes it possible to schedule a programme of many projects all together, in one combined multi-project calculation. This is especially important for organisations who are mostly engaged in project work.
- The software makes for standardisation. In organisations where project work is frequent, users benefit by being instantly familiar with the layout of project plans.
- Software tools can be linked to electronic contracts (including major project model form contracts for construction and engineering, such as NEC and FIDIC, discussed in Chapter 11): schedule or cost variances can automatically trigger remedial action, contract-appropriate claims for price variations, revised risk assessments and so on.

2.11   While these advantages are compelling, it is still worthwhile to mention some disadvantages of using software in general.

- It requires a financial investment. All personnel who are expected to participate significantly in the project will need to be provided with a copy of the software – and appropriate training.
- The project plans will reflect the perspective of the software manufacturer. Microsoft *Project*, for example, is said to be aimed at construction and civil engineering projects, and to be less suitable for other types of project.
- Software solutions may lack flexibility for the range of risks and issues that may be faced by a project – while fostering reliance, and potentially the erosion of human project management skills and risk awareness.

2.12   Some authorities would go farther than this in arguing against the use of software. Maylor, for example, is sceptical about its value. He cites the projects director of a large construction company as saying: 'I believe that computer-based project management software has set the subject back 20 years'. Maylor also refers to a UK plant of the Hewlett-Packard company, in which project planning at the highest level is based on whiteboards and post-it notes. This improves visibility of the overall project, while junior managers are free to use software to tackle their own particular area of the project.

The role of the project manager

2.13 The inherent challenge of project work places a considerable emphasis on the management of the project. The project manager must be able to successfully run the project and address barrier and risk issues.

2.14 The project manager leads the project team and is assigned the authority and responsibility for conducting the project and meeting the project objectives, on time and within budget. It is the project manager's job to direct and supervise the project from beginning to end – and to resist micro-management (excessively close supervision) from superiors in the project structure, which might stifle decisive action and flexibility.

2.15 CIPS summarises the project manager's role as follows.

- Shaping goals and objectives
- Obtaining resources
- Building roles and structures for the project team
- Establishing good communications
- Seeing the whole picture
- Moving things forwards (especially in difficult circumstances).

2.16 Meredith and Mantel argue that project managers need three key skill sets: competence in managing the project; leadership of the project team and stakeholders; and specific technical skills required by the project content. They also describe the desirable attributes of a project manager as follows.

- Someone with a strong technical background
- Someone hard nosed and mature
- Someone who has good relations with senior executives
- Someone who can keep the project team happy
- Someone who can walk on water!
- Someone with technical credibility
- Someone with administrative credibility
- Someone with sensitivity
- Someone with a strong ethical sense
- Someone able to handle stress

2.17 Meredith and Mantel highlight some of the special demands placed on the project manager: see Table 7.2.

Table 7.2 *Special demands on the project manager*

DEMAND	EXPLANATION
Acquiring adequate resources	Resources are often allocated to projects on the basis of optimism. Once the project is underway it may become clear that resources are insufficient. To keep the project on course, the PM must acquire additional resources
Acquiring and motivating personnel	Often personnel must be 'borrowed' from other functions, and must combine their routine jobs with their project work. The PM must be skilled in negotiating for release of staff and then in motivating the staff.
Dealing with obstacles	It is impossible to foresee the course of a project in every detail. Crises will emerge frequently. The PM must be adaptable enough to deal with this and must be able to call on his own experience and that of others in order to overcome the obstacles.
Making project goal trade-offs	We have already discussed the trade-offs between cost, time and quality. Decisions relating to these trade-offs of course fall to the PM.
Communication	We have also discussed the importance of keeping relevant stakeholders 'in the loop' by a systematic programme of communication. This too falls within the remit of the PM.
Negotiation	The PM must be a skilled negotiator to deal with each of the demands listed in this table, and in other areas of project work.

3   Project variables and outcomes

The cost-quality-time (CQT) triangle

3.1   A 'project objectives' triangle, also called the 'cost-quality-time' (CQT) triangle or the 'iron triangle' (because of the rigidity of the constraints it imposes) is often used to depict the interrelationship between the three key objectives of project management. Slack, Chambers and Johnston (*Operations Management*) illustrate this: see Figure 7.2.

Figure 7.2 *The cost quality time (CQT) or iron triangle*

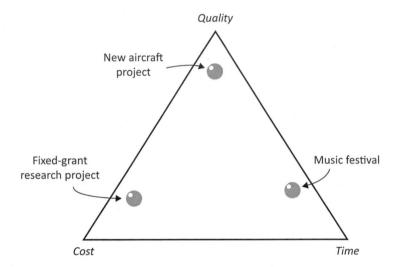

3.2   It is worth noting that, for the purposes of projects, 'quality' will often be defined and measured in terms of **scope or functionality**: in other words, all the work that was specified has been completed (scope) or all the outputs and deliverables have been achieved (functionality).

3.3   In an ideal world, we would like all projects to finish on time, within budget, and to the highest level of quality or functionality: all three objectives are important. However, as Figure 7.3 suggests, the **relative importance** of each objective may depend partly on the type of project concerned.

- In a project to construct a new type of aircraft, passenger safety is the overriding objective. The client cannot accept anything but the highest possible quality, regardless of the implications for cost and schedule.
- In a fixed-grant research project, the cost budget is totally inflexible. If money runs out, work will cease. The project managers must manage quality and schedule to fit in with the limited funds available.
- In a project to organise a music festival, customers will arrive at the scheduled time and 'the show must go on'. Regardless of quality and cost considerations, the time schedule is paramount.

3.4   The relative importance of the three objectives may alter over the life of the project. Conventional wisdom suggests that:

- Performance is the most important objective at the beginning of the project. In the planning phase, cost and schedule are regarded as less important: the crucial thing is to achieve the technical requirements of the project.
- As the project progresses, costs accumulate and the priority shifts to cost control. Project managers are ready to move the schedule and skimp on performance requirements if by doing so they can save costs.
- As the project nears completion, schedule is the overriding objective. Cost considerations (and perhaps performance) may be sacrificed in order to get the project completed by a specified date.

3.5   Research by Kloppenborg and Mantel, however, suggested that in fact:

- During the formation phase of a project, all three objectives are of high importance: reflecting the 'ideals' of the project.
- Schedule and performance objectives consistently take higher priority than cost – with the highest priority given to performance in the closing stage of the project. This reflects the fact that additional resources are often sacrificed to ensure that the project comes in on time, or at least delivers the desired outcome.

CQT trade-offs

3.6   In practice, project managers are generally faced with a trade-off between the three project objectives. Meredith and Mantel emphasise that 'a fundamental measure of the project manager's success is the skill with which the trade-offs among performance, time and cost are managed'.

3.7   In many cases it is possible, for example, to shorten the time taken on a project, or to get the schedule back on track, by investing additional resources (impacts on the cost objective) or by cutting corners on activities (impacting on the quality objective). Quality could be enhanced by taking more time or paying more. And so on.

3.8   Ideally, these decisions should be taken within a framework of stakeholder expectations. A stakeholder analysis should be part of the initial stages of the project: if the project manager has a clear idea of who the key stakeholders are, and what they regard as most important, he can make trade-offs that reflect their needs and priorities. The 'iron' part of the triangle can be a useful negotiating tool: if stakeholders can be made to accept that there really is an inflexible relationship between the three objectives, for example, the project manager may be able to negotiate additional resources if schedule or quality appears to be slipping.

3.9   We will look at a range of tactics for optimising time, cost and quality in Chapter 10, when we consider the project control process.

Other key variables

3.10   Not all commentators accept that the iron triangle is a valid model of project objectives. Some argue, in particular, that other objectives are present in most projects – and may become primary objectives for certain types of project. In community development and construction projects, for example, the project definition documents may include core objectives, outcomes and deliverables in regard to:

- **Safety:** the health and safety of workers, contractors and visitors to site operations
- **Sustainability:** the minimisation of environmental and social impacts of the project; reduction of wastes, pollution and congestion; support for SME subcontractors and so on
- **Stakeholders:** the minimisation of harmful impacts or costs on the community; the need for issues and reputation management, community consultation and grievance (issues handling) mechanisms; and so on.

3.11   Despite its limitations, however, most project managers would accept the usefulness of the CQT triangle model. It provides three clear targets that can be measured and controlled. It is at least a starting point for defining the objectives of most projects. And it is an easily understood tool for communicating with stakeholders.

4   Project-related risks

4.1   Sadgrove notes that, whatever diverse forms they take, projects have certain qualities in common: 'a big investment, a complex mix of people and assets, an uncertain outcome, and a high risk of failure.' Hence the focus of a whole section of your syllabus on the management of project-related risk!

4.2   Sadgrove continues: 'Many businesses are wholly project-based, whether management consultants or film studios. So their entire existence is routinely at risk. And failed projects have a devastating effect on corporate success. Whatever format they take, projects routinely overrun on cost and time, and don't work as they should. In many cases, the project is shelved.'

4.3   Certain key risks arise in all projects, owing to the nature of project working.

- The definition of a specific desired outcome from the project creates a failure risk: that is, the risk that objectives and deliverables will not be achieved. In some cases, a project may be cancelled or terminated before completion, because of emerging unacceptable risks, lack of resources, changing requirements or insurmountable performance problems.
- The non-routine or one-off nature of projects creates a high degree of uncertainty (that is: risk), since the particular set of circumstances and challenges has not been met before. This is particularly obvious in the case of engineering, technology and IT projects which typically make use of innovative (or experimental) processes and ideas. Uniqueness gives particular value to the capturing and transfer of learning from one project to another, as a form of risk management over time.
- The long time-scale and planning horizon of major projects (eg in construction) make them subject to contingencies: changes in stakeholder needs, circumstances, resource availability, external environmental factors and so on.
- The complexity of projects (with highly inter-dependent tasks, multi-organisational participation and multiple stakeholders) makes them vulnerable to risk, because of the difficulties of managing complexity.
- The multiple stakeholders of projects create a range of risks, including: delays or failure due to conflict, lack of support or lack of co-ordination between participant stakeholders (especially client, multiple contractors and suppliers, investors and users, say); stakeholder resistance to project aims or processes (including external secondary stakeholders, in the case of major projects such as construction).
- Projects typically have defined time, cost and quality targets, and a key source of project risk is variance from plan and missed targets. Cost and schedule overruns are very common – particularly where extra resources and time are required to achieve quality.
- Projects are often subject to changes to client specifications and contracts over time – especially where client expectations and project scope have not been negotiated, agreed and documented in detail in advance of work. This increases the risk of schedule or cost overruns, contract disputes and so on.

Causes of project failure

4.4   Because of their complexity, projects are inherently at risk of overrunning on time and/or cost, and/or failing to deliver their stated outcomes, and/or having to be abandoned because of external disruption or resource depletion. Such failures may be traced to some or all of the following shortcomings.

- Poor project definition by the project's owner (perhaps because of insufficient consultation with stakeholders or their failure to be specific about desired outcomes or deliverables), and changing specifications and milestones
- Lack of documentation of agreements in a formal project charter (usually because of haste to get a project 'up and running')
- Lack of ownership and personal accountability (especially, lack of senior management support, leaving room for escalating competition and conflict)

- Inadequately skilled or experienced project personnel
- Inconsistent understanding of required project activities, roles and responsibilities
- Inadequate reporting arrangements and feedback for decision-making
- Inadequate risk assessment in regard to disruption by contingencies and external factors, the use of unproven technology
- Untested assumptions made during the project initiation and planning phases (eg in regard to the availability of resources, supplier lead times and so on)
- Poor project management, which may emerge in: poor planning (eg unrealistic budgets or timetables, or illogical sequencing); poor control (lack of review at gates and milestones, lack of adjustment); poor handling of CQT trade-offs; poor team-building and management of the project team; and/or the appointment of technical specialists as project managers (where they lack the project management, leadership and communication skills).
- Lack of project risk management disciplines, such as risk identification and scenario planning; use of risk registers; allocation of risk accountabilities and ownership; and the management of environmental and supply chain risks which might affect the project.

Critical success factors for projects

4.5　Slack *et al (Operations Management)* give a detailed list of 'critical success factors' (CSFs) for successful project management.

- **Clearly defined goals**: which can include the overall philosophy or mission of the project, and the commitment to those goals from the project team members.
- **Competent project manager**: a project leader who has the necessary blend of interpersonal, technical and administrative skills.
- **Support of top management**: commitment that must be communicated to the project team. For cross-company projects, there may be nominated senior owners from each organisation involved in the project and its delivery.
- **Competent project-team members**: the selection and training of project teams who have the right blend of skills to successfully complete the project.
- **Sufficient resource allocation**: in the form of finance, personnel, logistics etc, which are available when required.
- **Clearly defined and visibly managed processes**, which are appropriate for the scale and complexity of the project.
- **Good communication channels**: between those involved on objectives, status, changes, organisational conditions and client needs – with timely decision-making supported by clear and short lines of reporting.
- **Control mechanisms**: put in place to monitor actual events and to recognise deviations from plan.
- **Feedback capabilities**: all parties concerned are able to review the project status and make suggestions and corrections.
- **Troubleshooting mechanisms**: a system or set of procedures which can tackle problems as they arise, trace them back to their root cause and resolve them. This enables the active management of risks and issues.
- **Project staff continuity**: the continued involvement of key project personnel through the project lifecycle. Frequent staff turnover can dissipate acquired learning and damage team morale.

4.6   Michael Greer similarly identifies 14 key principles for project success: Table 7.3.

Table 7.3 *Greer's 14 principles of project success*

1	Focus on three dimensions of success	These are the components of the iron triangle: cost, quality, schedule
2	Planning is everything	Planning must be thorough at the outset, and must be revised on an ongoing basis
3	Managers must transmit a sense of urgency	This is essential so as to maintain the project's momentum
4	Use a proven project lifecycle	The established models (discussed in Chapter 8) support quality and reduce work
5	Communicate in vivid detail	This applies to all project deliverables and all project activities
6	Deliverables must evolve gradually	To minimise risk and cost, build a little at a time, rather than 'jumping in with both feet'
7	Obtain clear sign-offs from sponsors	Anyone who has power to reject or demand revision of deliverables once they are complete must be required to examine and approve them as they are being built
8	Insist on a documented business need	Projects that correlate with a thorough analysis of the need for the project deliverables are more likely to succeed
9	Fight for time to do things right	Aim for a 'right first time' result rather than becoming resigned to later rework
10	Match responsibility with authority	Managers must have enough authority to acquire the resources needed to carry out their project responsibilities
11	Involve the sponsors and stakeholders	With authority to approve deliverables comes the responsibility to be an active participant in the project
12	Sell and re-sell the project	Sometimes the PM must function as a salesman to maintain commitment of stakeholders
13	Acquire the best people possible	The talents of skilled individuals can sometimes overcome shortage of other resources
14	Top management must actively set priorities	If there are too many projects to be completed successfully, top managers must prioritise

People risks in projects

4.7   Meredith and Mantel point out that 'meeting schedule and cost goals without compromising performance appears to be a technical problem for the project manager. Actually, it is only partly technical because it is also a human problem – more accurately, a technical problem with a human dimension'.

4.8   This is an important reminder that projects are achieved by people. No amount of sophisticated software and elaborate planning techniques will achieve success unless the project team have the necessary skills and motivation. The people aspects of projects are often identified as 'soft' aspects – in contrast to the 'hard' (or technical) aspects such as systems, technology, cost and scheduling. You might be familiar with this distinction from the McKinsey 7S model. Maylor adapts this for project management as follows:

- Soft factors: Staff, Skills, Style (culture), Stakeholders
- Hard factors: Structure (project lifecycle and management structure), Strategy and Systems (eg for project planning and control).

Resource constraints

4.9   Project managers will often have to cope with a constraint in resources (or possibly a bottleneck in the system generally). One approach to dealing with this is known as the **theory of constraints**, or TOC (EM Goldratt).

4.10   According to TOC, a five-step plan is required to deal with constraints.

- Identify the constraint – obviously!
- Exploit the constraint – this means making a virtue of the problem. For example, if the constraint is a certain type of machine, try to ensure that a back-up machine of the same type is available in case of breakdown.
- Subordinate everthing else to the constraint – it is pointless having everything else in top condition if the constraining factor is active. Therefore it is necessary to focus on the constraint, and make it the point around which schedules are based.
- Elevate the constraint – this means increasing the flow through this part of the system, in effect removing the constraint.
- Repeat the process.

Risks in product development and re-design projects

4.11   Lock (in *Project Management*) argues that 'development programmes aimed at introducing additions or changes to a company's product range are prone to overspending on cost budgets and late completion'. He highlights the risks of:

- Starting the project without an adequate project specification. To counter this, it is essential to begin with a detailed specification, covering expected performance, quality and reliability standards, styling guide-lines, size and weight limits, expected costs, expected commercial returns and time frame (with defined milestones).
- Introducing ill-thought out changes when the project is already under way. Tight control over progress, and in particular over proposed changes, is essential. Changes should not be introduced without adequate consideration from a dedicated 'change committee'.

Risks in process and systems development projects

4.12   As we have mentioned already, the output from a project is not necessarily a tangible product. Many projects are concerned with improving or re-designing operational processes, implementing new systems or technologies, or integrating existing systems (eg when introducing enterprise resource planning or ERP). Such projects clearly present a range of operational and technological risks.

4.13   We discussed risk mitigation measures for the introduction of new technology and systems in Chapter 3. One of the key risk mitigation measures is to either pilot test the new system (prior to wider roll-out) or to run the new system alongside the old system for a period (parallel running, or 'ramp up, ramp down'), in order to ensure that the new system functions as it should do.

Minimising risk in major projects: a process overview

4.14   Sadgrove suggests a basic nine-step process for managing project risk: Table 7.4.

Table 7.4 *A nine-step process for minimising project risk*

PLANNING FOR RISK	1	Obtain adequate information	• Undertake relevant market and technical research, including information about similar projects. • Quantify Value at Risk at each stage of the project, with sensitivity ('what if?') analysis. • Ensure flow of data on costs and timing at all stages of the project
	2	Examine all the options	• Evaluate alternatives to major project: eg make/do or buy options (outsource, acquisition, alliance), pilot project or staged roll-out
	3	Carry out a risk assessment	• Identify threats to the project, and its sensitivity to risk factors (eg rising costs, falling demand, disaster, contractor failure): maintain a risk register • Consider whether the organisation is financially and managerially equipped to carry out the project: risk avoidance or termination is an option.
	4	Allocate experienced staff	• Appoint a skilled project manager and/or consultants with experience in similar projects.
	5	Create a project plan	• Create the project plan (costs, milestones, people). • Modify the design, plan and contract, according to the identified risks.
RISK CONTROL	6	Invest one step at a time	• Where possible, stage costs and risks of investment. Review progress and risk at end-stage decision points (gateway reviews): go ahead or terminate?
	7	Build in flexibility	• Where possible, design flexibility into plant and equipment projects (in case market forecasts are inaccurate): eg for alternative uses, or capability for later expansion.
	8	Review progress regularly	• Continually reassess whether the business need is still valid: option to alter or halt the project. • Continually check milestones (compare progress against target) to identify where problems are occurring.
	9	Spread the risk	• Share project risks with other partners (equitably). • Utilise resources and competencies of partners • Lease equipment (minimise up-front investment) • Utilise insurances

4.15   Here are some of the key elements in project risk management (in addition to the discipline of risk identification, assessment and mitigation).

- **Project specification**: establishing an agreed statement of project *objectives* (cost, time and quality deliverables); *scope* (the boundaries of project tasks, outcomes and responsibilities); and *strategy* (the approach that will be taken to meet project objectives)
- **Project management plans**: objectives, schedules, cost budgets, health and safety and environmental policies, quality management plan, risk management plans (using the risk management cycle and a project risk register) and so on
- **Project control**: monitoring, end-of-stage reviews, milestones (key stage targets), gates (decision points at which each stage of work can be 'passed' or 'failed' for progress to the next stage), corrective action and/or plan adjustment – *plus* post-completion audit and review, and the capture of learning for the future
- **Tools and techniques**, such as budgetary control, variance reporting, Gantt charts, and network planning and control techniques such as critical path analysis.

We will explore all these aspects in detail in the following chapters of this Course Book.

5   Allocating project risks

Risk ownership in projects

5.1   As part of the risk management process the project manager should appoint an owner of each risk (as discussed in Chapter 2). It is the risk owner's responsibility to monitor the risk and update the risk management team regularly. Details of any changes to an existing situation should be formally recorded in the project risk register, with updates in control activity as required. The project manager has overall responsibility to monitor the risks and to ensure that procedures are being followed.

5.2   The following checklist on assignment of risk ownership should be used.

- Have owners been allocated to all the various parts of the complete risk process and have the future risks been catered for? For example, suppliers may be tasked with ownership of assessing risk as part of their contracts (as discussed later in this chapter).
- Are the various roles and responsibilities associated with ownership well defined?
- Do the individuals who have been allocated ownership actually have the authority?
- Have the various roles been communicated and understood?
- Are the nominated owners appropriate?
- In the event of change, can ownership be quickly and effectively reallocated?
- Are the differences between benefit and delivery risks understood?

Contractor relationships

5.3   Subcontracting and integrated project management are crucial factors in procurement for construction projects, in particular: enabling the prime contractor to access specialist expertise and incorporate specialist components (such as lifts or air-conditioning systems). An **integrated project team approach** is commonly used, bringing together multiple, integrated supply chains into one supply team (the primary or first-tier contractor) – which is then integrated with the client-side project team. This structure supports the management of the kinds of complex supply chains often employed in major construction projects.

5.4   **Supply chain relationships** are also crucially important, to support project working, co-ordination and co-operation over lengthy, complex projects. The UK's National Procurement Strategy argues that: 'Construction spend is the biggest single area of local authority external expenditure [especially on roads]. It follows that getting the procurement of construction, repair and maintenance right is likely to bring huge benefits. Benefits such as getting the job done right first time, and delivering it free of defect and dispute, also add real value. Many authorities have discovered that the best way they can secure those benefits is by developing long-term relationships with their contractors and the whole supply chain.'

Contract strategies

5.5   Once a decision has been made that a project is to be undertaken, a key issue to be addressed right at the outset is the overall management strategy. Should the client attempt to perform all or most of the work using internal resources, or should it rely on external contractors? In construction and engineering projects, for example, Peter Marsh (*Contracting for Engineering and Construction Projects*) identifies a range of options including: full turnkey, partial turnkey, client co-ordinated and management contracting strategies.

5.6   In a **full turnkey** approach, the external contractor takes entire responsibility for the project (design, engineering, procurement, construction, commissioning, testing, staff training and so on). Having specified its requirements and monitored progress, the client merely has to 'turn the key' to commence operation.

5.7   The contract underlying a strategy of this kind must obviously be very detailed and clear in its allocation of responsibilities and risks. The contractor must clearly bear the liability if the design fails to satisfy the client's requirements, and must also accept responsibility for all elements of the iron triangle.

5.8   Advantages and disadvantages of this approach, in terms of risk management, are summarised in Table 7.5.

Table 7.5 *Full turnkey contracting*

ADVANTAGES OF FULL TURNKEY	DISADVANTAGES OF FULL TURNKEY
Places maximum responsibility for the project in the hands of one organisation	Consequences are disastrous if an unsuitable contractor is selected
Probably achieves the quickest possible completion	In complex projects, the choice of possible contractors may be very limited
Encourages innovation in design, leading to improved quality and lower cost	Price must reflect the very high risk and responsibility assumed by contractor
Avoids diseconomies that arise when using multiple outside contractors	Contractor may skimp on areas beyond the strict contract terms (eg safety)
Minimises any claims for 'extras' as these are all a responsibility of the contractor	

5.9   In a **partial turnkey** approach, the external contractor assumes defined responsibilities, while leaving some activities (usually support activities) to the client, who also undertakes to co-ordinate the work of the various contributors. Client and contractor must negotiate the division of responsibilities and risks.

5.10   Marsh suggests that a common problem with this arrangement is that the client attempts to dictate how the turnkey contractor should perform the work – while holding it responsible for the outcome: an impossible situation. Another source of risk is where the client fails to perform its tasks on time, impacting on the schedule (and liability) of the turnkey contractor. Despite these issues, there are still turnkey-associated advantages. There is also the additional opportunity for the client to contract separately for activities outside the turnkey contract, taking advantage of specialist expertise, preferred supplier relationships or opportunistic price leverage.

5.11   In a traditional **client co-ordinated** approach, the client takes responsibility for design of the project works, while external contractors carry out the assigned works in line with the client's design and specification. The project may be split into separate 'packages' of work, with the client responsible for managing the different contractors in charge of each package.

5.12   This approach was for many years favoured by government and other public sector bodies, because of its perceived advantages of client control and price leverage (assigning work packages on the basis of competitive tendering). However, it has fallen out of favour in recent years. The benefit of early contractor involvement in project design has been recognised as contributing expertise and innovation. Project risk may also be created by:

• Lack of ownership in the project by contractors, leading to compliance-based conformance to specification *without* commitment to the real requirements and desired outcomes, or input to problem-solving and risk management
• Complexities of co-ordinating the work of two or more main contractors, whose only channel of communication will typically be through the client.

5.13   In a **management contracting** approach, the client appoints a professional project manager or consultants to direct the work, which will be carried out by one or more external contractors appointed by the project manager. The client has a direct contractual relationship with the project manager, and the project manager has a direct contractual relationship with the contractors. However, the project manager's liability for any breach of contract is usually limited to the amount(s) it can recover from the defaulting contractor.

5.14   The main advantage of this approach is leveraging project management expertise and resources. Marsh argues, however, that risk may arise from:

- The ambiguity in the role of the project manager, who is caught between the demands of the client and the contractors
- The client not knowing the full expected cost of the project at the outset, but having to rely on estimates provided by the project manager.

Project partnering

5.15   Here are some other options for structuring a project, accessing resources and sharing risks.

- **Joint ventures and consortia**. A joint venture is a formal arrangement by which two independent companies establish a new company which they jointly own (eg through shareholding, asset holding and profit distribution agreements) and manage. Their other businesses remain separate from this new, shared venture for the purposes of commissioning or undertaking a project. Where more than two companies enter this arrangement, it is called a 'consortium'. Joint ventures are often used to overcome barriers to entry in international markets, as well as pooling resources and expertise for major construction and infrastructure projects.
- **Public-private partnerships (PPPs).** In the UK, public-private partnerships (PPP) are schemes in which private sector firms and public authorities share capital and expertise, in various structured ways, with a view to building and operating major capital and infrastructure assets. Such structured partnerships were used to create national infrastructure such as the Channel Tunnel and the London Olympics facilities, as well as smaller projects such as hospitals, schools and barracks.
- A **Private Finance Initiative (PFI)** typically means that a private consortium raises the capital to design and build a public sector project. It is also contracted to maintain the buildings while a public authority uses them: eg providing cleaning, catering and security services. Once construction is complete, the public authority begins to pay back the private consortium for the cost of the buildings and their maintenance, plus interest. The contracts typically last for 30 years, after which time the buildings belong to the public authority.

5.16   The advantages of a PPP scheme for the public sector are claimed to be as follows.

- It can lower public sector costs (owing to the way service charges paid to the private sector operator are accounted for) – and can enable projects to be undertaken without having to cover capital costs from tax revenue, and without increasing public sector borrowing (the private partner incurs the borrowing)
- It can secure higher levels of capital expenditure and cashflow, owing to the potentially higher budget (and debt) capacity of the private sector partner. This may enable the public sector to undertake more large-scale projects than if they were prioritised under conventional public capital funding methods.
- It can tap into the creativity, expertise and existing capacity, capability and technology of private sector organisations, allowing higher levels of service to be provided to the public (supporting the objectives of the public sector partner) – especially where service levels are secured by appropriate KPIs, or where the private sector partner is putting its own capital at risk.
- It can therefore represent excellent value for money, especially if the private partner has already invested in the required equipment, technology and so on.
- Overall, a PPP scheme can enable a public sector body to complete projects, upgrade facilities and improve public services much faster than would otherwise be possible. According to healthcare think tank the Kings Fund, for example, the physical condition of most UK hospitals is now 'vastly improved' thanks to such partnerships.

7

5.17   On the other hand:

- Critics of PPP argue that the public sector may be surrendering control of the project, with the risk of lower levels of service, public accountability and consideration of environmental and social sustainability objectives.
- PFI contracts for PPPs can represent poor value for money and saddle the public sector with unsustainable financial commitments for decades to come. Some health authorities have found it too expensive to pay the annual charges to private sector contractors for building and servicing new hospitals, for example.
- The scheme may be unsustainably inflexible, because it ties public services into 20–30 year contracts – despite the fact that it is difficult to plan for changes in demand and service provision over such a long planning horizon.
- Trade unions have claimed that some PPP structures lead to poorer services, because private companies maintain facilities as cheaply as possible in order to maximise their profits.
- The pay and conditions of cleaners, catering and security staff in privately operated facilities are typically worse than their counterparts in the public sector.

5.18   From the private sector partner's point of view, the arrangement will only be successful to the extent that it gains a reasonable return on its investment (and perhaps also enhanced political influence). Some PFI consortia have seen profits soar: Octagon, the private consortium that financed and built the Norfolk and Norwich Hospital, refinanced the PFI deal so that the partners could take early profits, for example. But other firms, such as engineering firm Amey (with PFI contracts in education and road building) have been plunged into financial crisis.

Project pricing agreements

5.19   If the client wishes to allocate all cost-based risk to the contractor, it may seek to negotiate a fixed-price contract for the project. A **fixed-price agreement** is basically a firm agreement to pay a specified price when the items (services) specified by the contract have been delivered and accepted. Once agreed (on the basis of negotiation or competitive bidding), the price remains fixed for the duration of the contract. For major projects, such as construction or systems development, a firm price arrangement may be expressed in a **lump sum contract.** The principal and contractor agree a fixed sum for completing a specified programme of work by a given date.

5.20   The role and accuracy of the specification is paramount in awarding lump sum contracts, as it forms the basis for the contract. As with other forms of firm price agreements, a lump sum approach ensures a high degree of contractor motivation (since the contractor is liable for any cost blowouts) – but it can also lead to quality or performance concerns, if the supplier is forced to cut corners, to reduce its exposure to cost blowouts, towards the end of the contract. The project manager needs to monitor progress carefully (particularly on quality issues).

5.21   Some flexibility may expressly be permitted for adjustments to the price arising from changes in the scope of the contract: for example, if additional requirements are added (adding cost) or a project component is removed (subtracting cost). There may also be flexibility for the supplier to request some relief for losses arising from escalating costs, if the customer has contributed to those costs (eg by changing designs) – especially if the supplier is in a strong position (eg because no alternative suppliers are available at the right time or price to meet the need).

5.22   A fixed price may be set, but with **provision for upward or downward revision** on the occurrence (or non-occurrence) of specified contingencies, through the insertion of a contract price adjustment (CPA) clause. Such arrangements are used to recognise volatile labour or supply market conditions which make firm fixed pricing difficult – and would otherwise necessitate large 'contingency allowances' in the contract price. These may disadvantage the supplier if forecast price rises are greater than expected, or the buyer if they are less than expected.

5.23 The contract may stipulate that negotiated price adjustments are allowable, based on the following factors.

- **Actual increases or decreases** in material, labour, commodity or energy and fuel costs (depending on the cost vulnerabilities of the supply market) within the life of the contract, beyond the control of the supplier, and beyond a specified range of variation. Eligible costs and contingency events (eg exchange rate fluctuations outside an agreed range, or a rise in air freight costs due to new taxes, rising oil prices or carbon offset requirements) will have to be identified and closely defined, or subject to negotiation. The supplier's cost schedules and breakdowns will have to be monitored and verified to justify price adjustments.
- **Links to specified indices** relevant to supply market costs, for example commodities indices or the Labour Market Index.
- **The use of indexation and price adjustment formulae**, such as the British Electrotechnical and Allied Manufacturers Association (BEAMA) formula, which calculates the likely variation of labour and materials costs, based on industry average data, throughout the contract period, as a percentage of the total agreed contract price. The resulting industry-average cost variations can then be justified, as the basis of a claim for contract price adjustment.

5.24 If the buyer is unable to draw up a detailed enough specification to base the contract and pricing schedule on, it may agree a **schedule of rates or charges** (eg per hours worked, or per volume of materials used) associated with aspects of the anticipated work. (This is sometimes known as a 'measured form contract'.) Payment is then made against actual quantities, applying the agreed rates.

Risk/reward or incentivised contracts

5.25 Risk/reward or incentivised contacts are intended to give the contractor a meaningful stake in the project outcome, in the meeting of objectives, and in the management of project risks. Anywhere from 10–40% of the total value of the contract may be made part of the risk/reward element: contingent upon the contractor meeting defined KPIs and objectives for cost and budget, key milestone dates and completion date. Sadgrove suggests a structure where the client guarantees to pay 90% of the contract value, with an extra 20% if the supplier meets the objectives. The supplier thus stands to lose 10% for failure – but gain a 'bonus' 10% for success.

5.26 Here are some options for incentivised contracts, of different types.

- The establishment of a negotiated **target cost** for supply, on which a fixed maximum price (including a 'target profit' for the supplier) is based. The target cost will be an agreed amount that represents the most likely result under 'normal' business conditions. If the supplier achieves cost savings – ie comes in under the target cost – the amount of the savings will be shared with the buyer, on an agreed percentage or proportion basis.
- Staged payments (so that the supplier only gets paid in full on completion of the project) or contingency payments (eg part of the payment is linked to KPI performance or cost savings) or faster payment for early delivery (eg pay-on-receipt arrangements)
- Specified bonus payments (or incentive fees) added to the fixed price, linked to attainment of specific key performance indicators (KPIs), cost savings or improvement targets (eg for extra units of productivity, or each day or week ahead of schedule).
- Revenue, profit or gain sharing (eg allocating the supplier an agreed percentage or flat fee bonus for cost savings). Where supplier improvements create added value, revenue or profit for the buyer, the 'gain' is shared: a 'win-win' outcome.

5.27 In any form of incentive contract based on cost targets or reductions, the cost responsibility is shared by the buyer and supplier. As well as motivating the supplier to control costs, this may prevent the supplier from inflating or 'padding' the contract price to minimise the risks of cost uncertainty.

Self-test questions

Numbers in brackets refer to the paragraphs where you can check your answers.

1   List the seven key characteristics of projects identified by Meredith and Mantel. (1.2)

2   List stakeholder roles in a formally structured project. (1.9)

3   List differences between general management and project management. (Table 7.1)

4   What are the advantages of using project software? (2.10)

5   Describe how the relative importance of project objectives may change over the duration of the project. (3.4, 3.5)

6   Give examples of risks that arise in all projects. (4.3)

7   List the nine steps in Sadgrove's process for managing project risks. (Table 7.4)

8   What is meant by a full turnkey approach to project management? (5.6)

9   List criticisms of public private partnerships. (5.17)

10   Give examples of incentivised pricing arrangements. (5.26)

CHAPTER 8

The Project Lifecycle

Assessment criteria and indicative content

 2.2 Compare project lifecycle models that can mitigate risks in supply chains

- Staged models for project lifecycles
- Initiation and defining projects and risks
- Project planning
- Project organisation and implementation
- Measuring, monitoring, control and improvement
- Project closure

Section headings

1 Project lifecycle models
2 Project initiation and definition
3 Project planning
4 Organisation and implementation
5 Measuring, monitoring, control and improvement
6 Project closure

Introduction

In this chapter we give an overview of the main stages through which management of a project may progress. Projects typically go through a number of generic phases, which can be seen as the 'life' or 'lifecycle' of the project over time, from 'birth' to 'exit'. There are different ways of distinguishing such phases, and in this chapter we look at a number of models: broadly, however, they are talking about much the same activities, differently grouped and labelled.

We then go on to give an overview of the purpose and main activities of each stage – highlighting their contribution to risk management. Chapters 9 and 10 will follow up on this analysis by exploring the main stages in more detail – but this time, focusing on practical tools and techniques of project management at each stage.

1 Project lifecycle models

1.1 As we noted in our Introduction to this chapter, there are various staged models of the project lifecycle, and we will briefly survey some influential examples.

A four stage model: define, design, do, develop

1.2 Maylor puts forward a four-phase model of the project lifecycle, under the catchy title of the 4Ds: Table 8.1.

Table 8.1 *The 4Ds (four stage) model of project lifecycle*

PHASE	KEY ISSUES	KEY ACTIVITIES DESCRIPTION
D1: Define the project	Project and organisational strategy, goal definition *Key questions*: What is to be done? Why is it to be done?	*Conceptualisation*: Generate explicit statements of needs *Analysis*: Identify what has to be provided to meet needs: is the project feasible?
D2: Design the project process	Modelling and planning, estimating, resource analysis, conflict resolution and justification *Key questions*: How will it be done? Who will be involved? When can it start and finish?	*Proposal*: Show how needs will be met through project activity *Justification*: Prepare and evaluate financial costs and benefits from the project *Agreement*: Go-ahead is agreed by the project sponsor
D3: Deliver the project (do it!)	Organisation, control, leadership, decision making and problem solving *Key question*: How should the project be managed on a day-to-day basis?	*Start-up*: Gather resources, assemble project teams *Execution*: Carry out defined activities *Completion*: Time or money constraint reached or activity series completed *Handover*: Output of the project passed to the client or user
D4: Develop the process	Assessment of process and outcomes of the project, evaluation, changes for the future *Key question*: How can the process be continually improved?	*Review*: Identify the outcomes for all stakeholders *Feedback*: Put in place improvements to procedures, fill gaps in knowledge, document lessons for the future

1.3 Maylor argues that there is no 'most important phase'. All phases are important, because the eventual outcome will only be as good as the weakest link in the chain. This means that all phases must be carried out effectively if the project is to succeed. In this respect, even Maylor's final phase is critical because of its impact on future projects.

1.4 Another important point noted by Maylor is that the project manager is often not involved in the early stages of this process. Instead, he is handed a brief once the D1 phase has been completed by another party. This means that the project manager is not involved in problem avoidance measures at the earliest possible time, which can store up difficulties later in the project.

A five-stage model

1.5 Weiss & Wysocki (*5-Phase Project Management: a Practical Planning and Implementation Guide*) propose a five-phase lifecycle model: Table 8.2. Note that the general lifecycle is essentially the same as a four-phase model, but distinguishes more clearly the 'do'/implementation processes of 'organisation' and 'control'. This is arguably helpful for risk management, in separately highlighting the need for measuring, monitoring and control of project progress and performance.

Table 8.2 *Weiss and Wysocki's five-phase lifecycle*

PHASE	ACTIVITIES	DELIVERABLES
Definition	State problem Identify goals List objectives Obtain preliminary resources Identify assumptions and risks	Project overview
Planning	Identify project activities Estimate time and cost Sequence activities Identify which activities are critical Write project proposal	Work breakdown Project network Critical path analysis Project proposal
Organising	Obtain resources Recruit project leader Recruit project team Organise project team Assign work packages	Criteria for success Work description Work assignments
Controlling	Define management style Establish control tools Prepare sit-reps (situation reports) Review project schedule Issue change orders	Variances from targets Sit-reps Staff allocation
Closing	Gain client acceptance Install deliverables Document the project Issue final report Conduct review of the project	Final report Audit Recommendations for future projects

The PRINCE2 model

1.6   In 1989 the UK government issued a standard guide to the management of IT projects (PRINCE: Projects In Controlled Environments) and in 1996, PRINCE2 was released as a generic project management methodology. PRINCE2 is now widely used in the public and private sectors, for major projects which justify the scale and complexity of the structure and administrative requirements.

1.7   The PRINCE2 methodology is based on eight project processes: Figure 8.1. Whether or not PRINCE2 is adopted as a framework, this offers a best-practice view of the kinds of processes and structures required for effective project management.

8

Figure 8.1 *An overview of PRINCE2 processes*

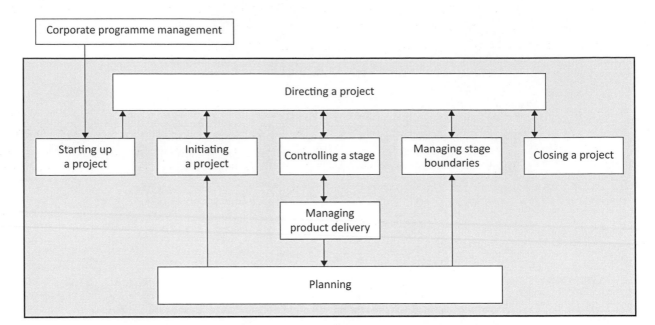

1.8   Briefly surveying each of the elements or processes of project management in turn:

- **Directing a project** is carried out by a senior management team, referred to as the project board. It involves: defining the project; allocating resources to it; overseeing the project throughout its duration on a 'management by exception' basis; and taking responsibility for both project assurance (ensuring achievement of objectives while managing risk factors), and project support (providing a technical and managerial resource for the project team).
- **Planning a project** involves the use of structured tools throughout the project, but especially at the beginning. The aim is to provide a model of the project activities, their sequence and duration, the resource requirements and any associated risks
- **Starting up a project** concerns the development of infrastructure and organisation. A project team must be appointed. Objectives should be assigned to the individuals involved. A project brief is prepared. Decisions are taken on the overall approach to be adopted. It is important at this stage to ensure availability of all information required for the project team.
- **Initiating a project** (usually carried out by the project board) involves development of the project brief as a fully-fledged business case for the project. Decisions are taken on the project controls to be adopted and the methods to be used to ensure quality.
- **Controlling a stage** involves authorising work, monitoring progress, monitoring changes and taking any necessary corrective action to stage progress in line with objectives. (The PRINCE2 methodology is based on breaking down the overall project into stages, which are further broken down in order to derive 'work packages' which can be assigned to individuals or teams.)
- **Managing product delivery** means ensuring that each work package is appropriately accepted, executed and delivered. Managers must ensure that all work is done according to specification and in line with the project objectives. Outputs must meet accepted quality criteria and must be subject to a defined approval process.
- **Managing stage boundaries** is about managing the transition from one project stage to the next: conducting 'gateway' reviews; ensuring that all outputs from the stage have been delivered; providing information to enable the project board to authorise continuation to the next stage; and recording any information or lessons learned that may help with the following stage or later stages.
- **Closing a project** involves shutting down the project systems, reporting on project completion, establishing that project objectives have been achieved, and identifying areas for improvement in future projects.

1.9   PRINCE2 also specifies a number of key documents (in addition to mainstream project plans and control reports), including: a quality log (recording any checks carried out on the product or the process); issue log (recording any problems experienced and any changes made as a result); and risk log (recording the main risks associated with the project and the control actions performed so as to manage them).

Mapping the project lifecycle

1.10   The lifecycle can be mapped to show the effect of the investment of different levels of resource and effort at successive stages of a project: in other words, the time distribution of project effort. A broadly typical project lifecycle would reflect a relatively slow start-up phase; a middle phase in which rapid progress is made, as resources are deployed productively; and an end phase in which progress slows (as 'loose ends' are tied up) and effort and resources are withdrawn: Figure 8.2.

Figure 8.2 *A typical time distribution of project effort*

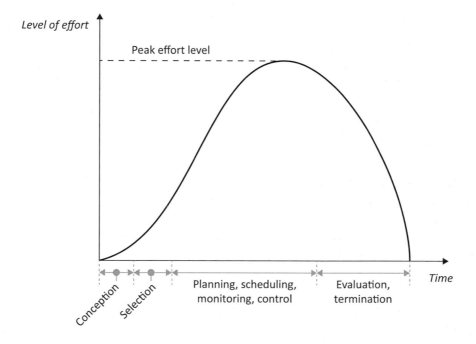

1.11   Another approach to lifecycle mapping is to map momentum for project completion over time. A typical construction project, for example, might exhibit a slow start (initial planning, permissions and contracting); followed by a period of swift momentum when the work begins in earnest; and a slower move towards completion (finalising and clearing up): Figure 8.3.

Figure 8.3 *A typical 'S curve' project lifecycle*

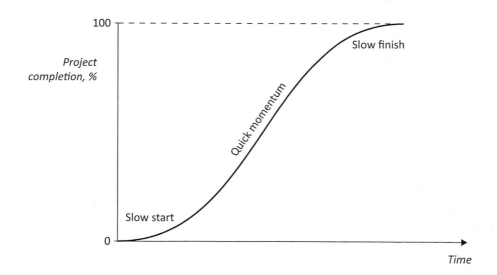

1.12   You might be able to see how other patterns could emerge in different types of project.

- The curve for some types of software development might reflect the fact that most of the life of the project is in planning and conceptualising: the bulk of outputs and deliverables are achieved in a relatively short, steep curve towards the end.
- The curve for a project to install new technology, or to introduce a sustainable procurement policy, say, might reflect the fact that the client wants 'quick wins': beginning with deliverables that provide the biggest benefits, and momentum for change. This will mean rapid progress in the earlier stages, with slower gains later on.
- Some projects may show rapid initial progress, followed by a lull or plateau (eg as changes are consolidated), culminating in a final push to completion: an inverted 'S' curve.

1.13   Awareness of such patterns will help the project manager to assess the resource levels required at different phases of the project – and to manage the momentum expectations of the project client and key stakeholders.

Risk management focus through the lifecycle

1.14   Different risks may be a priority at different stages of the lifecycle. For example:

- **Define/initiation:** the key risks may be excessively rigid definition; failure to involve key stakeholders in definition; conflict between stakeholders; and failure to obtain sponsorship and commitment.
- **Design/planning:** the key risks may be lack of information; lack of planning; excessively detailed, inflexible planning; over-optimism (lack of slack time, contingency plans); inadequate resourcing; lack of project management, specialist and/or teamworking skills; and unclear structures of authority and reporting.
- **Do/execution:** the key risks may be inadequate monitoring, review and control; lack of flexibility in responding to contingencies and trade-offs; missed milestones and targets (cost, time, quality); failure to pass to the next stage at gateway review; losing sight of overall objectives; health and safety, technology and other operational risks; and/or environmental (STEEPLE) factor risk, as relevant to the particular type of project.
- **Develop/exit:** the key risks may be failure to complete the project; failure to recognise when outcomes have been achieved; and failure to audit the process and capture learning for future projects.

1.15   It is also worth noting that estimates of risk are much more prone to error in the earlier phases of a project. Meredith and Mantel illustrate this by considering an estimate of project cost made at three different times: Time 1 (the start of the project), Time 2 and Time 3: Figure 8.4.

Figure 8.4 *Estimates of project cost made at Times 1, 2 and 3*

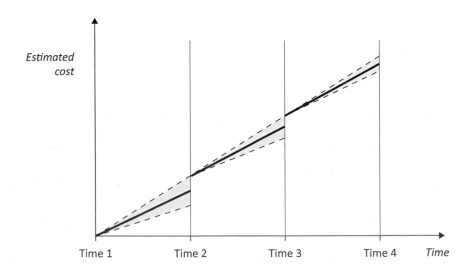

1.16 The solid line in the centre represents our best estimate of the expected costs. The shaded areas indicate the extent of our uncertainty: costs may be slightly less than expected, or considerably more. The important point is that the shaded area reduces as the project progresses. At the beginning of the project, we have considerable uncertainty about the possible costs. As time progresses, we become more sure of our ground as various project deliverables are already 'in the bag'.

Conflict risk through the lifecycle

1.17 Influential research by HJ Thamhain & DL Wilemon ('Conflict management in project lifecycles'; *Sloan Management Review*) focused specifically on the risk of conflict arising between project stakeholders at different stages of the project lifecycle. The study showed that different issues were a source of conflict at different phases of the project, and that conflict varied in intensity over the life of the project: Figure 8.5.

Figure 8.5 *Conflict intensity over the project lifecycle*

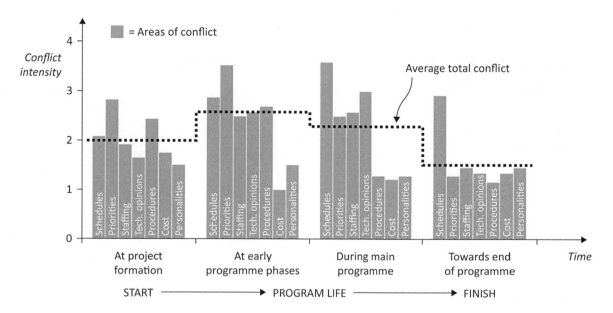

1.18 Interpreting this diagram:

- Intense conflict over schedules and priorities is virtually a constant over the project lifecycle. The same can be said about staffing issues, at a slightly lower level of conflict.
- Conflicts over cost are at their most prominent in the very early stages of the lifecycle, but tend to be well below average in intensity.
- Conflict over procedures takes place mainly in the earlier stages: once they have been agreed, there is a greater likelihood of straightforward compliance.
- Technical issues are an important source of conflict, particularly during the main phase of the lifecycle – when the real work is being done.

Using project lifecycle (PLC) models

1.19 The value of the PLC to project planning and control lies, broadly, in allowing project managers to:

- Understand the distinct phases that all projects go through, and the risks, resource requirements, priorities and challenges of each phase
- Manage the expectations of stakeholders at each stage, based on identified risks and resource requirements, progress patterns and so on
- Break down the project in a rational manner, to facilitate planning and control of distinct phases of activity
- Apply 'stage'-based planning and control tools, such as 'gates' (approval points), end-stage reviews

and end-stage approvals, so that the project does not move to the next stage until the previous stage has been satisfactorily completed.

1.20 We will now attempt to give an overview of the key stages of the project lifecycle, using the phases identified in the syllabus. All but the project initiation and definition stages are covered in more detail in separate learning outcomes, and will accordingly be explored in Chapters 9 and 10.

2 Project initiation and definition

Project selection

2.1 An initial decision may have to be taken on which projects to undertake: in other words, whether to accept or avoid project risk.

2.2 Meredith & Mantel identify the following non-numerical (qualitative) approaches to project selection.

- The **sacred cow**: a project is suggested by a senior and powerful leader in the organisation – and others have no option but to implement it.
- The **operating necessity**: if a business-critical system is threatened with collapse, a project to rescue it is a necessity, with little further formal justification.
- The **competitive necessity**: an organisation may need to take action to maintain its competitive position (eg by modernising its IT or re-designing products).
- The **product line extension**: a project to develop and distribute new products may be judged on the degree to which it fits the firm's existing product line.
- The **comparative benefit model**: projects are ranked by reference to the added value benefits they bring to the organisation, and those offering the greatest benefits are selected for implementation.

2.3 Alternatively or additionally, quantitative or numerical methods of project evaluation may be used, generally based on calculations of profitability, using investment appraisal techniques such as payback period, accounting rate of return and discounted cashflow. Meredith and Mantel also suggest project 'scoring' methods.

- The **unweighted factor model**. A list of relevant evaluation criteria is established (eg consistency with current operations, or potential increase in market share). Each project is then scored according to the number of criteria it satisfies. A problem with this is that it does not identify the *extent* to which a project matches a particular criterion.
- The **unweighted factor scoring model** remedies this problem by identifying (on a scale of 1 to 5) how closely each project matches particular criteria. A further problem remains, however, since neither of these methods distinguishes between criteria of high and low importance.
- The **weighted factor scoring model** additionally weights each criterion to reflect its importance to the organisation. A project that matches highly-weighted criteria is preferable to one that only scores well on low-weight criteria.

Business case

2.4 The formulation and approval of 'business case' is an important part of procurement authorisations in the public sector, and PRINCE2, for example, places considerable emphasis on definition of the business case of a project, at the project initiation stage. Organisations are forced to focus on doing the right projects, at the right times, for the right reasons, by making the start of a project and its continued existence (at review stages) dependent on a valid ongoing business case, and delivery of business case outcomes.

2.5 The term 'business case' is used for the justification of a project in terms of its identifiable business benefits, balanced against any recognised constraints, costs and risks involved in obtaining those benefits. Business benefits may take the form of increased revenue, reduced costs, enhanced profitability or value for money (especially in public sector contexts); increased capacity or capability; improved performance; enhanced shareholder value; improved brand equity; and so on.

2.6 Developing a business case involves comparing a range of business options for delivery of project objectives (eg partnering or subcontracting), and recommending a preferred option for approval by the executive board, whose role it is to ensure that business case outcomes are delivered through the life of the project. (The business case will contain target costs and benefits, and agreed variations, which will be scrutinised at key decision points in the project lifecycle.)

2.7 A full-scale business case may require detailed project cost-benefit analysis and investment appraisal, using financial and commercial modelling techniques (such as payback period, accounting rate of return and discounted cashflow).

2.8 Since business case development is a time-consuming and costly exercise, it may be preceded by a project feasibility study, which considers high-level objectives and possible options, with ballpark figures for costs and benefits. The feasibility study will be used to assess whether the initial proposals are robust enough to take forward to developing a full-scale business case.

2.9 It is worth noting that a project may be a 'technical success' (ie it conforms to specification in terms of project deliverables) but a 'business failure' (ie it fails to achieve the wider contribution specified in the business case). For example:

- A construction project may be completed on-budget, on-time and to specification – but may still fail to deliver planned business benefits (eg flow-on future revenue from a build-and-operate contract, enhanced shareholder value, gain in reputational capital, learning and capability development, partnership development – and so on).
- A technical success in developing and launching a new product may be a business failure if planned financial and commercial benefits (product adoption, revenue, return on investment, profitability, market share, brand development) are not achieved.

Project definition and specification

2.10 A project requires a clear and unambiguous statement that encompasses three aspects.

- **Its objectives**: the end result that the project is trying to achieve. The objectives provide a focus to the project team. Good objectives will be clear, measurable and quantifiable. This may be made easier if they are broken into smaller staged sets of objectives that will come together to meet the overall objective at the end. Common objectives would be cost, time and quality.
- **Its scope**: the exact range and responsibilities covered by project management. The scope of the project serves to identify the work content and outcomes: what is included and what is not. A firm grasp of the agreed scope of the project must be maintained throughout its life. The scope of the project also helps to define project participants, time periods including start and end dates, the commercial and legal responsibilities of those involved and the resources to be employed.
- **Its strategy**: how the project management role will ensure that the objectives will be met. The strategy enables an overview of the project and allows for phases of the project to be identified which then allows for milestones to be set. These can then be conveyed to those involved so as to provide a common understanding.

2.11 A **project specification** is one form of project definition. The draft specification will usually need clarification with everyone concerned with the project (from originator, through the workers, to the end-customer) to ensure everyone is working with the same understanding. The outcome of this deliberation should be a written definition of what is required, by when; and this must be agreed by all involved.

2.12 The work on the specification can be seen as the first stage of quality assurance – and a crucial activity in risk management – since we are looking for and countering problems at the very foundation of the project.

Developing a project initiation document (PID)

2.13 Different authorities describe different procedures and documentation for getting a project off the ground. One model often referred to in the literature is the exchange of a project brief and a project initiation document.

- The client prepares the **project brief** or terms of reference, specifying the deliverables it requires.
- The project organisation replies by sending a **project initiation document (PID)** or specification.

2.14 A PID should include the following elements.

- Project vision, goals and objectives
- The business case for the project
- The critical success factors by which achievement of the objectives will be judged
- Details of the project scope (organisation, functional areas, timetable etc)
- A risk assessment
- Roles and responsibilities within the project team
- Project control mechanisms
- Reporting lines and procedures
- A list of planning milestones
- The project budget

3 Project planning

The project management plan

3.1 The project management plan is the document that embodies the project. It is the most important document in the overall planning, monitoring, and implementation of the project and should be 'owned' by the project manager and his or her team.

3.2 Meredith and Mantel list the elements of a project plan: Table 8.3.

Table 8.3 *Elements of a project plan*

ELEMENT	DESCRIPTION
Overview	A short summary of the project objectives and scope, as discussed already above
Objectives	A more detailed statement of technical and profit goals
General approach	Describes both the managerial and the technical approaches to the work
Contractual aspects	Lists all reporting requirements, customer-supplied resources, liaison arrangements, review and cancellation procedures etc
Schedules	Lists all tasks and milestones with estimated dates
Resources	The budget, and cost monitoring and control procedures
Personnel	The skills and expertise needed for the project
Risk management plans	Identifying potential threats, planned responses and risk owners, and specifying the use of a project risk register
Evaluation methods	Standards should be established at the project's inception against which its eventual success or failure can be evaluated

Detailed project planning

3.3 More detailed project plans will be developed from the overview project plan. The PRINCE2 hierarchy of plans, for example, includes the project plan, a stage plan (for each stage of the project), detailed plans (if more detail is needed at any point in a stage) and individual work plans (guiding the activity of each project team member).

3.4 Maylor identifies the need for integrated plans for:

- Time (scheduling) – including the use of critical path networks and Gantt charts
- Cost – including cost estimates and budgets
- Quality management
- Risk and contingencies.

It may also be necessary to integrate a **resource plan** (matching human, physical and other resources to the planned workload) and a **communication plan** (where there are multiple stakeholders with differing information needs).

3.5 Most projects are too involved and complex to be planned effectively unless they are broken down to a manageable size. The 'work breakdown structure' (WBS) is a key component of project planning. The project is progressively broken down to derive discrete work packages which can be allocated, monitored and managed effectively.

3.6 A range of project planning techniques is typically used to establish the **sequence** in which project activities must be performed, showing which can be done concurrently (at the same time) and which consecutively (one after the other) – and which activities are dependent on the completion of previous activities before they can start. This analysis can be used to establish a precedence network – which in turn (once the likely **duration** of each activity has been estimated) can be used to identify **critical activities**: activities on which other activities depend, for which there is no 'slack time' in the schedule. A late start, or late completion, in a critical activity will cause an overrun in key stage deadlines or the overall completion date of the project.

3.7 We will discuss critical path analysis, together with Gantt charts and other project planning tools, in Chapter 9.

Estimating cost

3.8 It is vital to ensure that adequate resources are available for each stage and activity. Lack of resources (financial, physical, informational or human) available at the right time can derail a project. Cost estimating, and related risk management, requires preparation of a detailed budget, authorised in advance by senior management.

3.9 The budget is both a planning tool and a method of control. The control aspect operates by means of continual or periodic comparison between budgeted costs and actual costs as the project progresses. Where deviations from plan are noted, corrective action may be taken. By examining the pattern of deviations it may be possible to identify in advance that significant overspends are likely. It is sometimes said that the major aim of project management is to avoid nasty surprises: good budgeting helps to achieve this objective.

4 Organisation and implementation

Project governance and communication mechanisms

4.1 Mechanisms and structures will be set up to ensure that:

- The project board or steering committee represents senior management (responsible for the business interests of the organisation), users (often responsible for the specification), main contractors and/or technical specialists (responsible for implementing the project)
- Defined responsibilities and accountabilities have been allocated for all tasks, deliverables and risks
- Periodic progress and exception reports flow upward, via the project manager, to the project client or board/steering committee, for management by exception
- Information on progress, resources and risks flows freely and efficiently between client and contractor(s) and between all project participants, in such a way as to co-ordinate activity and maintain the visibility of risks
- All activities are monitored and evaluated at key points. Project plans usually incorporate milestones (key stage targets) and gates (measurement points where each stage of work 'passes' or 'fails' against acceptance criteria)
- Appropriate authorisations and approvals are obtained for key expenditures, variations to plan or contract, and progress through to next project stages.

Project structure

4.2 There are three basic ways in which projects may be accommodated within an organisation.

- **Functional structure:** the project is accommodated within a function (eg a supplier rationalisation project within the procurement function), alongside the ongoing work of the function. This takes advantage of available expertise and resources, and provides continuity if individuals leave the project team. However, there is a risk that the project (and its internal client) may take lower priority than the 'business as usual' of the host function – and there may be less input from cross-functional stakeholders.
- **Matrix structure**: project team members are drawn from different functions, reporting both to their departmental managers (for ongoing work) and to a project manager (for work pertaining to the project). This is a preferred approach for organisations which undertake projects on an occasional basis, as it facilitates cross-functional collaboration, while optimising the use of available resources.
- **Pure project structure**: the whole organisation is permanently structured for project work, facilitating a horizontal business process focus, and softening (or eliminating) boundaries between functions. The project manager has full line authority over participating staff. Such a structure ensures accountability and authority for project management, increases project visibility, and develops project management maturity (through continuity of project management).

Determining personnel needs

4.3 Selecting a **project manager** with the right blend of expertise, experience and interpersonal skills is clearly a key element in ensuring project success.

4.4 **Project teams** are typically cross-functional teams set up on a short-term basis, and empowered to take action within the limited remit of the project specification and terms of reference. It is important systematically to identify the skills required for key project tasks, and to make arrangements to source and deploy the required skills at the appropriate time. This may involve arranging to have existing staff seconded to a project team, or sourcing external expertise through recruitment, external consultancy, contracting or outsourcing.

Operational and supply issues

4.5 Individual projects and types of projects will face their own operational issues of quality, health and safety, supply and logistics, which will require effective management in order to mitigate risk. At every stage, there will be issues of management and leadership; control of time, cost, quality and changes; and problem-solving and contingency-handling.

4.6 In the case of major **construction projects**, for example, there is typically a high degree of risk in regard to the following issues.

- Reputation, with a typically poor reputation for quality, delivery, cost control and health and safety
- Environmental sustainability and impacts (such as energy and water usage and waste generation) and pressure to contribute to sustainability targets – particularly in construction projects commissioned by the public sector
- An adversarial supply chain climate, and fragmented supply chains, due to entrenched competitive relationships with subcontractors and suppliers, and a trend towards contractors unilaterally imposing price reductions on suppliers, in order to keep bids competitive. This has created pressures for integrated project teamworking (to support more innovative, sustainable, buildable, client-focused solutions) and more integrated supply chains ('joined up thinking'), so that learning and development can be carried forward from one project to the next.
- The use of outsourced, subcontracted and casual labour, creating problems for health and safety (no time for ongoing training), capability development (no continuity) and sustainability (no opportunity to secure 'buy in'). This may also be a procurement issue, with the need to drill down through the supply chain to monitor and enforce ethical and safety standards.
- Logistical complexity, with construction sites often far distant from the procurement unit, and supplies often needing to be transferred from one site or construction project to another
- Security issues (theft, pilferage, vandalism and damage) on construction sites, which may lack storage facilities – creating pressure for just in time supply scheduling
- Architects, site engineers or project managers having discretion to arrange for the supply of materials and services, requiring strong communication, liaison and co-ordination with the project's procurement officer (or the contractor's procurement unit)
- Community and secondary stakeholder issues (eg in regard to noise, congestion, environmental impacts, fly-in-fly-out workers and so on)

5 Measuring, monitoring, control and improvement

5.1 **Project monitoring** recognises that the progress of the project must be continually measured and compared against milestones, targets and other indicators of quality, time and cost. Inspection rejection rates, costs against budget, and activities not started on time are examples. The project manager must ensure that a robust monitoring infrastructure and mechanisms are in place and that prompt and accurate feedback is gathered and given. Monitoring is the only way to ensure that resources can be reallocated effectively and judiciously when required.

5.2 **Project control** is the administrative interface that ensures that the project is progressing as intended. 'Controlling' means taking the appropriate action in the light of the information gained from monitoring: project control is put in place to make sure that the criteria detailed in the project plan are being met and (if not) to instigate remedial action.

5.3 This is obviously a crucial area in the management of project risk – particularly in regard to the risk of project variances (in cost, schedule or quality) and project failure. Meredith and Mantel argue that the two fundamental objectives of control systems are: (a) the regulation of results through the alteration of activities, and (b) the stewardship of organisational assets.

8

5.4 There are two key elements to the control of a project.

- **Milestones:** clear, unambiguous targets of what needs to have been achieved and by when. A mllestone includes a clear definition of deliverables or other performance measures; a scheduled target date by which a milestone should be achieved (in order to identify time variance); a budgeted target spend at the point of milestone achievement (in order to identify cost variance); a sequential project plan or critical path network showing the interdependencies of milestones (to identify risks and priority activities for contingency planning and 'crashing' of activities); and acceptable variances for quality, time or cost at milestones (triggering exception reporting, if variances are outside agreed tolerances).
- Mechanisms for **feedback gathering, reporting and communication** on milestone attainment.

5.5 Milestones are 'scheduled events signifying the completion of a major deliverabale or set of related deliverables', specifically used as 'checkpoints' to measure and validate progress, and as 'decision points' for corrective action. For the project manager milestones are a key mechanism to monitor progress. For those involved in the project, they represent tangible and motivating short-term goals. Milestone definition and management offers an audit checkpoint for risk management:

- A checkpoint for measuring project progress against plan
- A checkpoint for identifying critical issues and risks for escalation and problem-solving
- A decision point for authorising next stages, in the light of current risk status.

5.6 A project reporting system should be designed so as to meet the needs of all stakeholders: the client, senior managers and lower-level project personnel. Reports should be carefully framed so as to include the appropriate level of detail for the intended audience. They should also be closely tied in with the work breakdown structure (WBS), so that reports are relevant to the control of specific tasks being carried out to a specific schedule. The timing of reports should generally correspond to the timing of project milestones.

6 Project closure

6.1 The final phase of project management is essentially two-fold.

- **Project completion**: finishing work, completing documentation, closing down systems and handing over deliverables
- **Review**: identifying immediate needs such as remedial action for project shortfalls; and capturing learning for future projects, to develop project management capability and maturity

Project completion

6.2 The completion phase may involve a number of activities.

- The finishing of work and 'tying up of loose ends' – often under time or resource pressure. Effort must be put into contractor performance management, new system testing, user training and so on.
- The completion of documentation: eg for quality or sustainability certification, or where the client and users are to be provided with operating documentation or policy guidelines as part of the project deliverables. All contracts, correspondence, budgetary control and accounting records and other documentation must be carefully filed for follow-up reporting, and in case of subsequent disputes.
- Project systems (eg for control and accounting) must be closed down, once their task is complete (eg all costs have been posted). Project and contract management structures may be disbanded.
- Where the project has been managed for a client, under contract, its deliverables will need to be formally handed over to the client. The client must formally accept that the contract has been completed, and take responsibility for any further action (such as operation and maintenance of a facility or system): this may happen at a formal project closure meeting. Depending on the project, handover may be a systematic, risk-managed process of 'ramp-up, ramp-down', phased

implementation, parallel running and so on, in order to manage learning curves, teething problems and other risks.

Project review

6.3 Project review is a crucial process. Because of the unique and episodic nature of projects, continuous improvement of project performance over time is difficult – particularly where organisations only manage occasional projects on an *ad hoc* basis. Skills and knowledge developed during a project may dissipate after completion, or disperse with project teams – unless systematic effort is made to capture and document learning. What worked well? What didn't work well? What template processes and documents can be carried forward? What benchmarks have been set?

6.4 We will consider all these elements in more detail in the following chapters of this Course Book.

Chapter summary

- Staged models of the project lifecycle include Maylor's (define, design, do, develop), Weiss and Wysocki's (definition, planning, organising, controlling, closing) and the PRINCE2 model.
- An initial decision is required as to which projects should be accepted. Such decisions should be supported by a fully developed business case.
- Project planning should cover the key aspects of timing, costs, quality and risk.
- Projects should be formally structured in terms of management levels, progress reporting, and authorisations.
- Two key elements in control of a project are defined milestones and mechanisms for feedback and reporting.
- A project review following completion is an important source of learning for future projects.

Self-test questions

Numbers in brackets refer to the paragraphs where you can check your answers.

1   Describe the four stages in Maylor's model of the project lifecycle. (Table 8.1)

2   List the eight project processes in the PRINCE2 model. (1.8)

3   What are the benefits of using a project lifecycle model? (1.19)

4   Describe quantitative methods of project evaluation. (2.3)

5   What are the typical contents of a project initiation document? (2.14)

6   List typical elements of a project plan. (Table 8.3)

7   Describe possible structures for accommodating a project within an organisation. (4.2)

8   What is meant by a milestone in the context of project management? (5.4)

9   List activities included in the project completion process. (6.2)

CHAPTER 9

Project Planning

Assessment criteria and indicative content

 Evaluate the contribution that project planning can make to managing risks in supply chains

- Planning: identifying activities, estimating timings and costings
- Sequencing activities
- Applying critical path analysis
- Developing Gantt charts and baselines

Section headings

1   The importance of project planning
2   Planning and sequencing activities
3   Critical path analysis (CPA) and PERT
4   Gantt charts and baselines

Introduction

This chapter focuses in detail on the important planning stage of the project lifecycle, which was mentioned in overview in Chapter 8. This is the area usually most readily identified as 'project management', as it concerns practical tools and techniques for setting out what needs to be done, when, how and with what resource requirements.

We start by briefly highlighting the role and contribution of project planning in risk management and project success. We then explore the use of some essential project management tools such as work breakdown, critical path analysis (CPA) and Gantt charts. Although the syllabus focuses on 'evaluating the contribution of project planning to managing risks', you should be prepared to utilise (prepare and interpret) such tools in response to exam case study scenarios.

1   The importance of project planning

1.1   Project planning contributes to the management of supply chain and project risks in a range of ways.

- It forces those involved to consider potential risks and vulnerabilities, and how they can be mitigated — especially where risk management is explicitly part of the project planning process.
- It identifies the deliverables, likely duration and cost of the project, supporting decisions on whether the project will be feasible and worthwhile in cost/benefit and return on investment (avoid or accept risk).
- It determines the resources that will be required at each stage of the project, enabling proactive planning to ensure those resources are available when required (minimising resource-related risk).
- It allows time for an examination of costs quoted, challenging of business need and over-specification and so on, managing financial and specification risks.
- It identifies the tasks to be undertaken, the sequence and timing within which they need to be undertaken, and any dependencies between tasks (where one task must be completed for another to begin). This enables the identification of vulnerabilities, such as peak resource requirements,

bottlenecks and tight spots in the schedule (where there is no margin for error). It also enables the co-ordination of effort and resources, minimising the risk of 'gaps' (ineffective) and 'overlaps' (inefficient) in the work.

- It underpins control processes such as setting phases and milestones, defining responsibilities and requiring authorisations. Control – the monitoring, evaluation and adjustment of progress against plans – is essential in managing all areas of risk (especially time, cost and quality), since it enables the correction of deviations and errors, and the triggering of remedial action and contingency plans.
- It provides for end-stage or gateway reviews, at which project risk and viability can be re-assessed in the light of emerging risks and changes.
- It specifically establishes expenditure budgets, quality and output targets, and timescales and deadlines, against which project activity and progress can be measured (as a way of identifying variances which may present project risk).
- It provides tools and outputs (such as project plans, charts and risk registers) which make project success factors, milestones and risks visible to all project participants and stakeholders.
- It supports management by exception (escalating issues on the basis of deviation from agreed plans), making senior management oversight, for risk management, more feasible and efficient.
- It allows the needs, views and interests of project stakeholders to be taken into account in planning processes and deliverables – and allows for the establishment of mechanisms to handle stakeholder communication and conflict.

2 Planning and sequencing activities

Identifying activities

2.1   It is important at the outset of a project to identify and 'capture' all of the activities that will be needed in order to complete the work. One tool for determining and organising activities in a methodical way is a **work breakdown structure** (WBS). This document can take a variety of forms, but its main purpose is to list the tasks to be completed, usually with assignment of responsibility for each task. The WBS can allow for several levels of 'disaggregation' of work, starting with major project phases, and gradually breaking them down into major activities, sub-activities – and finally discrete tasks or 'work packages' that can be assigned to individuals or teams.

2.2   An example of how a product development project might be analysed is illustrated by Meredith and Mantel: Figure 9.1.

Figure 9.1 *Work breakdown structure*

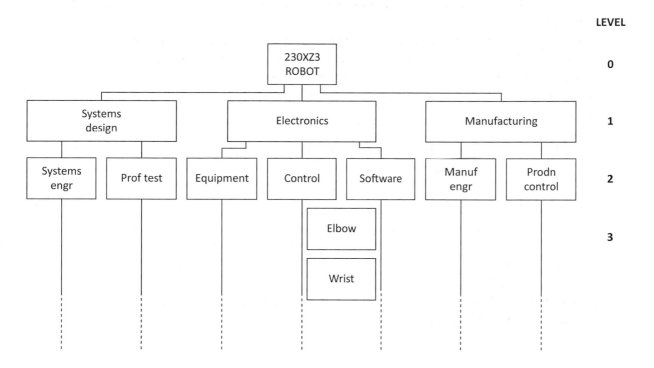

2.3   A breakdown by activity (as illustrated above) is not the only possible way of organising the WBS.

- Maylor suggests that another possibility would be to organise it by **functional area**: the top level of the chart then represents the different functions that will be involved (eg finance, manufacturing, IT and so on).
- The PRINCE2 methodology uses a **product breakdown** approach: directing management attention to what is to be achieved (outputs) rather than how to do it. This may be helpful in complex projects, where the processes and activities involved may be less clear, initially, than the desired outcomes. PRINCE2 divides project products into three groups: technical products (deliverables to be provided to users); quality products (quality standards to be achieved); and management products (the project management structure, planning documentation, reports and so on).

2.4   Meredith and Mantel suggest the following six-stage approach to using a WBS.

- Using information from the project action plan, list the task breakdown in successively finer levels of detail, to derive discrete 'work packages' which can be effectively managed
- For each work package, list the personnel and/or organisations responsible for completion.
- Review this with the people responsible to ensure accuracy and acceptability.
- Calculate the cost of each activity (discussed further below).
- Aggregate the information into a project master schedule.
- As the project is carried out, continually examine resource usage and timing in the light of the WBS.

Sequencing activities

2.5   Once all activities of a project have been identified, they should be analysed to establish the order in which they will be undertaken. This will depend on various factors.

- **Dependencies** between activities: some activities will have to be completed before others can start, because they provide inputs to the subsequent activities. Determining dependencies between project activities is a key aspect of project planning, because it is the main constraining factor in sequencing activities.
- **Interactions** between activities: some activities are linked to other activities (though not necessarily

dependent) – for example, because of the shared use of a limited resource. Two activities requiring the same expert, or the same equipment, cannot run concurrently: their order of priority (based on importance, urgency or dependencies) will have to be established.

- **Resource requirements** of activities: if resources (including human resources and machine time) are available, some activities may be undertaken concurrently – while if resources need to be transferred from one activity to another, they will have to be undertaken consecutively (one after the other)
- **Durations or timings** of activities, which affects the extent to which activities can be carried out concurrently (eg you can accomplish two 3-day activities while another 6-day activity is in progress); the sequence of activities that will give you the shortest project duration; and the sequence of activities that determines the total project duration (and therefore the project completion target). This should become clear when we look at critical path analysis and Gantt charts.

2.6 Activity sequences may be plotted in a simple precedence network or flowchart. This might look much like a 'skeleton' critical path network shown in Figure 9.3 later in this chapter: simply depicting which activities flow on from (or depend on) other activities, in order.

Estimating activity timings

2.7 The timings or duration of each activity will have to be estimated, in order to develop schedules. Particularly for unique project activities, this is obviously an inexact science, but schedule estimates can be drawn from past experience on the same or similar activities; past documented schedules; and the expert opinion of planners, in consultation with experienced workers. The Mind Tools website (www.mindtools.com) suggests the following techniques for estimating time accurately: Table 9.1.

Table 9.1 *Techniques for estimating time*

Bottom-up estimating	Break larger tasks down into detailed tasks, and then estimate the time needed to complete each one – and add individual task timings together to derive a time for the project as a whole. Estimating should be more accurate, because it is easier to estimate for individual tasks incrementally.
Top-down estimating	Develop an overview of the expected timeline for the whole project, using past projects, previous experience or expert opinion as a guide. It may be helpful to compare top-down estimates against bottom-up estimates, as a 'reality check'.
Comparative estimating	Use the time taken to do similar tasks, on other projects (or in business as usual working) to estimate the time for tasks.
Parametric estimating	Estimate the time required for one deliverable (eg the time to deliver one page of a website) then multiply it by the number of deliverables required (total number of pages to be delivered).
Three-point estimating	Develop a best-case, worst-case and most-likely-case estimate, in order to take account of uncertainties and contingencies. This takes more effort to develop, but allows the project manager to set more reasonable expectations, and to build risk factors into outcome estimates.

Estimating project costings

2.8 The main principle involved in controlling costs is to estimate in advance what the costs are expected to be; compare the estimate with actual outcomes; and investigate any significant discrepancies or variances. This is the process of budgetary control.

2.9 You should be familiar with the basic techniques of cost estimation, based on historical data, current operational data, expert input (including quotes from contractors and suppliers) and cost research.

- Various statistical techniques (including simple moving averages, weighted averages, time series analysis, regression analysis and the use of published indices) can be used to extrapolate from historical cost data to forecast future costs of project inputs, such as materials and labour.

- An activity schedule costing approach may be used to build up project cost estimates, by estimating the costs of each of the component activities. The planner needs to estimate what resources will be required, in what quantity, and at what unit cost. These estimates are naturally subject to uncertainty, but some items will be more uncertain than others. Meredith and Mantel compare building a brick wall (where an experienced builder can calculate the number of bricks required very accurately) with writing a piece of software (where the number of programming hours may be very difficult to estimate in advance).

- Bills of quantity (BOQ) may be used as the basis of cost estimation in construction projects. Specification of construction supplies will often take the form of a 'bill of quantities': a document prepared by a quantity surveyor from drawings and specifications prepared by architects or engineers. The BOQ sets out the detailed requirements of the work and the quantities involved, as 'priceable items': items against which tenderers can quote a price per unit – so that the grand summary will provide the tender price for the contract. This should avoid large 'contingency' amounts (padding) built into tenders, and should assist in calculating price variations due to subsequent changes in design.

- From a client's point of view, the total cost of a project may also be determined by the estimate of the project contractor(s), the negotiation of the contract pricing agreement and/or the award of a contract at a particular price via competitive tender. For example, a project contract may be negotiated on the basis of fixed lump sum pricing, target costing, risk/reward pricing or cost-reimbursable contract – as discussed in Chapter 7.

2.10   All cost estimates are – by their nature – subject to inaccuracy and change. In order to manage financial risk effectively, all estimates should be accompanied by some indication of expected accuracy (such as a +/− range). The accuracy of estimates can be improved by learning from past over-estimating or under-estimating mistakes, and working with specification information that is as detailed, specific and accurate as possible.

2.11   There are two main approaches to establishing project budgets: 'top-down' budgeting and 'bottom-up' budgeting.

2.12   In **top-down budgeting**, senior managers estimate the overall project cost based on their judgement and experience of similar projects in the past. They may extend their analysis by estimating the overall cost of major sub-projects making up the total project. They then hand their estimates to lower-level managers, who continue the breakdown of cost by allocating amounts to each of the activities identified in the project plan.

- An advantage of this approach is that, in the experience of many project managers, the overall project budget may be quite accurate. For example, many project managers in the construction industry feel able to predict quite well how much it will cost to build an office block, based on their experience that total costs usually work out to about $X per square foot.

- A disadvantage is that at the more detailed level there may be quite serious inaccuracies. Moreover, this system can lead to intense competition among junior managers fighting for their share of a predetermined budget. Experience suggests that junior managers often perceive the amounts they have been allocated as inadequate to achieve the required deliverables.

2.13   **Bottom-up budgeting** works the other way round. Once the project has been planned in detail, and all projected activities are known, the people responsible for each task are asked to estimate the relevant resource requirements. These are then converted to monetary equivalents. During this process there may be discussions and disagreements between the managers concerned. The project manager may also become involved in order to ensure accuracy in the estimates. The project manager will also add an estimate of indirect costs, not specifically attributable to any particular task, and perhaps also a contingency allowance to cover unexpected developments. All of these sums must be aggregated to arrive at the overall budget.

9

- An advantage of this approach is the greater accuracy of costing individual activities. There is also a behavioural advantage: managers involved in setting budgets for their activities will feel more commitment to achieving them. By contrast, managers who have budgets forced upon them without their own involvement may be resentful and demotivated.
- A disadvantage of bottom-up budgeting is that it is critical to ensure that every single activity is included, and this is a difficult task. Another drawback is that junior managers tend to overstate their resource requirements in the expectation that all proposed budgets will be cut.

2.14 Meredith and Mantel believe that top-down budgeting is much more common in practice than bottom-up budgeting. 'Senior managers see the bottom-up process as risky. They tend not to be particularly trusting of ambitious subordinates who may overstate resource requirements in an attempt to ensure success and build empires. They are understandably reluctant to hand over [the key project control tool] to subordinates whose experience and motives are questionable.'

3 Critical path analysis (CPA) and PERT

Network analysis

3.1 Projects frequently comprise a large number of separate activities which are related to each other in terms of their timetabling. For example, it may be that Activity C can only be commenced after Activities A and B have been completed. Network analysis is the process of analysing the relationships between activities and exhibiting them in a diagrammatic form. In order to draw a network diagram it is necessary to have estimated durations of each activity.

3.2 Nowadays, the creation of a network diagram invariably involves the use of a computer. The project planner can enter data about the activities (eg the duration of Activity C, and the fact that it can only begin after completion of Activities A and B). The computer program can then draw a precedence network diagram, as well as producing various items of management information useful to the planner. For example, the software can calculate:

- Which activities are on the **critical path**: the activities where any delay will lead to a delay in the overall completion of the project.
- Which activities have 'float' (activities which take less time than is available) and how much float or 'slack time' they have
- Probabilities that particular activities will overrun, and/or that the project as a whole will overrun.

3.3 The use of network analysis to identify the critical path is referred to as **critical path analysis (CPA)** or the critical path method (CPM).

3.4 Key benefits of using network analysis include:

- The enforced need to think clearly about project activities, their interdependencies and estimated durations
- The focus of attention on 'critical activities': those for which there is no 'slack time'. If a critical activity runs late, the project will run late. It is helpful to identify these activities in order to prioritise the allocation of resources so as to avoid overruns on critical activities – and to avoid wasting resources on non-critical activities. It may also be possible to shorten the total project timetable by directing extra resources to critical activities, in order to complete them more quickly. Again, it would be wasted effort and cost to do this in the case of activities that already have 'float' or slack time.
- Allowing project managers to maintain a constant check on project progress, with cross-project visibility of the dependencies of all key activities.

Preparing a network diagram

3.5   There are various notations that may be used in the preparation of a network diagram. We will illustate the **activity on arrow** diagram, in which each activity is represented by a line (or arrow) joining two circles (usually called nodes). The duration of the activity is written by the arrow representing it. This is illustrated in Figure 9.2.

Figure 9.2 *A basic 'activity on arrow'*

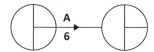

3.6   In our example, Activity A has a duration of six (days, hours, weeks or whatever). The nodes representing the beginning and end of Activity A are divided into three parts; the reason for this is explained later.

3.7   The best way to understand the preparation of network diagrams is to do an example. Project Alpha consists of nine activities, named as A, B, C, D, E, F, G, H, J. The table below shows which preceding activities must have been completed before a subsequent activity may begin, and also the estimated durations of each activity.

Activity	Preceding activities	Duration in days
A	—	3
B	—	3
C	—	7
D	A	1
E	D, J	2
F	B	2
G	C	1
H	E, F, G	1
J	B	1

3.8   This information can be shown in a skeleton network: Figure 9.3.

Figure 9.3 *A skeleton network*

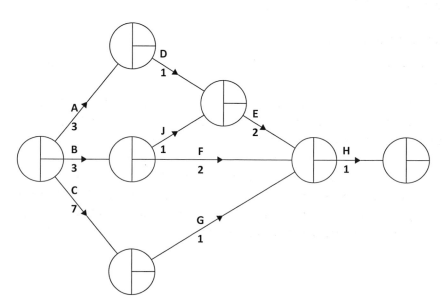

3.9 Next, we number the nodes, beginning at the left with number 1, and moving across the page to the right: Figure 9.4.

Figure 9.4 *Numbering the nodes*

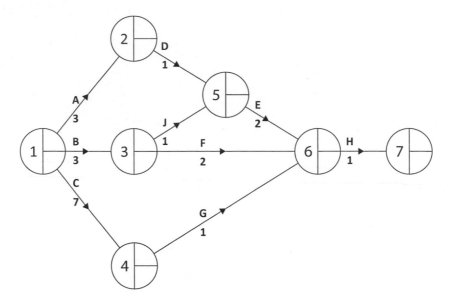

3.10 We now work forward through the network (ie from left to right), *adding* activity durations to calculate the **earliest starting time** (EST) for each activity, which is inserted in the upper right quadrant of each node. An activity cannot start until all preceding activities have been completed. If there are no preceding activities (eg for Activities A, B and C in our example) the EST is conventionally called Day 0 (ie immediately). If there *are* preceding activities, we must allow time for them to be completed. ESTs have been inserted in Figure 9.5: make sure you can see where our numbers come from.

Figure 9.5 *Earliest starting times*

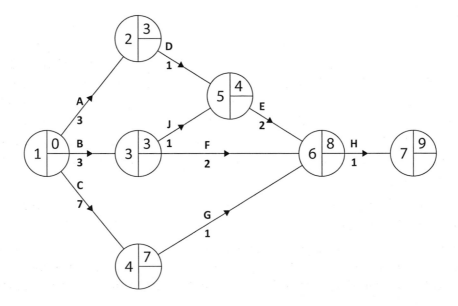

3.11 Note that where there is more than one activity coming into a node, it is the *longest* accumulated time that must be entered, because *all* activities ending on the node must be completed before the next activities can begin. For example, the EST on Node 6 is Day 8: although it only takes six days to reach Node 6 via Node 5, the route via Node 4 takes *eight* days, which means that Activity H cannot begin until after Day 8.

3.12 We now work *backwards* through the network (ie from right to left), *subtracting* activity durations to calculate the **latest finishing time** (LFT) for each activity, which is inserted in the lower right quadrant of each node. The LFT is the time by which all activities ending at a node must be completed if the schedule is to remain on target. This is illustrated in Figure 9.6.

Figure 9.6 *Latest finishing times*

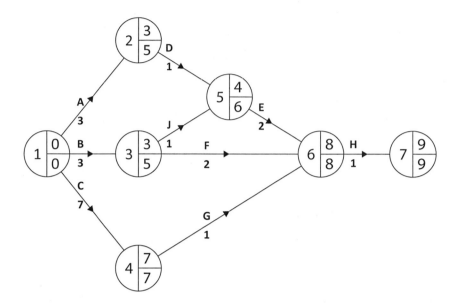

3.13 Again, care is needed where more than one activity/arrow is emerging from a node, as for Node 3. To go from Node 3 to Node 6 requires two days, so it may look as though the LFT for Node 3 is Day 6, leaving time for Activity F to complete by Day 8. But that would leave no time to complete the longer path E–J. To allow the three days for Activities E and J, the LFT for Node 3 must be Day 5.

Analysing the network diagram

3.14 Once the network diagram has been drawn, we can derive useful information from it.

- It is clear that the project will take nine days to complete (assuming no slippage).
- By comparing the EST and LFT at each node, we can see how much 'float' or slack time an activity has. At Node 2, there is float of two days. In other words, although we are expecting Activity A to take three days, it could take as much as five days without damaging the overall schedule.
- Where the EST and the LFT are identical, there is no float: any delay to the activity will mean delay to the overall project – so such nodes are on the critical path. The critical path in our example runs from Node 1, through Nodes 4 and 6 to Node 8: Activities C, G and H are critical to achieving the nine day project timetable.

3.15 This simple example should be enough to show how a network diagram can be prepared and how to analyse the information it discloses.

- To **identify the critical path**, look for the nodes for which the EST and the LFT are identical: there is no float (or slack time) in these activities, and any delay in the activity will therefore delay the overall project. Note that the critical path is by definition the *longest* path to project completion, not the shortest.
- Where the EST and LFT differ, there is a **float** in the preceding activity. A float is the amount of time a non-critical task can be delayed without impacting the overall duration of the project. (By definition, all critical path activities have zero float.)

Crashing activities

3.16 Sometimes the network diagram will reveal that the project is taking too long. We then need to consider how to 'crash' activities: that is, to shorten their duration by applying additional resources. The procedure is as follows.

- Identify activities that may be 'crashed'.
- For each activity, establish cost.
- Estimate activity duration with resources added.
- Determine revised completion date and cost.
- Recalculate critical path and costs.
- Compare various options to determine most effective solution.

3.17 There may be various options for crashing activities to shorten project duration, eg: redeploying staff from other tasks; contracting or subcontracting resources from suppliers; authorising overtime working; increasing shift working; or hiring or leasing additional equipment. This will be discussed further in Chapter 10.

Program evaluation and review technique (PERT)

3.18 In our discussion of critical path analysis we have assumed that the times required for each activity are known. In practice, these times are obviously subject to uncertainty. This causes problems for the project manager, which to some extent can be addressed by statistical analysis. The aim is to establish within probable limits what the actual time may be for each activity.

3.19 Project (or programme) evaluation and review technique (PERT) is an application of probability theory to cope with uncertainties in the estimated activity durations of a network analysis. Instead of estimating a definite duration for each activity – which is very prone to error – planners can define an optimistic duration (a), a pessimistic duration (b) and a most likely duration (m). These are used to calculate the mean time (μ) and the standard deviation (σ), using the following formulae:

$$\mu = \frac{4m + b + a}{6}$$

$$\sigma = \frac{6 + a}{6}$$

3.20 Using these calculations, we can extend our use of CPA to cater for the uncertainties inherent in our estimates of activity durations. For example, we can calculate the probability that an activity on the critical path will overrun its allotted time and therefore endanger the timely completion of the project as a whole. This kind of calculation is invariably carried out using appropriate computer software. All you should need for the examination is general awareness of the underlying principles.

Problems with time scheduling

3.21 As any review of case histories will tell you, projects frequently suffer from schedule overruns. Maylor identifies various causes of schedule variances.

- Time estimates for activities contain uncertainties.
- A given activity usually takes *at least* the time allowed for. This is an application of Parkinson's Law: 'work expands to fill the time available for it'.
- 'A delay in one step is passed on in full to the next step, whereas an advance in one step is usually wasted' (Goldratt). This is because people tend to defer action until the time they had expected to begin – rather than rushing to begin early.
- Most people are required to multi-task, increasing the lead time for all of the activities they are engaged in (because of the time lost in switching from one task to another: eg re-familiarising oneself with a broken-off task).

- People include safety margins (or 'padding') in their scheduling estimates: deliberately exaggerating the amount of time estimated to be required for an activity, to minimise the risk of overruns ('just to be on the safe side'). However, the sense of 'safety' actually *demotivates* project teams from striving to meet tight deadlines: they tend to delay starting, in the confidence that they 'still have time' – ignoring the possibility of the contingencies they originally allowed for.

Critical chain project management

3.22 Critical chain project management (CCPM) is a modern approach that seeks to address problems of time scheduling which arise with more conventional project tools. It takes a radically different approach to estimating times.

- No importance is attached to adhering to a planned sequence of activities. 'Time plans establish precedence relationships but should be treated as overviews only. The nature of project management needs to reflect the dynamic of the actual situation, and accommodate changes as they occur' (Maylor).
- Time estimates do not include padding. This requires the education and buy-in of project planners. It also requires recognition that many timings will be underestimated: managers should specify in advance that they are expecting 50% of activities to overrun, while 50% will be completed early.
- When time becomes critical on a project, the traditional management approach is based on 'crashing' activity 'floats' (slack time). CCPM instead uses 'buffers': defined quantities of time applied to a project schedule to protect the promised due date from variations. A 'feeding buffer' protects non-critical tasks when they feed into critical tasks, improving the chance that the critical task can begin on time. A 'capacity buffer' is used in a multi-project environment to protect each project from variation in resource use in other projects. And a 'resource buffer' protects against the possibility that a key resource will be in short supply when needed.

4 Gantt charts and baselines

Gantt charts

4.1 Henry Gantt (1861–1919) was one of the pioneers of scientific management, an approach to production management that emphasised the importance of analysing tasks into sub-tasks and measuring them in terms of resource usage. He has given his name to a type of chart that measures the progress of project activities over time. Often, both actual progress and scheduled progress are indicated, so that any time overruns are immediately apparent.

4.2 A good example of a simple Gantt chart is shown in Slack, Chambers and Johnston (*Operations Management*), illustrating work undertaken by a small specialist furniture manufacturer: Figure 9.7.

Figure 9.7 *Gantt chart for job progress*

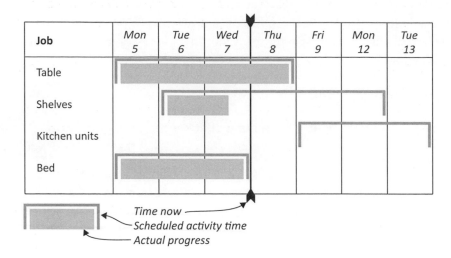

4.3 The vertical line indicates that it is now close of business on Wednesday 7th. The table is already complete (indicated by the complete shaded region), which means the manufacturer is a day ahead of schedule. By contrast, the shelves are behind schedule (the shaded area should reach as far as the present time, but in fact falls short of that). Scheduled work has not yet begun on the kitchen units. The bed has been completed on schedule.

4.4 The use of Gantt charts can be extended beyond this very simple illustration. For example, a scheme of colour coding can be used to indicate what types of resource are in use on particular days (blue to represent an electrician, brown for a carpenter etc). Or there may be a resource chart at the foot of the Gantt chart. This would indicate the number of units of a particular resource expected to be needed on a particular day. This has obvious relevance to resource planning: by shifting tasks from one day to another we may be able to even out demand for particular resources, avoiding days when the resource is overloaded and days when it is not utilised in full.

4.5 For example, the number of staff (or other resources) required for each task can be written below each line or bar of the chart. Where a 5-person task overlaps with a 3-person task, it is easy to see that, for the duration of the overlap, 8 people will be required. An extra item line can therefore be drawn for the whole duration of the project, divided into segments identifying resource requirements: Figure 9.8.

Figure 9.8 *Gantt Chart showing resource requirements*

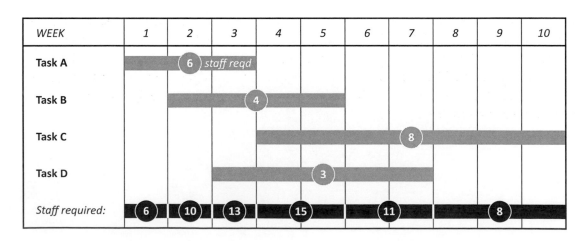

4.6   In this example, you can see that at the peak period of the project, when activities B, C and D are running concurrently, you will need 15 staff – while in other weeks, you will have idle time. You could smooth out your resource requirements, for greater efficiency, in various ways (depending on the relationship between the various tasks).

- You may be able to start Task D earlier or later. (You may like to try this, and recalculate the staff requirements line at the bottom of the chart.)
- If this chart reflects the critical path network, on the other hand, you may choose to keep 10 or 11 people on yoru project team and draft in extra staff for the peak period, minimising idle time.

Baselines

4.7   In risk management, baselines are sets of assumptions and methods that are used as the base evaluation of risk. In project management, a baseline is the project's original plan: that is, the 'starting' schedules and milestones. This allows progress to be measured against the original project plan – highlighting cumulative deviation and variances – as well as against updated or edited versions of the plan, as the project develops.

4.8   Some Gantt chart software and project management software applications offer the option of:

- Highlighting the baseline plan, so that it can easily be compared with the current version of the plan
- 'Locking' the baseline plan, so that it does not change when the schedule is edited.

Optimising resource allocation

4.9   There may be two main problems with resource allocations.

- Resources may be *over-allocated,* or over-stretched (eg an individual with an unrealistic daily or weekly work load, or a shortage of technicians): the quantity of resource required by the project plan exceeds its availability. This is a significant source of worker stress, and project delays. Solutions to the problem include redeploying staff from other tasks; subcontracting; using temporary agency staff; or increasing productivity (eg through improved training or use of ICT).
- Resources may be *under-allocated,* or under-utilised (eg a project team with insufficient work to do): people or equipment has been assigned to the project, but insufficient task-related work is available or assigned. This may be tolerated in the short term, or in the interest of flexibility, but represents poor value for money (especially if the idle or under-utilised resource is paid a high daily rate). Options include: matching of assignments and tasks as closely as possible; part-time, flexible and short-contract working; accelerating the project schedule, taking advantage of available resources; or re-assigning underutilised resources (eg to preparatory work on future tasks).

4.10   Often, project plans (such as Gantt charts) will indicate unavoidable peaks and troughs in the requirement for resources from one task or week to the next, and this creates the challenge of **resource smoothing**, or **resource levelling**: deploying resources efficiently across the life of the project, to avoid under- or over-allocation as far as possible. The most obvious approach to this is manipulating the timing of non-critical tasks (within available float times, so that overall deadlines are not affected), to smooth out peaks and troughs of resource requirements.

Chapter summary

- Project planning is a critical aspect of controlling projects and ensuring successful achievement of objectives.
- A work breakdown structure is used to organise project activities in a methodical way.
- A key aspect of project control is systematic estimation of activity timings and costs.
- Critical path analysis is a method of sequencing project activities in diagrammatic form. It assists in determining which activities are on the critical path.
- A Gantt chart is another diagrammatic technique to aid in project control. It highlights the level of resources expected to be in use at different times within the project.

Self-test questions

Numbers in brackets refer to the paragraphs where you can check your answers.

1 List reasons why project planning is important. (1.1)

2 List six stages in using a WBS. (2.4)

3 Distinguish between top-down budgeting and bottom-up budgeting. (2.12, 2.13)

4 List benefits of using network analysis. (3.4)

5 List the steps involved in a decision to 'crash' activities in the network diagram. (3.16)

6 How does CCPM differ from conventional project management approaches? (3.22)

7 In the context of project management, what is meant by a baseline? (4.7)

CHAPTER 10

Project Implementation and Control

Assessment criteria and indicative content

 2.4 Evaluate how the organisation, implementation, monitoring and control of projects mitigate risks in supply chains

- Organising and assigning work packages
- Determining the needs of personnel
- Health and safety issues in the workplace
- Establishing performance review mechanisms
- Implementing remedial actions
- Issuing change control orders
- Project closure
- Obtaining client acceptance
- Conducting audits/learning from experience

Section headings

1 Project organisation and implementation
2 Project team management
3 Health and safety issues
4 Monitoring and control
5 Project closure
6 Audit and learning

Introduction

In this chapter we complete our coverage of the syllabus section focusing on project management, by surveying in more detail the organisation, implementation, control and closure phases of the project lifecycle introduced in Chapter 8.

There is a lot of practical information to cover here, but much of the groundwork has already been laid in earlier chapters. This material is highly relevant to the management and mitigation of risks, since the operational phase of the project highlights the full range of operational risks; the monitoring and control phase is explicitly aimed at identifying and correcting risk factors (such as time, cost and quality variances); and the audit and learning phase is aimed at supporting risk management in future projects.

Note that, unless otherwise specified, the law discussed in this chapter is that of England and Wales, as exemplar.

1 Project organisation and implementation

1.1 Much of the work of project 'organisation', at a high level, will already have been accomplished at the project planning stage, in terms of:

- Establishing a project management and governance structure
- Establishing project responsibilities and accountabilities
- Establishing project communication and reporting mechanisms
- Establishing work breakdown structure, defining manageable work packages and allocating work packages to relevant functions, working groups and risk owners.

Organising and assigning work packages

1.2 As a result of work breakdown planning, and similar techniques, discrete work packages should be identified, which can be assigned to working groups, project teams or individuals. Efficient organisation of work packages involves grouping activities so that:

- They form meaningful manageable 'chunks' of the whole project for the designated individual or team
- They optimise the use of available resources (including expertise, knowledge and equipment) by grouping together tasks that share resource requirements and required shared specialist expertise
- They minimise the need for co-ordinating mechanisms within work packages (eg by centring work within a team or function) – allowing attention to be given to co-ordination between work packages (ie linkages between project areas)
- They can be regarded as a single area of accountability, as the responsibility of a single manager or team leader (ensuring that outcomes are within their control).

Determining the needs of personnel

1.3 The syllabus refers to the 'needs of personnel', but this can be divided into two key organising processes.

- Determining the needs of personnel – for information, resources, time and authority to implement their part of the project plan adequately. In other words, resourcing project implementation.
- Determining needs *for* personnel: in other words, determining the human resource and skill requirements for each work package. How many people hours will be required, at what skill level, and under what conditions? What contingency plans (eg for subcontracting, temporary agency or contract labour, or staff redeployments) may need to be made for risks such as loss of key personnel, schedule variance, unexpected demand, lack of skills, or staff sickness, absence or turnover?

1.4 We will focus on two key implementation issues – project team management and health and safety issues – in the following sections of this chapter.

2 Project team management

Project teamworking

2.1 Project teams are typically cross-functional teams set up to handle specific strategic developments (such as the introduction of a just in time approach), tasks relating to particular processes (such as the computerisation of inventory control), tasks relating to particular 'cases' or accounts (such as co-ordination of traffic with a particular supplier) or special audit or investigation of procedures or improvement opportunities (such as a review of order parameters or supplier ethical codes). Project teams are examples of task force or problem-solving teams. They are often short-term in nature, and empowered to take action within the limited remit of the project specification and terms of reference.

2.2 Cross-functional teams are particularly valuable in increasing team members' awareness of the big picture of their tasks and decisions – and therefore dovetailing functional objectives with overall strategy. They enable a wider pooling of viewpoints, expertise and resources, and represent a wider range of interests (which may both enhance the quality of the decision-making and minimise the potential for conflict and resistance at the implementation stage). This can help to generate innovative and integrative solutions to problems, and suggestions for performance or process improvements, by contributing more pieces of the overall puzzle.

2.3   Cross-functional working often requires different leadership roles.

- There will be a designated team leader or project manager, who has primary responsibility for building and managing the team and for delivering project outcomes on time and within budget.
- There is likely to be a project sponsor: a key stakeholder who has primary responsibility for the achievement of the project's business objectives, and who provides and is accountable for the resources invested into the project. For projects there is usually a defined individual or group who initiates the project, and ensures that the human and other resources are available to support its objectives. The sponsor's role is to act as an integrator and facilitator of the team's efforts.
- The team may effectively be autonomous or self-managing. Self-managed teams contract with management to assume various degrees of managerial responsibility for the team's task activity (day-to-day planning and control) and internal people management functions (selection, coaching, development and so on). Team members learn and share management tasks: no immediate manager is visible, although the team may report to a sponsor.

2.4   When a manager selects project team members, a mix of attributes, competencies and resources should be secured to match the needs of the project. Specialist skills and knowledge may be required (perhaps from different areas in the organisation); experience may be helpful (particularly to guide less experienced members of the team); organisational influence or access to resources (including information) may help to champion the team in its competition for limited resources.

2.5   In addition to the specific requirements of its objectives (which may be called **content** roles), an effectively functioning team requires its members to adopt various task and team-maintenance (or process) roles. You may, for example, be familiar with Belbin's nine team process roles, from your studies in *Management in Procurement & Supply:* an effective team needs a mix and balance of leaders, ideas people, big picture and detail people, implementers, critics and challengers, and so on.

International project teams

2.6   Given that projects may be multi-functional, multi-site, 'virtual' or even multi-organisational, they are increasingly likely to involve cross-cultural or international teams, with members from (and/or located in) different countries. This presents several additional management challenges.

- Decisions must be made as to which countries will be represented on the team (and at what levels), and how to get the best from these various sources. In addition to considerations such as the individual expertise and team member process roles required (Belbin), there may be political issues (whose interests or voices are represented), language issues (what will be the dominant and common language of the group) and so on.
- The organisation of the team will need to be related to key project locations. One option is to gather the team together in a project office which moves from key site to key site as required. Another is for team members to be permanently based at (but dispersed between) the different key sites. This may raise issues of different time zones for communication, problems of frequent travel, 'culture shock' for members posted to foreign sites and so on. ICT links are increasingly used to facilitate virtual project teamworking, across international borders.
- Multi-national/multi-cultural teams pose particular leadership challenges, owing to differences in values and behavioural norms, business customs, language, and relationship and communication styles. You may be familiar with the Hofstede model, for example, which suggests that cultures differ on certain key dimensions, including their acceptance of authority and leadership; their preference

10

for security, order and control; their preference for individualist or collectivist styles of working; and their dominant relational values. You should also be able to think of more specific examples of cultural differences: gender roles and attitudes to equality; negotiating and decision-making styles; respect for status and seniority; the importance of 'face'; work ethics and working patterns; and so on.

- An international project manager will require highly-developed cross-cultural competencies: not necessarily in-depth knowledge of all cultures involved, but sensitivity to differences and dynamics, flexibility and adaptability, and the ability to facilitate discussion and (where necessary) conflict resolution to bring differences and assumptions into the open.

Project team development and team building

2.7   Teams are not static. They mature and develop. Four stages in this development were identified by Bruce Tuckman ('Developmental sequences in small groups': *Psychological Bulletin).*

- **Forming** is the first stage, in which members try to find out about each other and about how the group is going to work: its purpose, composition, leadership and organisation are still being established. There will probably be a wariness about introducing new ideas: members will 'toe the line' in order not to make themselves unacceptable to the group. This cautious introductory period is essential, but not conducive to task effectiveness.
- **Storming** is the second stage, in which members begin to assert themselves and test out roles, leadership, behavioural norms and ideas. There is more or less open conflict and competition around these areas – but this may also be a fruitful time, as more realistic targets are set, open communication develops and ideas are generated.
- **Norming** is the real settling-down stage, in which agreements are reached about work sharing, individual requirements and output expectations. Group procedures and customs will be defined and adherence secured. The enthusiasm and brainstorming of the second stage may have died down, but methodical working can be introduced and maintained.
- **Performing** is the stage at which the group focuses on executing its task: the difficulties of group development no longer distract from performance.

2.8   A project team may progress through these stages quickly or slowly, may overlap stages, or may get stuck at a given stage (particularly 'storming'). Tuckman and Jensen ('Stages of small group development revisited': *Group & Organisation Studies*) added further stages to the original model.

- **Dorming**: the team has been performing successfully for some time and has grown complacent. It goes into a semi-automatic mode of operation, with efforts devoted primarily to the maintenance of the team itself.
- **Mourning or adjourning**: the team sees itself as having fulfilled its purpose, and the group disbands – either physically (eg in the case of a temporary project team) or psychologically (as the team turns to new goals, renegotiates membership roles, and returns to the forming stage for its next phase).

2.9   Teams are not generally left to develop by themselves. One of the tasks of leadership is the 'building' of the team: initiating or accelerating the stages of development, to support progress towards mature performance. So, for example, a leader may not act to stifle or prematurely resolve conflicts in a new team: these may be encouraged, and brought into the open, in order to progress the team healthily through the storming stage.

2.10   Team building poses a particular challenge for leaders in loosely structured, physically dispersed (eg on multi-site projects) and matrix-structured teams – including supply chain partnerships and virtual teams. Additional challenges of such teams include the establishment of roles and shared goals, and the monitoring and control of work.

3 Health and safety issues

3.1 The syllabus raises the issue of health and safety in the workplace under the heading of project-related risk – but of course there are health and safety hazards in 'business as usual' operations as well as in projects, and this is a major category of operational risk. In 1972, the UK's Royal Commission on Safety and Health at Work (the Robens Report) reported that unnecessarily large numbers of days were being lost each year through industrial accidents, injuries and diseases, because of the 'attitudes, capabilities and performance of people and the efficiency of the organisational systems within which they work'.

3.2 Wider attention has subsequently been given to health and safety issues, with consumer demand for social responsibility by organisations (underpinned by the competitive need to attract and retain quality labour) and widespread exposure of abuses through disasters such as the Bhopal chemical plant and Piper Alpha oil rig explosions. So why should organisations plan to minimise health and safety risks in the workplace?

- To protect people from pain and suffering (obviously, we hope)
- To comply with relevant legal and policy standards
- To minimise the costs of accidents and ill-health (including disruption to work, sickness benefits, repairs, replacement staff, legal claims and compensation etc)
- To enhance their ability to attract and retain quality staff
- To avoid negative PR and enhance their brand and reputation for corporate social responsibility

3.3 Management of workplace health and safety is now one of the most developed risk disciplines. Supported by law, there is a long history of risk assessment and management related to the control of hazards, and minimisation of risks, in the workplace. Since the Robens Report, major legislation has been brought into effect in the UK.

The legal framework on health and safety

3.4 The UK's Health and Safety at Work Act 1974 (HSWA) is foundational legislation which places general duties on all people involved in work, including employers, employees, contractors, controllers of premises, and suppliers. The Act extends across all businesses, sectors and workplaces (including delivery vehicles, which are regarded as the workplace of drivers).

3.5 The HSWA is an enabling Act, giving rise to many of the regulations, approved codes of practice and guidance notes which provide the risk management and compliance framework for organisations. A number of additional regulations have been formulated to implement EU directives on health and safety.

3.6 Each country, and industry, will have its own occupational health and safety (OHS) regime – and you should try to develop your awareness of the provisions in your own region and areas of interest.

Hazards in the project environment

3.7 Here are some examples of typical workplace hazards.

- Incorrect or irresponsible use of equipment, machinery and tools (especially, ignoring available safety guards and rules, failing to use protective equipment etc)
- Hazards of movement associated with confined or cluttered spaces, stairs, poorly maintained flooring or wet and slippery floors
- Storage, handling and use of hazardous materials and chemicals
- Operation of machinery (eg with sharp or moving parts)
- Inadequate lighting, heating, ventilation or hygiene
- Poor ergonomic design of work spaces, equipment and furniture, putting strain on workers (eg eye or back strain from long hours at poorly-designed workstations)

10

- Heavy lifting (particularly using incorrect techniques or failing to use mechanical assistance or protective equipment where required)
- Risk of fire (particularly where electricity, cluttered spaces and flammable materials are involved)

3.8   Sadgrove suggests a template for health and safety risk identification and assessment: Figure 10.1.

Figure 10.1 *Health and safety risk identification and assessment*

Risk	Question	✓
Machinery	Do staff work with dangerous machinery or pressurised systems?	☐
Hazardous substances	Do employees work with hazardous substances?	☐
Electrical safety	Do staff work with electrical tools or equipment?	☐
Slips, trips and falls	Is the work environment ever wet? Do employees work at heights? Can staff trip over wires or other obstructions?	☐
Lifting and handling	Does the business store a lot of stock? Does anyone manually lift goods?	☐
Computers	Do any staff spend long periods working at computer monitors?	☐
RSI	Do employees carry out repetitive tasks?	☐
Noise and vibration	Is the work place noisy? Is vibrating equipment in use?	☐
Confined spaces	Does anyone work in confined spaces?	☐
Vehicles	Does the work involve vans, lorries or forklift trucks?	☐
Total points [score one point for each box ticked]:		
[Score: 0–3 points: low risk. 4–6 points: moderate risk. 7–10 points: high risk.]		

3.9   Risk mitigation methods will therefore consist of a mix of:

- Risk assessment
- Preventive measures and safeguards (both physical, as in machine safety guards and protective clothing, and procedural, as in safe storage and handling protocols)
- Ecological and environmental controls (such as maintenance of hygiene and ergonomic design)
- Employee information, training, instruction and supervision (to minimise risk-taking behaviours) and the creation of a health-and-safety-aware culture. Some industries, in which health and safety are a priority concern, have mandatory training, induction and certification requirements.

In Australia, for example, a Construction White Card is compulsory for all workers carrying out construction work. In order to qualify for the card (which must be shown for access to work sites), employees must be able to identify workplace health and safety (WHS) legislative requirements; identify construction hazards and control measures; identify WHS communication and reporting processes; and identify WHS incident and emergency response procedures.

Exposure to hazardous materials

3.10   Exposure to hazardous materials (including adhesives and cleaning agents) and substances generated during the work process (such as gases, fumes or dust) is a major identified hazard in some work settings. Exposure can result in problems such as burns, allergic reactions, skin irritations, infections, lung damage (from inhalation) and long-term health problems (such as cancers or asbestosis).

3.11   Under the UK's Control of Substances Hazardous to Health (COSHH) Regulations, employers are required to make a suitable and sufficient assessment of health risks created by work, and the measures to be taken to reduce those risks. Measures to reduce exposure risks might include the following

- Storage in restricted access areas, under controlled conditions
- Control measures: ventilation systems, hygiene regimes, time-exposure limits or protective clothing

- Clear labelling of hazardous substances, with warnings, instructions for use, and instructions in the event of exposure
- Adequate information, instruction, training and supervision of staff (particularly new recruits) in safe handling, usage, storage and emergency procedures
- Health surveillance monitoring (where the residual risk of exposure is high)
- Arrangements to deal with accidents, incidents and emergencies, including first-aid facilities, warning systems, evacuation procedures (practised using drills) and so on.

The management of health and safety risk

3.12 Under the Health and Safety at Work Act 1974, every UK employer has a general duty to ensure the health, safety and welfare at work of all employees, so far as is reasonably practicable. Various aspects of this responsibility, included in the Act and subsequent Regulations, are set out in Table 10.1

Table 10.1 *Employer and employee duties in managing health and safety*

EMPLOYEE'S DUTIES	EMPLOYER'S DUTIES
Health And Safety At Work Act 1974	
<ul><li>To take reasonable care of himself and others affected by his acts or omissions at work</li><li>To co-operate with the employer in carrying out his duties (including enforcing safety rules)</li><li>Not to interfere intentionally or recklessly with any machinery or equipment provided in the interests of health and safety</li></ul>	<ul><li>To provide safe systems (work practices)</li><li>To provide a safe and healthy work environment (well-lit, warm, ventilated, hygienic and so on)</li><li>To maintain all plant and equipment to a necessary standard of safety</li><li>To support safe working practices with information, instruction, training and supervision</li><li>To consult with safety representatives appointed by a recognised trade union</li><li>To appoint a safety committee to monitor safety policy if asked to do so</li><li>To communicate safety policy and measures to all staff, clearly and in writing</li></ul>
The Management Of Health And Safety At Work Regulations 1992	
<ul><li>To inform the employer of any situation which may pose a danger</li></ul>	<ul><li>To carry out risk assessment, generally in writing, of all work hazards, on a continuous basis</li><li>To introduce controls to reduce risks</li><li>To assess the risks to anyone else affected by their work activities</li><li>To share hazard and risk information with other employers, including those on adjoining premises, other site occupiers and all subcontractors entering the premises</li><li>To initiate or revise safety policies in the light of the above</li><li>To identify employees who are especially at risk (other legislation cites pregnant women, young workers, shift-workers and part-time workers)</li><li>To provide fresh and appropriate training in safety matters</li><li>To provide information to employees (including temporary workers) about health and safety</li><li>To employ competent safety and health advisers.</li></ul>
Health And Safety (Consultation With Employees) Regulations 1996	
	<ul><li>To consult all employees on health and safety matters (such as the planning of health and safety training, changes in equipment or procedures which may substantially affect health and safety at work, or the health and safety consequences of introducing new technology)</li></ul>

10

Compliance risk in health and safety

3.13   It is worth noting the additional compliance risks arising from health and safety issues. The Health and Safety at Work Act 1974 contains detailed provisions for enforcing, by use of criminal proceedings, all of the duties imposed by all health and safety legislation.

3.14   The **Health and Safety Executive** has the general duty of monitoring health and safety at work and formulating government policy. It also monitors the health and safety of particular workplaces. HSE inspectors have wide powers of inspection, and enforcement of legislation through:

- Issuing prohibition notices requiring the shut down of hazardous processes until remedial action has been taken
- Issuing improvement notices requiring compliance within a certain time
- Seizing hazardous articles for destruction or rendering harmless
- Prosecution of offenders, who are liable to fines and even imprisonment in serious cases.

4   Monitoring and control

Control systems

4.1   To ensure adequate control over project objectives, project boards need to decide on key features of the control system.

- At what points in the project will we try to exert control?
- What factors are we trying to control?
- How do we measure the factors we seek to control?
- How much deviation do we tolerate before we intervene?
- How can we spot potential deviations before they occur?

4.2   Meredith and Mantel identify three different types of control processes.

- Cybernetic control (automatic detection and correction of deviations from plan, eg in measuring the output from a production process)
- Go/no-go controls (testing to see whether a condition has been met before allowing progression to the next step, as in the use of project 'gates')
- Post control (review after the event with a view to improving future performance).

4.3   **Cybernetic control systems** are the most common approach to project control. Such a system is based on measuring the outputs from a process, comparing them with a predetermined standard, and automatically reporting deviations to a decision maker, who determines corrective action: Figure 10.2.

Figure 10.2 *A cybernetic control system*

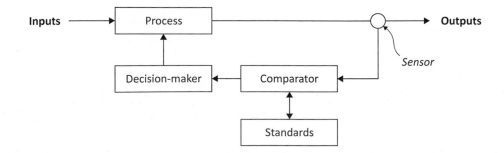

4.4   The aim in such a system is invariably to reduce deviations from the predetermined standards. When a movement away from standard is detected, the system acts to bring it back into line. This is referred to as a **negative feedback loop** (meaning that the system applies a force in the opposite, negative, direction to the deviation detected).

4.5   It is easy to see how this can apply to a project. Typically, there are predetermined standards relating to cost, time and quality, as part of the original project specification. By regular comparison with actual outcomes – actual expenditures, completion dates and deliverables – deviations from plan should come to light, and project managers can make decisions to correct the variances. However, application of cybernetic control is not straightforward in project work.

- Even if we spot a deviation, we may not identify the underlying cause.
- Even with the cause identified, we may not be able to rectify it. For example, the required action might take us outside budget.
- We may not necessarily be able to apply the desired improvement. For example, we may identify that a particular workgroup needs to make up for lost time by working longer hours. But it may not be easy to persuade them of this, and even if we do, their morale and quality of work may suffer.

4.6   A **go/no-go control system** is based on checking whether a particular condition has been met. If it has, we proceed to the next step. If not, progress is held up and a decision maker determines how to proceed. Once it is determined by a 'gateway' or 'checkpoint' review, for example, that there is a performance shortfall at an end-stage review point, the project manager must take action to rectify it – or there will be no authorisation to proceed to the next stage. Meredith and Mantel cite the example of a new jet engine, in which each part must pass its own go/no-go test. Either it exhibits the expected quality, or it fails.

4.7   This kind of control must be exercised with care in the context of project work. Some factors are critical in the sense that even a small deviation from plan is enough to halt progress. With other factors, more generous tolerances apply, and minor deviations can be ignored.

4.8   **Post-control** is exercised after a project is complete. It may well be too late to do anything about what has happened during the project, but this is a vital tool in planning for future projects. Meredith and Mantel recommend that post-control is applied through a relatively formal document in four distinct sections.

- The project objectives, identifying the extent to which objectives were met and the causes why they were not met in full.
- Milestones, checkpoints and budgets. Significant deviations from these predetermined targets should be identified and explained.
- The final report on project results. This should highlight significant deviations from plan, both good and bad (ie things that went unexpectedly well in addition to problem areas).
- Recommendations for performance and process improvement. This is a valuable tool for improving future project performance.

Performance review mechanisms

4.9   Regular performance and progress review should be a central part of the project control system. A performance measurement and reporting system must:

- Adopt simple performance measures that are easily understood by the project team
- Ensure that managers measure only what is really important (critical factors affecting cost, time and quality)
- Set appropriate control limits, tolerances or acceptable variances: when these are exceeded, the system flags the need for action
- Report by exception only.

4.10 Project management uses a range of control methodologies, in order to keep the complex and interrelated elements of the project 'on track'.

- **End stage assessments** are carried out at completion of each stage of a project, using reports from the project manager and representatives of user groups. Plans for the following stage are reviewed and approved, and management issues (including stakeholder communication and relationships) can be raised if necessary.
- **Highlight reports** are submitted regularly by the project manager to the steering committee or project board. These are the principal mechanism of regular feedback control: they are often submitted monthly (or at intervals agreed at project initiation). They are basically progress reports, with brief summaries of the status of the project in regard to schedule, budget and deliverables.
- **Checkpoints** are used for feedback and control by the project team: they involve progress review meetings, often held weekly (more frequently than highlight reports) for continuous monitoring by team members and leaders.
- Project plans typically include **milestones** (key stage targets) and **gates** (measurement points where each stage of work 'passes' or 'fails' against acceptance criteria) as review points.
- Techniques such as project budgets, Gantt charts and network analysis can be used to monitor progress against specific quality, cost and schedule targets.
- Complex project management software (such as Microsoft Project) may be used to co-ordinate planning, progress tracking and reporting data.

Project reporting

4.11 Meredith and Mantel identify the following benefits of detailed, timely reports on progress, delivered to the proper people.

- Mutual understanding of project goals
- Awareness of the progress of parallel activities
- More realistic planning
- Understanding interrelationships between different tasks
- Early warning signals of problems and delays
- Reducing delays in communicating any changes deemed necessary
- Faster management response to defective work
- Higher visibility to top management
- Keeping the client and other interested parties up to date

4.12 Meredith and Mantel also identify common problems in the preparation of reports.

- There is usually too much detail to be useful, with the result that what is useful is obscured by what is not.
- Often there is poor interface between the project information system and the parent firm's information system.
- Often there is poor correspondence between the planning systems and the reporting systems. Reports may relate to issues not directly arising from the project plan, which means that they will be useless as control tools.

Earned value analysis

4.13 We have already discussed the principles of budgetary control in Chapter 9 since they are so closely linked with the planning process of budgeting. One common pitfall, however, is to measure funds spent in relation to time rather than in relation to results and deliverables. For example, a project may spend money in Month 1 that is within the expected outgoings for that month. However, the expenditure should still not be authorised unless it leads to accomplishment of Month 1 goals: otherwise, the project expenditure would appear on target, but may actually be out of control (because the activities that were supposed to have been performed have not been completed).

4.14   This difficulty has led to the development of an integrated measurement tool known as **earned value analysis (EVA)**. Using this method, project controllers can calculate the 'earned value' of the work completed, and compare it to the amount of money actually spent. For example, if a project team has completed 50% of a task that was budgeted to cost $1,000 then it has achieved earned value of $500. If $750 has been spent, this would look good from a budget point of view – but not so good from an earned value point of view.

4.15   Meredith and Mantel identify a number of methods used in practice to estimate percentage completion of project activities.

- The 50–50 rule: any task in progress is counted as 50% ('half') complete. This has the merit of simplicity, but clearly is not very scientific.
- The 0–100 rule: any task unfinished is regarded as 0% ('not yet') complete. This is clearly a very conservative rule: it encourages personnel to strive for completion, as – until they complete – reports will show them to to be in arrears.
- The critical input rule: you identify the critical input for each task (eg Grade X labour) and calculate what percentage of that input has so far been used. This gives an estimate of how near completion the task is.
- The proportionality rule. If a task is supposed to take ten days, and we have so far been occupied on it for three days, we regard the task as 30% complete.

Progress tracking metrics

4.16   Similar simple metrics which may be used to track and measure progress (controlling the 'time' element) of a project, include the following.

- **Percentage complete values**: frequent collection of data on the percentage of each activity which has been completed (as discussed above) – ie 'how far have we come?'
- **Estimated remaining durations**: estimating the remaining duration of each activity in working days – ie 'how far have we got to go?'
- **Actual start/finish times**: recording an actual start and actual finish date (when completed) for each activity – ie 'are we there yet?'

4.17   The advantages and disadvantages of these metrics are summarised in Table 10.2.

Table 10.2 *Progress tracking metrics*

METRIC	ADVANTAGES	DISADVANTAGES
Percentage complete	• Easy to understand by everyone • Lends itself to aggregation, resource management and EVA approaches	• Can be subjective, inviting 'creative' reporting and conflict
Remaining durations	• Practical approach • Motivational: puts pressure on the estimator (eg team leader) to live up to the estimate	• Carries no implications for resources or costs deployed • Arguably, simplistic and difficult to aggregate
Actual start/finish	• Very simple to use • No room for subjective assessment • Easy to collate information	• Little or no precision in relation to tasks in progress: unacceptable for any significant task

4.18   Project management software can be used to support progress tracking via any or all of these metrics.

- It helpfully provides an integrated central source of progress data, which can be appropriately formatted and disseminated to different users for different purposes. This helps to facilitate rapid and effective communication within the project team and with relevant stakeholders.
- It allows the creation of charts and graphs (eg Gantt charts) which highlight planned progress against

actual progress for ease of review. Other flexible report formats may be generated, including tabular reports (or checklists) of tasks that are behind schedule, tasks that are in progress and so on.

- It may also support managerial decision-making, eg by creating exception reports: notifying the controller when progress falls too far behind. More sophisticated systems also allow 'what if?' scenarios and spreadsheet analysis, so that potential rescheduling or additional-resource solutions can be modelled, evaluated and (if approved) incorporated in new plans.
- It allows similar systems to be used for progress control as are used for budgetary control (monitoring budget against actual expenditure) for more integrated control measures.

Problem solving in projects

4.19   Project management makes use of a range of techniques for tackling the problems that arise in project working. Maylor highlights five categories of problems, which align neatly with ideas about risk management.

- A problem may require an immediate response or 'conditioned reflex', perhaps because someone is threatened with physical danger.
- A problem may rank as a crisis – unless we do something very soon there may be serious adverse consequences.
- Some problems rank as 'emerging' – something undesirable seems likely to happen unless we take action in advance.
- Some so-called problems are actually opportunities – we can take advantage and convert potential loss into gain.
- Some problems have a long time scale. By formulating a long-term strategy we can forestall adverse consequences and/or take advantage of opportunities.

4.20   In practice, a project manager will always be faced with a number of problems (however they are defined or identified). A key skill is then to decide on which problems to tackle first: in other words, to prioritise the problems that arise.

4.21   A problem is likely to have high priority if it has any or all of the following characteristics, which should be familiar from our wider consideration of risk management.

- There is a tight deadline attached to it, with little margin for error (ie urgency).
- Other issues or activities depend on its resolution (ie dependency).
- The adverse consequences if we fail to deal with it are serious (ie importance).

4.22   Various techniques exist for assigning priorities.

- **Pareto analysis** (based on the '80/20 rule') suggests that you can save 80% of adverse consequences if you can eliminate just 20% of the problems: by finding the small number of high-impact, critical, recurring problems, and tackling their root causes, you can dramatically reduce the overall risk.
- **Paired comparison analysis** is a tool for weighing the relative importance of different options, so that you can choose the most important problem to solve, or select the solution that will leverage your resources most effectively to give you the greatest benefits. In essence, you list all the problems you want to compare in a grid, enabling you to compare all options in pairs. For each pair, you decide which is more important and by how much (allocating a score), and then add up the scores for each of the options to rank them by priority.
- **Risk (probability/impact) analysis** can be used to evaluate which of the problems presents the greatest risk to successful completion of the project.

4.23   A further range of tools and techniques is commonly used for problem-solving in project management, including brainstorming (or thought showers) and mind-mapping; Ishikawa (cause and effect analysis or 'fishbone') diagrams; decision trees (discussed in Chapter 5) and so on.

4.24   Maylor illustrates the use of Ishikawa diagrams, for example, to explore a problem concerning late delivery of software to clients: Figure 10.3. The problem is broken down into four main causes of the problem: management of the team, specification of the software, the people in the team, and the hardware. Each of these is then analysed further by adding branches to the original diagram. In this example, the key problem has been identified as the software specification, and in particular the fact that this was changed during development.

Figure 10.3 *Ishikawa/fishbone diagram applied to late delivery problem*

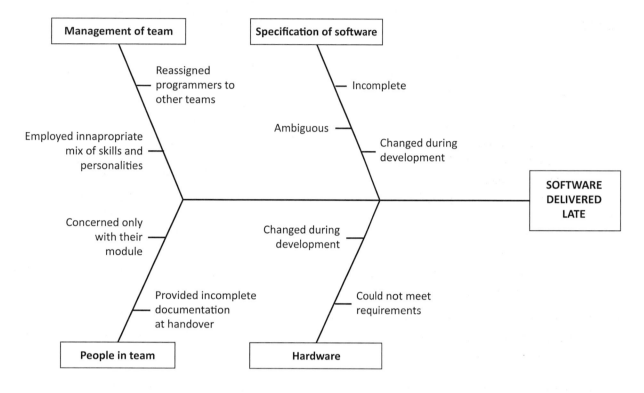

4.25   Such techniques can be incorporated into a systematic process model for solving problems. Maylor outlines such a model, involving the following steps.

- Identify problems.
- Seek alternative definitions.
- Select definition.
- Evaluate possible solution.
- Select solution.
- Implement.
- Check and amend.

Implementing remedial action

4.26   There are various options for **reducing the overall duration** of a project, if the current version of the project plan does not meet the stated project deadline, or if the project is running behind schedule. Here are some possibilities.

- Reviewing and challenging individual task durations – especially for tasks on the 'critical path' (tasks on which the overall duration of the project depends). If unnecessary delays and time-estimate 'padding' can be overcome, shortening critical task durations will reduce the overall project duration. (This will have to be done consultatively and sensitively, to avoid pressuring staff.)
- Analysing the logic of activity sequencing, to see if some tasks can be carried out in parallel, or if the project can be simplified or reduced in scope (eg by rationalising the number of tasks: removing tasks, or combining tasks to remove the effects of padding estimates of each component task).

- Authorising overtime, additional work shifts and so on – so that staff accomplish more in each working day. (This may have significant cost, employee relations and possibly health and safety implications, and should be used as an emergency resort.)
- Increasing resources: either deploying more staff, or seeking additional people or equipment where capacity has been reached (eg by subcontracting). This is a reasonable tactic to consider, if the benefits of shortened duration justify the extra costs – and if the application of extra resources directly and reliably shortens duration.
- Reducing quality (eg if products are over-specified or tolerances are unnecessarily strict) without impacting on fitness for purpose – where this would have the effect of reducing task duration.

4.27 The optimising of time may have a knock-on effect on cost: either positive (shortened duration requiring expensive human resources over a shorter period) or negative (shortened duration requiring additional expense of resources). However, again, there may be a range of tactics available to **reduce overall project costs**.

- Reducing the scope of the project by deleting tasks, or reducing the resources assigned to tasks (if cost is deemed more important than other objectives at a given stage)
- Challenging initial resource estimates, to identify 'padded' quantities and qualities where possible (again, with consultation and sensitivity, as this can be threatening to project teams)
- Challenging project overheads (costs not incurred by tasks directly connected to project deliverables: eg accommodation charges, office equipment, transport and travel, communication, administration and so on)
- Negotiating competitive market rates for contracted staff and establishing a competitive bidding environment for subcontracts (bargaining power permitting)
- Planning and mobilising resources over longer periods (eg longer work contracts) for economies of scale, where possible

4.28 **Quality** is primarily defined for a project as 'fitness for purpose': the accepted level of optimal quality – neither too high (over-specified and over-assured, leading to higher costs), nor too low (impacting on project success and acceptability). The concept of fitness for purpose also raises a range of issues, over and above 'product quality', such as ease of use, user training, supporting documentation, installation and handover procedures and so on. 'The best' software or equipment, for example may be over-specified for a small organisation or a simple task – and may also turn out to be less than 'fit for purpose' if it is difficult for users to operate and adopt, or if lack of user consultation at the development stage means that it fails to meet a key user requirement.

4.29 While approaches such as total quality management are designed for repetitive process work, the principle 'get it right first time' can be effectively applied to projects. Excessive checking, testing, repair and rework is unnecessarily costly and time-consuming – as well as frustrating for the project team. The culture of quality should be one of quality *assurance* (establishing controls and systems to prevent or minimise defects) rather than quality *control* (defect detection).

Issuing change control orders

4.30 Change is a fact of life in projects. Other than in the simplest of projects, it is likely that many circumstances will arise which were not contemplated at the planning stage. In particular, the client frequently changes plans and thinks of improvements that could be added in to the schedule. Unless such changes are closely controlled, there is a risk that the project may be disrupted. Usually control is based on the issuing of **change orders**.

4.31 Maylor proposes a somewhat complicated model of change control: Figure 10.4. (If you find it difficult to navigate around this, the key is to start in the middle with the change co-ordinator, then follow the numbered boxes 1–10.) This model is quite complicated, and would not apply to minor changes. For minor changes, it is more important to empower individuals to take appropriate action themselves, within predetermined limits.

Figure 10.4 *Change control system*

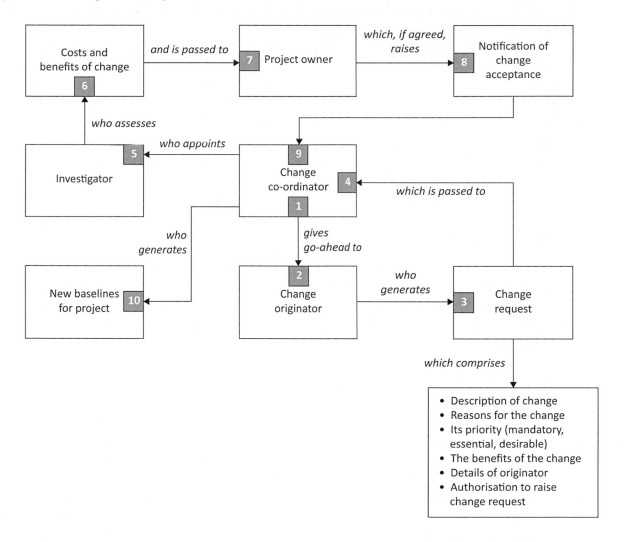

4.32 Once changes have been made, it is vital to record them. Failure to log changes appropriately can mean that the project team is unknowingly working towards objectives that no longer apply.

4.33 **Change control procedures** should be included in the project contract. The respective roles and responsibilities of both parties in the change control process must be clearly identified, along with the procedures for raising, evaluating, costing and approving change requests.

4.34 A single change control procedure should apply to all changes, although there may be certain delegated or shortened procedures available in defined circumstances (eg delegated budget tolerance levels within which a contract manager would not have to seek senior management approval). Flexibility should be built into this procedure to deal with emergency variations (eg additional, urgent requirements, or an agreement to pay instalments in order to support a supplier in cashflow difficulties).

5   Project closure

Obtaining client acceptance and installing deliverables

5.1 Many projects terminate earlier than anticipated. There are various reasons why this may happen.

- The project may fail. If this happens, the project team must be disbanded and re-allocated to other tasks. There may still be useful lessons to be learned, and possibly successes to be celebrated, even though the overall project was not a success.

- The objective of the project may be superseded. For example, the organisation may be taken over by another body which already possesses the system or asset that was being developed.
- Funding may run out.

5.2 However, assuming a project is completed a key final step is to obtain sign-off by the client. The client may be an internal department or it may be another organisation. Either way, the client will not accept completion until everything has been done to satisfaction. This will include installation of any 'hard' deliverables. For example, if the project was to create a computerised system, the client will not accept until he has seen the system installed and running effectively.

5.3 While this is perfectly reasonable behaviour on the part of the client, the project manager must ensure that it does not go further, to the point where the client is insisting on changes and refinements not contemplated in the original project plan.

5.4 Maylor emphasises that 'an ounce of image is worth a pound of performance'. This observation means that it is important to 'sell' the successes of the project to the client. This will enhance the image of the project organisation in the eyes of the customer and more generally among the public. This kind of favourable publicity can have beneficial effects internally, as it is seen that good performance is both looked for and recognised.

Documenting the project

5.5 Maylor suggests that this is the least exciting part of a project. There is therefore a danger that it will be overlooked or skimped. However, there are important reasons why project documentation should be carried out thoroughly.

- To provide evidence that the project has been completed in a proper manner. This is an important part of satisfying the client, and is also an aid to avoiding disputes.
- To give the client guidance on operation and maintenance of the output provided (a computer system, an office building or whatever).
- To provide a good starting point for any similar project in the future.

5.6 It is best not to leave documentation until the final stage. This is because much information may have been forgotten by then, and relevant team members may have moved on to other projects. The ongoing preparation of documentation should be included in the activity schedule along with all other project activities.

5.7 To assist in the process, individuals should maintain their own log books of events, discussions and agreements. The project documentation should include all contracts, permissions, letters and memos. It is particularly important to include all documents with legal implications.

Issuing the final report

5.8 Meredith and Mantel describe the final project report as 'the history of the project, a chronicle of the life and times of the project, a compendium of what went right and what went wrong, of who served the project in what capacity, of what was done to create the substance of the project, of how it was managed'.

5.9 The information required for the report will be found in the project master plan, a document that includes the proposal, all action plans, budgets, schedules, change orders etc. This is supplemented by all audits and evaluations conducted throughout the project, and by the reflections of the project manager.

5.10 Meredith and Mantel suggest that the final report should contain the following elements.

- Project performance – a comparison of what the project achieved with what it tried to achieve
- Administrative performance – a summary of how well the administrative aspects of the project were handled (which is often wrongly regarded as just a minor factor in the success or failure of the project)

- Organisational structure – including comments on how the structure helped or impeded the progress of the project
- Project and administrative teams – a confidential summary of the performance of individuals
- Techniques of project management – a summary of how well the team performed in the areas of forecasting, planning, budgeting, scheduling, resource allocation, risk management, and control

5.11   For each element in the final report, recommendations for improvement should be included. This reflects the ultimate purpose of the final report, namely to improve the management of future projects.

Final steps

5.12   The following final steps are needed before the project can be regarded as complete.

- Frequent reviews and project meetings in the final stages to maintain urgency on the way to completion
- Classifying project outcomes in three categories: 'good enough' (could be improved, but have little impact on overall success); not good enough but not worth persevering with; important to project success and therefore to be prioritised in the final stages.
- Changing the project manager, to reflect that project closure requires different skills compared with ongoing project management
- Measuring the results
- Communicating success, both to the client and to the team
- Embedding the results (including training of end users)
- Dissolving the team quickly, and allocating them to fresh tasks
- Celebrating successes

6   Audit and learning

6.1   There are further opportunities for feedback gathering and reporting at the end of each project. The project manager should produce a completion report, summarising the project objectives and outcomes achieved; budget and schedule variances; and any ongoing issues or unfinished business (and how these will be followed up).

Post-completion audit

6.2   A post-completion audit is often used as a formal review of a programme or project, in order to assess its impact and ensure that any lessons arising from it are acknowledged and learned. Such an audit may be carried out using a survey questionnaire of all project team members and key stakeholders, or meetings to discuss what went well and what didn't.

6.3   The focus of a post-completion audit (and resulting audit report) is as follows.

- Assessing whether and how far the project outcomes met the expectations of the sponsor and other stakeholders: were the deliverables up to standard, were they achieved on time and within budget and so on?
- Assessing the effectiveness of the management of the process: the effectiveness of the plans and structures set up for the project; the performance of individuals and teams; what problems (communication lapses, conflicts, errors, delays) might affect similar projects in future, and how they can be avoided.

6.4   Maylor is somewhat cynical about the project audit process, sometimes described as 'praise of the unworthy followed by punishment of the innocent'. Despite this, a project audit is an important part of improving performance on future projects. Appropriate resources must be allocated to the task.

6.5 The project manager should be involved in the audit process, but it will usually be sensible to appoint an auditor from elsewhere in the organisation. This will improve impartiality, and may in any case be necessary if the appropriate skills are to be deployed. For example, audit of the financial aspects of the project may well require an auditor with financial expertise.

6.6 The audit process involves the following steps.

- Establishing the procedures (ie establishing how activities should have been carried out in terms of financial impact, performance aspects, environmental effects etc)
- Checking documentation to ensure that the procedures were followed
- Reporting on any areas where it appears that shortcomings arose

6.7 Maylor highlights the areas that should be subjected to audit and performance review: Table 10.3.

Table 10.3 *Review and audit criteria*

CRITERIA	AUDIT	REVIEW
Financial	Accounting systems	Return on investment, cost variances
Time	Conformance to plan	Customer satisfaction
Quality	Quality procedures	Customer perceptions
Human resources	Conformance to policy	Team spirit, motivation
Environmental	Conformance to policy	Environmental impact assessment
Planning	Conformance to plan	Cost, techniques used
Control	Systems for control	Basis for improvement

6.8 Meredith and Mantel regard the audit process as an ongoing one, not just a procedure to be carried out at the end of the project. In this light, an audit report should cover the following points.

- Current status of the project
- Future status – are significant schedule changes likely?
- Status of crucial tasks
- Risk assessment
- Information pertinent to other projects
- Limitations of the audit
- Lessons learned; communication, evaluation and learning

Capturing learning for future projects

6.9 An important outcome of the project should be to obtain ideas for improvement. Maylor points out that we can learn both **by doing** and **before doing**: see Figure 10.5.

Figure 10.5 *Performance improvement*

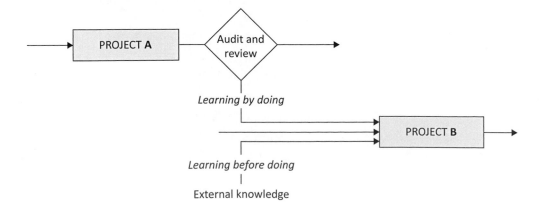

6.10 The diagram indicates that in entering Project B, we can draw on our experience of Project A (learning by doing), and also on our prior preparation (learning before doing).

6.11 Another model that is helpful in this context is the **experiential learning cycle** devised by David Kolb. This shows how everyday work experiences can be used for learning, personal development and performance improvement, through the process of 'learning by doing': Figure 10.6.

Figure 10.6 *The experiential learning cycle*

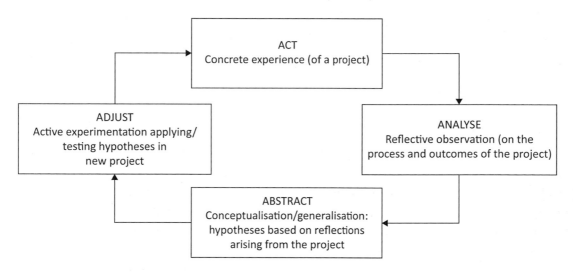

6.12 Working through the learning cycle:

- The learner has a concrete experience of the technique or concept to be learned. (For example, a team engages in a project.)
- The learner reflects on the project, project stage or critical incident that happened during the project – perhaps using a journaling process, or learning group discussion. What went wrong? What could be done differently next time?
- Using theory and experience, the learner develops some abstract concepts (eg explanations for performance problems and possible solutions), and develops action plans which will allow possible solutions to be tested in practice at an identified future opportunity.
- The learner applies and tests planned ideas and solutions during the next project stage or project – providing material for further reflection: was the changed approach or behaviour successful, or what could be done differently *next* time?

Chapter summary

- A key aspect of organising a project is to devise a work breakdown structure that groups tasks together in a logical way.
- Projects are typically carried out by cross-functional teams. The management of such teams calls for different leadership roles as compared with 'business as usual' management.
- A major category of risk is the area of health and safety. This is the case not only in project work, but also in 'business as usual' activities.
- Projects are typically controlled by a cybernetic approach, in which outputs are measured against a predetermined standard and variances are investigated. Remedial action will be taken if necessary.
- A key final step in project completion is to obtain written sign-off by the client. This is also the stage when full documentation of the project should be completed.
- A post-completion audit can help to establish lessons learned from the project, which can be carried forward to later projects.

 ## Self-test questions

Numbers in brackets refer to the paragraphs where you can check your answers.

1   List principles by which activities may be grouped into meaningful work packages. (1.2)

2   Describe ways in which leadership roles for a project differ from 'business as usual' leadership. (2.3)

3   Describe Tuckman's stages of group development. (2.7, 2.8)

4   List reasons why organisations should plan to minimise health and safety hazards. (3.2)

5   Give examples of typical workplace hazards. (3.7)

6   Describe a cybernetic control system. (4.3)

7   List benefits of detailed and timely progress reports during a project. (4.11)

8   Describe methods of prioritising project problems. (4.22)

9   Give reasons why projects should be thoroughly documented. (5.5)

10   What are the steps in the process of auditing a project? (6.6)

CHAPTER 11

Contractual Remedies for Managing Risks

Assessment criteria and indicative content

 3.1 Analyse the use of contractual remedies for managing risks in supply chains

- Indemnities and liabilities
- Ownership of IPR (Intellectual Property Rights)
- The use of *force majeure* clauses
- Clauses for testing, inspection and acceptance
- Global sourcing considerations and ensuring compliance to standards
- Model Form Contracts such as the NEC and FIDIC: provisions for the use of risk registers, notices and compensation events

Section headings

1. Managing risks through the contract
2. Liability, indemnity and insurance
3. Contract performance
4. Intellectual property protection
5. International sourcing contracts
6. Model form contracts

Introduction

In this chapter, after our sequence of chapters focusing in detail on project management, we return to other 'key processes' in managing risk in supply chains, as identified by the syllabus. These are generic risk mitigation approaches which may be applied to a range of specific risks, as appropriate: the use of contractual remedies, the retaining of third party services, the 'hedging' of risk using insurances, and the discipline of contingency planning (including business continuity and disaster planning).

In this chapter we focus on how risks can be managed through contract terms and provisions, as well as through contract administration and management. Obviously, this is a vast area of study in its own right – and the focus of major syllabus sections in other units. Here, we will focus on the areas highlighted by the syllabus, but you should also be able to draw on your learning from other units with a more substantial legal aspects component.

One area which you might be surprised to find missing from the list is contractual protections in regard to subcontracting and outsourcing. We mention subcontracting and assignment clauses under the heading of 'contract performance' here. Express provisions for outsourcing contracts were surveyed briefly in Chapter 7, where the issue of risk allocation for outsourced work and services is included by the syllabus.

Note that, unless otherwise specified, the law discussed in this chapter is that of England and Wales, as exemplar.

1 Managing risks through the contract

1.1 The role of a contract is to set out the roles, rights and obligations of both parties in a transaction or relationship. For the purposes of the management of contract performance, a contract is basically a statement of:

- Exactly what two or more parties have agreed to do or exchange (specifications, prices, delivery and payment dates and so on)
- Conditions and contingencies which may alter the arrangement (eg circumstances under which it would not be reasonable to enforce certain terms, or agreement that if party A does x, then party B may do y)
- The rights of each party if the other fails to do what it has agreed to do ('remedies' for 'breach of contract')
- How responsibility or 'liability' will be apportioned in the event of problems (eg who pays for damage or loss of goods)
- How any disputes will be resolved (eg by arbitration).

1.2 Contract terms are statements by the parties to the contract as to what they understand their rights and obligations to be under the contract. They define the content of the 'offer' (or counter-offer) which becomes binding once accepted by the other party.

1.3 There are a number of important distinctions in regard to types of contract terms.

- **Express terms** (which are explicitly inserted into a contract by either or both of the parties) and **implied terms** (which are automatically assumed to be part of a contract, by virtue of relevant statute, custom or business and other factors).
- Implied terms, such as those implied in the UK by the Sale of Goods Act 1979, are designed primarily to protect the buyer from basic risks, such as relying on descriptions or samples of goods in making the purchase decision: in such circumstances, it is implied that the goods supplied should conform to the description or sample. Similarly, it is implied that goods supplied should be of satisfactory quality and fit for purpose.
- Many of the terms most important in the management of contractual risk are *express* terms. The most common examples would be where the parties specify price, delivery dates, how carriage and insurance costs will be shared, and so on. Another example is an exclusion or exemption clause, which states that one party will not be liable (or will have only limited liability) for some specific breach of contract, or a *force majeure* clause which specifies special circumstances in which a party will not be liable for failure to fulfil its contract obligations.
- **Conditions** (vital terms of the contract, the breach of which entitles the wronged party to cancel or 'repudiate' the contract) and **warranties** (non-vital terms of the contract, the breach of which only entitles the wronged party to damages, with the mutual obligations of the contract otherwise remaining in place). This is an important distinction in managing the risk of non-performance or breach of contract.

Caveat emptor

1.4 The common law principle *caveat emptor* (Latin for 'let the buyer beware') states that a buyer cannot claim damages for defects which make goods or services unfit for ordinary purposes, unless the seller has actively concealed these defects. In other words, the buyer must take responsibility for inspecting and choosing wisely before entering into contracts.

1.5 Now, under implied statutory terms in regard to 'satisfactory quality and fitness for purpose', the buyer is much better protected – but he still has responsibility to do due diligence, and make reasonable investigations, inspections and choices.

Contract development and risk management

1.6 For a broad – non-technical – overview of how contracts can be used to minimise or mitigate a range of supply risks, Table 11.1 sets out some typical procurement-related risks, and how contract provisions might be used to mitigate them.

Table 11.1 *Contract provisions to mitigate or remedy risks*

POTENTIAL RISK	CONTRACT PROVISION
The supplier delivers the wrong quantity.	The quantity to be supplied, how the quantity delivered should be established, and who in the supplier's organisation should deal with any query.
The product is not made to the correct specification.	The contract provides the product specification, and sets out how rectification should be made in the event of the product not being supplied to specification.
The buyer fails to pay a supplier invoice.	The contract specifies when payments should be due, and perhaps provides for an 'interest payment' if the buyer pays after the due date.
The supplier is late with delivery.	How potentially late deliveries should be dealt with; whether 'time is of the essence' in delivery, entitling the buyer to additional remedies.
There is disagreement about who should pay for transportation charges.	The contract will specify how the goods should be delivered and who is responsible for the cost.
The service might be performed or installation carried out by individuals who are insufficiently qualified.	The contract will specify the qualifications or experience of anyone carrying out a service or making an installation, and will state how the qualifications or experience of the individuals will be established.
The product might be dangerous to handle.	The contract will specify how the product should be delivered and packaged, or what type of containers it should be delivered in, so as to avoid health and safety risk.
Changes may be required to the contract, relating to the specification, the provision of new services, design or performance measurement.	A variation clause, detailing the procedures that should be followed if changes are needed which will ensure value for money.
The parties may wish to vary the prices charged.	A price variation or contract price adjustment (CPA) clause, possibly based on a mutually agreed cost index.
A dispute arises	A dispute resolution clause, detailing the procedures that should be followed, such as mediation or arbitration.

1.7 We will look more technically at the key contract remedies highlighted by the syllabus in the rest of this chapter.

Passing of risk in contract

1.8 Risk generally (or *prima facie* – 'unless proved otherwise') passes with property or title in the goods, but this may not always be the case. The passing of risk determines who is responsible for insuring the goods, and who bears the cost of any loss or damage to the goods.

1.9 This is particularly important in international contracts, where delivery is likely to comprise several stages, and goods are in the hands of various parties along the way. Who is responsible for insurance and loss at each step along the way? The standard terms for international commercial contracts – Incoterms 2010 – provide expressly for risk to pass at a number of different stages in the journey from the supplier to the buyer.

Remedies for contract failure

1.10   Many contractual terms are designed to minimise risk by clarifying expectations and obligations, and acting as a disincentive to non-performance, by providing for legal 'remedies' (redress) for the injured party. However, there will inevitably be cases when a party is unwilling or unable to perform all of its obligations under the contract, and in such cases the resulting damage or loss to the injured party must be provided for by legal remedies for breach of contract.

1.11   Breach of contract is an unjustified failure to perform all the terms of the contract. There are various remedies for breach of contract, depending on whether the breach is actual or anticipatory (a party shows an intention not to perform the contract), and whether a condition or warranty has been breached.

1.12   In appropriate cases, the party who has suffered a breach of contract may have any of the following 'remedies' in law.

- **Damages:** financial compensation for losses suffered as a result of the breach. Where the amount of damages is stipulated in the contract, as a genuine estimate of the amount of the injured party's loss, this is referred to as 'liquidated damages'. If no amount of liquidated damages is stated, the issue of compensation will be referred to the courts, which will decide whether to pay 'unliquidated damages', and in what amount.
- **Specific performance:** a remedy whereby the court orders the defendant to carry out his obligations under the contract, if damages would not be an adequate remedy (eg if the claimant wanted to buy a particular property)
- **Injunction:** a remedy whereby the court orders a person to do something (mandatory injunction) or not to do something (prohibitory injunction), in order to avoid a breach of contract. An example may be an injunction restraining a supplier from breaking an exclusivity contract.
- *Quantum meruit:* a remedy available when a contract has been partly performed, entitling a party which has provided a benefit, or performed work, to be paid a fair amount for it.

Contract management and risk management

1.13   It is important to bear in mind that the legal aspects are not the *only* factor in identifying non-performance of a contract. The buyer (or contract manager) will also have to monitor and interpret a range of financial, technical and performance data to establish whether a supplier is complying – or likely to comply – with price, time, quality and other express and implied terms; whether the goods delivered conform to specification; whether services comply with agreed service levels and so on. These are key aspects of project management, contract management, supplier management and supplier performance management: all important aspects of risk management in their own right.

1.14   Many of the risk mitigation measures (and cost savings and improvements) available from procurement are achieved by how buyer and supplier work together *after* the contract has been awarded. If contract performance is not proactively or effectively managed by the buying organisation, the following adverse outcomes may occur.

- The *supplier* may be obliged to take control of contract performance and problem-solving, resulting in unbalanced decisions that do not serve the buyer's interests.
- Decisions may not be taken at the right time (or at all) to protect or optimise performance.
- Buyer and/or supplier may fail to understand their contractual obligations and responsibilities, creating poor conditions for performance.
- There may be misunderstandings and disagreements, and too many issues may be escalated inappropriately, damaging the relationship.
- Progress may be slow (because un-expedited) or there may be an inability to move forward.
- The intended benefits from the contract may not be realised.
- Opportunities to *improve* performance, add value and secure competitive advantage may be missed.

1.15 On the other hand, there are important benefits of positive and proactive contract management.

- Improved risk management in developing and managing contracts (particularly in dynamic supply environments where minimal inventory is held, putting pressure on reliable, risk-managed supplier performance)
- Improved compliance and commitment by the supplier
- Incentives and momentum for ongoing relationship and performance improvement
- Added value (arising from efficient contract administration and performance).

2 Liability, indemnity and insurance

Liability

2.1 Liability, in a legal context, is in essence the legal and financial responsibility or obligation of an entity in a situation. Organisations are 'liable' for debts, in the sense of having a legal obligation to pay. They may also be 'liable' to pay compensation or damages to other persons or entities who suffer loss as a result of their actions, under legal concepts such as the tort (common law 'wrong') of negligence and damages for breach of contract.

- **Strict liability** is a situation in which an entity is legally responsible for the damage or loss caused by acts or omissions – regardless of fault (such as malicious intent or negligence). The law imputes strict liability to situations it considers inherently dangerous, in order to encourage entities to take all possible precautions. Strict liability exists in **product liability**, for example: manufacturers, distributors, suppliers, retailers and others who make products available to the public are held responsible for any injuries they cause.
- **Vicarious liability** is a situation in which a superior bears responsibility for the acts of the subordinate: organisations are generally liable for the conduct of their employees, in the course of their work.

Litigation risk

2.2 Sadgrove cites an AXA survey which found that the biggest perceived threat to small and medium-sized businesses (SMEs) arises from increasing litigation: the threat of being sued for compensation, stimulated by the rise in 'no-win, no-fee' legal services. 'More businesses will be damaged by mundane risks such as fire or lack of sales than litigation. Nevertheless, businesses are right to be concerned and should take steps to prevent it.'

2.3 Companies may be sued by employees (over wrongful dismissal, discrimination or health and safety incidents); by consumers (over product or service failures, or failure to make premises accessible to disabled people); by customers or suppliers (over breach of contract, including failure to pay); by competitors (over infringement of intellectual property rights or unfair competition); or by pressure groups (over CSR or environmental violations).

2.4 Risk mitigation measures will be focused on ethical and compliant conduct; staff training; record keeping and so on. However, *contractual* remedies include ensuring that legal contracts are clear, sound and signed by both parties.

Indemnity clauses

2.5 An indemnity clause is designed to secure an undertaking from the other party that it will accept liability for any loss arising from events in performance of the contract, and will make good the loss to the injured party or parties. In other words, it assigns primary liability to the other party in the contract.

11

2.6   An indemnity clause might include costs or debts (eg reimbursement of rectification costs or legal claims incurred as a result of breach of contract terms or product liability issues); loss or damage to the buyer's property as a result of negligent or defective work; business losses incurred by a supplier's poor professional advice; or injury to the buyer's staff, customers or third parties (eg visitors) caused by the negligence of the other party's personnel – especially if they are performing work at the buyer's premises (eg in the case of a cleaning service) or at a customer's premises (eg in the case of outsourced service delivery).

2.7   A general indemnity clause, designed to protect a buyer, might be as follows.

'The supplier indemnifies the buyer against all costs and claims incurred by the buyer as a result, direct or indirect, of the supplier's breach of any obligation contained in this contract.'

Insurance clauses

2.8   A buyer will usually wish to confirm that the supplier has the ability to pay compensation in the event of any indemnities or legal claims arising against it, and will usually make it a requirement of the contract that the supplier has the necessary insurances to cover them. We discuss different types of insurance in Chapter 12.

2.9   A comprehensive **indemnity and insurance** clause might be as follows.

'Without prejudice to any other rights or remedies available to the Buyer, the Supplier shall indemnify the Buyer against all loss of or damage to any Buyer property to the extent arising as a result of the negligence or wilful acts or omissions of the Supplier or Contract Personnel in relation to the performance of the Contract; and all claims and proceedings, damages, costs and expenses arising or incurred in respect of:

(a) death or personal injury of any Contract Personnel in relation to the performance of the Contract, except to the extent caused by the buyer's negligence;

(b) death or personal injury of any other person to the extent arising as a result of the negligence or wilful acts or omissions of the Supplier or Contract Personnel in relation to the performance of the contract;

(c) loss of or damage to any property to the extent arising as a result of the negligence or wilful acts or omissions of the Supplier or Contract Personnel in relation to the performance of the Contract.

'The Supplier shall at its own expense effect and maintain for the Contract Period such insurances as required by any applicable law and as appropriate in respect of its obligations under this Contract. Such insurances shall include third party liability insurance with an indemnity of not less than [$2m] for each and every claim.'

Health and safety

2.10   In addition to the insurance and indemnity provisions discussed earlier, in the UK for instance there is additionally a statutory requirement for both buyers and suppliers to observe the Health and Safety at Work Act 1974 and related regulations.

2.11   It is common for buyers to use contract terms to remind suppliers of the statutory requirements imposed on the parties by the Health and Safety at Work Act 1974; of the supplier's responsibility for compliance; and of the supplier's duty to ensure that staff working at the premises of the buyer (or the buyer's customers) comply with the health and safety requirements of those premises. The buyer may also require the supplier to indemnify him against any liability, costs, losses or expenses sustained by the buyer if the supplier fails to comply with the legislation.

2.12   A simple clause of this type may be formulated as follows.

'All goods shall have all necessary safety devices fitted. You are responsible for compliance with the Health and Safety at Work Act 1974 in relation to Goods and Services and will indemnify us against any liability, costs, losses or expenses we may sustain if you fail to do so.

When you are working at our premises or the premises of our customer in the performance of any services or installation of the goods you shall ensure that your staff comply with our or our customer's requirements at the premises.'

Limitation of liability

2.13   The term 'exclusion clause' is applied to contract clauses which:

- Totally exclude one party from the liability which would otherwise arise from some breach of contract (such as the supply of goods of inferior quality); or which
- Restrict or limit its liability in some way; or which
- Seek to offer some form of 'guarantee' in place of normal liability for breach of contract.

2.14   Such clauses used to be very common in printed contracts and conditions of sale put forward by manufacturers, distributors and carriers of goods. However, the tendency of modern statutes is to limit the use of exclusion clauses – especially in dealings involving private citizens or consumers, who frequently do not read or understand the effect of the 'small print' put before them for acceptance.

2.15   In regard to **negligence**:

- A person in business cannot exclude or restrict his liability for death or personal injury resulting from negligence, and any clause purporting to do this is prohibited.
- A person in business cannot exclude or restrict liability for negligence causing loss (other than death or personal injury), unless the exclusion clause is 'reasonable'.

2.16   In regard to **breach of contract**, any term purporting to exclude or restrict liability in a standard term contract (whereby one party deals on the other party's written standard terms of business) or in a consumer contract (between a business and a consumer for the sale of goods for ordinary private use) is effective only if it is 'reasonable'. The burden of proving **reasonableness** of the exclusion clause is on the party wishing to rely on the clause to limit its liability. The term's inclusion must be fair and reasonable, in the light of the circumstances which were, or ought reasonably to have been, known to or anticipated by the parties when the contract was made.

3   Contract performance

3.1   A number of express terms may be inserted to define key aspects of contract performance, in regard to quality, price and time.

Testing, inspection and acceptance clauses

3.2   Inspection and testing clauses may be used to stipulate:

- That the buyer is not legally bound to accept delivery of goods (which may imply the transfer of possession, title and risk) before inspection and/or testing of the goods to ascertain that they conform to specification and are fit for purpose
- That the buyer is to be allowed a reasonable time to inspect and test incoming goods.

3.3   A related acceptance clause may stipulate the right of the buyer to reject goods for various reasons, such as quality defects or lateness of delivery (ie stating that 'time is of the essence' of the contract).

3.4   A range of clauses may be used to support performance management, especially in outsource contracts, to ensure supplier performance of specific KPIs and critical success factors. Here are some examples.

- A rights of inspection clause, giving the outsourcer rights of access to inspect the supplier's premises, processes or performance to monitor compliance
- A schedule performance clause, making it a condition of contract that certain tasks (eg systems maintenance or data back-up in an IT outsource contract) be performed according to a defined schedule, or within defined timescales or response times
- Penalties for specific non-performance (eg liquidated damages), and incentives for performance or improvements (eg gain sharing arrangements, bonus payments).

Passing of title

3.5   As a general principle, property in goods passes from the seller to the buyer at whatever time the parties *intend* it to pass. If the parties do not indicate their intentions, s18 of the Sale of Goods Act 1979 lays down various rules for when property passes. However, the contract may expressly stipulate an appropriate point at which the buyer assumes title.

- A buyer may wish to stipulate that ownership passes when the goods have been delivered and formally accepted, following inspection, testing or other procedures.
- A supplier may wish to stipulate that ownership passes only when goods have been paid for in full, so that it can repossess the goods if the buyer does not pay for them (or becomes insolvent). This is called a retention of title clause, or a Romalpa clause. A standard retention of title clause might appear as follows.
  'All goods supplied under this contract will remain the property of the supplier until the buyer has paid for them in full.'
- A buyer may secure ownership of the goods upon inspection and payment, but may ask the supplier to retain *possession* of some or all of the goods, in order to reduce its own stockholding.

Price

3.6   Contract clauses may be used to stop or limit the supplier from increasing the price through the life of the contract, or adding 'extras' not included in the original quotation or tender. Examples (mentioned briefly in Chapter 7) include:

- A fixed price clause for the duration of the contract: essentially, allocating all cost-related risks to the supplier or contractor
- A contract price adjustment clause, detailing how new prices or price changes will be determined and jointly agreed: essentially, sharing cost-related risks with the supplier or contractor – but also mitigating some risk, by relating price adjustments to actual cost rises (or falls), rather than agreeing an up-front price with an inflated 'contingency' element.
- Dispute resolution clauses, detailing how disputes on price will be resolved.

Time of performance

3.7   Express stipulations as to time of performance (such as dates of shipment, transfer or delivery) are normally treated as *conditions* in commercial contracts and other contracts where time lapse could materially affect the value of the goods.

3.8   Such time stipulations are generally treated as part of the essential description of the goods, and are governed by implied terms in relation to sale by description (s 13 of the Sale of Goods Act 1979). However, it is common to note expressly that 'time is of the essence of the contract', so that the buyer can insist upon the delivery date specified in the contract. In such cases, if there is a delay in performance, the injured party may treat it as breach of condition and pay nothing (and also refuse to accept late performance if offered).

Subcontracting and assignment

3.9 Since buyers have a key interest in assuring the quality of the goods produced, or the services performed, by suppliers, they will generally not want the supplier to hand over the contract to a third party – at least without the opportunity to pre-qualify and approve the subcontractor. The original supplier will remain liable for any failures on the part of the third party, but the risk may still be unacceptable to the buyer.

3.10 The general rule is that a contract can be assigned or subcontracted unless it is evident in all the circumstances that a supplier was specifically *chosen for its unique qualities* (and it would therefore not fulfil the buyer's intentions to have the work done by another party).

3.11 A subcontracting and assignment clause may be used to prevent any assignment or subcontracting without prior written consent. A typical clause might be as follows.

'The supplier shall not assign or transfer the whole or any part of this contract, or subcontract the production or supply of any goods to be supplied under this contract, without the prior written consent of the buyer.'

Liquidated damages

3.12 A liquidated damages clause is used to guarantee the buyer damages against losses arising from a supplier's late or unsatisfactory completion of a contract – and to motivate the supplier to perform the contract. Such clauses are often used in large contracts (eg for construction works or capital equipment).

3.13 The purpose of *damages* is to put the injured party into the position it would have been in if the contract had been properly performed: they are a 'compensatory', not a 'punitive' (or punishing) remedy. So if a seller has failed to deliver goods, for example, the buyer's measure of damages will be the difference between the agreed contract price and the price the buyer needed to pay in order to get the goods elsewhere at prevailing market price.

3.14 As a proactive form of dispute and relationship management, the parties may agree a sum to be paid in the event of breach of contract – or they may not discuss this point at all.

- Where the contract does not make any provision for damages, the court will determine the damages payable. Such damages are referred to as 'unliquidated damages'.
- Where the contract provides for the payment of a fixed sum on breach, this is known as a 'liquidated damages' clause.

3.15 The clause specifies the damages which will be payable for breach, at a predetermined amount (eg $x per day late) which is designed to be a *genuine estimate of the damage or loss which would be caused by the non-performance of the contract*. It will be enforceable if a breach occurs, usually without action in the courts: if both parties have agreed to the clause, the buyer can simply deduct the damages from its payment to the supplier in breach.

3.16 Even if the actual damages suffered are greater than the liquidated damages provided for in the contract, the claimant can only claim the liquidated amount.

3.17 If a liquidated damages clause is framed as a disincentive or deterrent to breach of contract – as an attempt to minimise the risk of contract non-performance – it may be defined as a 'penalty clause' (regardless of the name given to it in the contract). Such clauses are not enforceable in law: they are void in the event of breach. The injured party will have to prove the actual loss suffered in court, and unliquidated damages will be assessed and awarded by the court. Generally, a clause will be presumed to be a penalty clause if it does *not appear to be a genuine attempt to estimate the potential loss*, eg if:

- The sum stipulated appears unreasonably large.

- A single sum of damages is payable on the occurrence of one or more breaches, not distinguishing between breaches that are trivial and those that are serious
- A sum is stipulated for breach by non-payment – but is greater than the amount of the payment owed.

Force majeure clauses

3.18   The general rule is that, unless otherwise agreed, a party which fails to perform its contractual obligations is in breach of contract and liable for damages – whatever the excuse for non-performance. The legal doctrine of 'frustration' was designed to reduce the severity of the general rule, by allowing for genuinely good excuses for non-performance.

3.19   The purpose of *force majeure* (major force) clauses is to release the parties from liability in circumstances where their failure to perform a contract results from circumstances which were unforeseeable, for which they are not responsible, and which they could not have avoided or overcome.

3.20   Examples of such circumstances include 'act of God'; flood, earthquake, fire, storm and other natural physical disasters; war, revolution, riot or civil disorder; general industrial disputes (not limited to the employees of the supplier or its subcontractors); and so on. Such circumstances do not automatically frustrate or end a contract, but may cause late delivery or non-delivery for which liability needs to be waived.

3.21   A *force majeure* clause should (according to the CIPS model clause):

- State the events that will constitute *force majeure*, as relevant to the industry or market
- Oblige either party to notify the other if *force majeure* events have occurred which may materially affect the performance of the contract
- State that a party will not be considered in default of its contract obligations, as long as it can show that full performance was prevented by *force majeure* events
- Provide for the contract to be suspended for up to 30 days, if performance is prevented by *force majeure* for this period
- Provide for the termination of the contract, by mutual consent, if the *force majeure* event continues to prevent performance for more than 30 days (with provisions for transfer of work done so far, in return for reasonable payment).

3.22   A very simple clause might be as follows.

'Neither party shall be regarded as being in breach of its obligations if it can show that it was prevented from performance by any circumstances of force majeure *which arose after the date of the contract. Such circumstance may include, but is not limited to, war and other hostilities, terrorist activity, revolution, riot, earthquake, flood or other natural disaster, and industrial disputes (not limited to the employees of the parties or their subcontractors).'*

Grievance mechanisms

3.23   Grievance mechanisms (or dispute mechanisms) are structured processes to address grievances, problems or disputes that arise between two or more parties engaged in contractual or commercial relationships. A range of grievance mechanisms is commonly provided for in contracts, in order to ensure that performance and relationship issues can be dealt with – ideally *without* recourse to costly and relationship-damaging litigation (pursuing the dispute through the courts).

3.24   In buyer-supplier relationships, supply contracts will often include clauses setting out the methods that will be used to settle disputes between the parties, and how they will be 'escalated' (taken further or to a higher level) if necessary.

3.25   In 2001, the UK Office of Government Commerce (OGC) produced guidance on dispute resolution, noting that:

Dispute resolution techniques can be viewed as a continuum that range from the most informal negotiations between the parties themselves, through increasing formality and more direct intervention from external sources, to a full court hearing with strict rules of procedure.

3.26   The grievance mechanisms provided for in contracts are generally 'non-judicial' (not resolved within the court of law) and embrace a range of 'alternative dispute resolution' (ADR) mechanisms such as the following.

- **Consultation**: a form of 'issues' management, in which potential causes of conflict are discussed, and the other party has an opportunity to give its input, before the problem arises (or as soon as possible, once it has arisen). A buyer may, for example, commit himself to formal or informal consultation with suppliers about the need to vary the terms of a contract.
- **Negotiation**: often used as an official mechanism for the resolution of contract disputes and relational problems with suppliers. The contract may provide for an 'escalation ladder': typically commencing with buyer-supplier negotiation, and progressively escalating to a joint forum made up of senior management representatives from the concerned organisations.
- **Conciliation**: a process where conflicts or grievances are aired in a discussion, facilitated by an impartial conciliator, whose role is to manage the process and make constructive suggestions (and *not* to make a judgement for one side or the other). There is negotiation towards a mutually acceptable position – and, if possible, a 'win-win' outcome.
- **Mediation** may follow conciliation, if a voluntary settlement has not been reached. It involves the appointment of an independent person (or panel) who will consider the case of both sides and make a formal proposal or recommendation (not binding on either party) as a basis for settlement of the dispute.
- **Arbitration**: the appointment of a mutually acceptable independent person (or panel) who will consider the arguments of both sides, in formal, closed proceedings, and deliver a decision or judgement which is legally binding on both parties. Because of the costs and other disadvantages of litigation, it is increasingly common for buyers and suppliers to treat court proceedings as a last resort, and to stipulate in their contracts that disputes must first be referred to arbitration: an **arbitration clause**. It is also usual for the arbitration agreement to contain *time limits* during which the arbitration must begin, in the event of a dispute. The arbitrator may be identified in the contract, or may be appointed once a dispute has arisen. Another important part of such an arrangement is that both parties agree to be bound by the decision of the arbitrator, which can be enforced as if it were the decision of a court.

3.27   In addition, a contract may include specific provisions for the handling of grievances, contract variations and 'claims': we will consider these in relation to model form contracts in Section 6 of this Chapter.

4   Intellectual property protection

Intellectual property rights (IPR)

4.1   Businesses often expend considerable time and money developing ideas, processes, designs and other intangible assets that will enable them to generate profits. Once they have done so, they are naturally concerned to ensure that they reap the benefits without disturbance from others. The law assists them in this by providing a range of measures to protect such 'intellectual property'. These laws derive from both common law and statute (in the UK, especially the Copyright, Designs and Patents Act 1988).

4.2   Various legal provisions are made for the ownership and protection of intellectual property rights.

- **Technological inventions** may be protected by the law relating to patents (such as the Patents Act

2004). To secure protection for an invention, the owner applies to the Intellectual Property Office for the award and registration of a patent, which lasts for 20 years. The right given by the patent is that of control over the use and commercial exploitation of the invention (including granting usage licences to other parties). If a patent is infringed, a civil action may be brought to seek an injunction to prevent further abuse, as well as damages or an account of profits.

- Products carrying a **distinctive design** (shape, pattern or ornament) may be protected by the law relating to registered designs. Designs may be registered at the UK Intellectual Property Office, and protected for five years (extendable in five-year periods to a maximum of 25 years). An automatic 'unregistered design right' in any case applies for 10 years from the article's first marketing or 15 years from its first design – whichever period expires sooner. During the last five years of this period, anyone may obtain a licence to make the article by paying a royalty to the owner. If any design right is infringed, the remedies are an injunction, plus damages or an account of profits.

- The goodwill attaching to a particular mark or logo used by a business may be protected by the law of **trade marks** and service marks (Trade Marks Act 1994). In the case of abuse of an *unregistered* mark, the main recourse for the owner is to bring an action for the common law offence (tort) of 'passing off': deceiving the public by deliberately causing confusion with another (better known) brand or organisation. A *registered* trade mark (one formally registered with the Registrar) is protected against use of any 'similar' mark on goods or services 'similar' to those covered by the registered mark (causing the possibility of public confusion).

- Protection of original literary, dramatic, musical and artistic work (including graphic work and computer programmes) is afforded by the law of **copyright** (Copyright, Designs and Patents Act 1988). The right to protection arises automatically and expires 70 years from the end of the calendar year in which the author (or other assigned owner) dies. Infringement of copyright usually means that someone has copied or adapted a work created by someone else.

4.3   Issues of IPR risk have been highlighted in recent years by questions raised about:

- The adequacy of existing IP law to cope with new digital formats, particularly in view of the popular practice of downloading, sharing and utilising digital content – with strong consumer and activist pressure to maintain 'freedom of the internet' from restrictive IP controls. The Intellectual Property Act 2014 addresses many of these concerns.

- The licensing of patented technologies for applications such as smartphones and tablet computers, with escalating legal battles between companies such as Samsung and Apple to protect the value of patents, while enabling technological innovation.

4.4   **IPR clauses** are designed to enforce statutory protection for designs, patents and copyrights owned by either party to a contract.

4.5   It is important for the buyer to ensure that adequate protection is included in contracts for goods and services where these matters are likely to arise. An example clause is given below, providing protection for the buyer. (A more complex clause may also seek an indemnity from the supplier against any claims or costs arising from infringement of intellectual property rights.)

All Intellectual Property Rights in all documents, drawings, computer software and any work specifically prepared or developed by the Contractor in performance of the Contract shall vest in the Client.

All Intellectual Property Rights developed by the Contractor and used in the performance of the Contract which do not vest in the Client shall be vested in the Contractor. The Contractor hereby grants to the Client a royalty-free, worldwide, non-exclusive licence to use the same.

Copyright in all documentation and Intellectual Property Rights in all other items supplied by the Client to the Contractor in connection with the Contract shall remain the property of the Client to the extent that they are in the ownership of the Client.

The Client hereby grants the Contractor a non-exclusive, non-transferable licence to use all the Intellectual Property Rights owned (or capable of being so licensed) by the Client required by the Contractor or any of its employees, subcontractors or agents to provide the Services. Any such licence is granted for the duration of the Contract solely to enable the Contractor to comply with the obligations of this Contract.

The Contractor shall reimburse the Client's reasonable costs incurred in complying with the provisions of this Clause.

Confidentiality clauses

4.6   Confidentiality clauses are designed to protect either party, in cases where they need to give the other party access to information about their operations, in the course of the contract.

4.7   A confidentiality clause should define 'confidential information' (eg information that would appear to a reasonable person to be confidential or is specifically stated to be confidential) and should provide that the other party will take all proper steps to keep such information confidential.

4.8   In certain cases requiring stricter confidentiality, one party may require the other to sign a separate **non-disclosure agreement**, to be appended to the main contract.

5   International sourcing contracts

Opportunities (upside risks) in international sourcing

5.1   Some of the opportunities available from a 'gamble' on international sourcing can be identified as follows.

- Access to required materials, facilities and/or skills, which may not be available (or available at the right price) in local supply markets
- Access to a wider supplier base, with opportunities to select the most competitive offering – and the flexibility to switch sources of supply, if requirements are not reliably available in any single market
- Opportunities for cost savings. Historically, this has been the prime motivator of international sourcing. Certain overseas countries have been strongly price competitive with domestic supply markets, because of cheap wage rates, sourcing economies (eg easy access to abundant supplies of local raw materials), scale economies, government export subsidies or beneficial exchange rates.
- Competitive quality, arising from suppliers' ability to take advantage of raw material quality, skill and technology specialisation, or quality values and management techniques in other cultures
- Reduced regulatory and compliance burden. Some overseas countries may have more lax regulatory regimes in relation to quality standards, health and safety, minimum wages, environmental protection, or the protection of intellectual property. Although this may be a source of reputational and compliance risk for the importer, it may also enable it to 'cut corners' on costs.
- Leveraging available ICT developments for virtual organisation, e-sourcing and e-procurement, contract management and supplier relationship management and communication
- Ability to compete with competitors who are benefiting from any or all of the above advantages

Downside risks in international or global sourcing

5.2   International sourcing and trading imposes a distinct set of risks for businesses. Depending on the particular circumstances, they may include any of the following.

- Socio-cultural differences (including business customs, consumer behaviour, communication and negotiation styles, management styles, and social values) – creating potential barriers to communication; difficulties in attempting to transfer marketing, sourcing and managerial strategies across cultures; and, in some areas, increased risk of bribery and corruption

11

- Language barriers – with potential for misunderstanding (in a legal sense, affecting the validity of a contract, as well as in general communication)
- Legal issues, such as which nation's legal rules apply in determining contract disputes
- Logistical and supply risks, arising from long-distance supply lines, long lead times for supply; the risks of loss, damage or deterioration of goods in transit; and the potential ambiguity of the passing of risk and title, and responsibility for insurance, in such circumstances
- Technical risk: lack of technical expertise, supplies and resources, infrastructure
- Increased security risks to personnel and operations: kidnap, extortion, terrorist activity, civil unrest
- Exchange rate risk, due to potential fluctuations in foreign currency values during the contract period (requiring measures such as forward exchange contracts)
- Payment risk, due to limited direct contact between the parties, different legal systems, and the possibility of currency restrictions
- Difficulties of monitoring and assuring quality, environmental and ethical standards in overseas supplier operations (especially in areas where local standards, regulation and legislation are less stringent) – creating quality, compliance and reputational risk
- General STEEPLE factor risks in the overseas environment: political instability; nationalisation of businesses by regimes; economic instability; inflationary climates; protectionist policies (tariffs, quotas etc); poor technological infrastructure; poor education infrastructure and skilling; and so on

Price and cost risks

5.3   International sourcing creates a number of risks in relation to cost – despite the strong cost advantages available.

- Additional costs of identifying, evaluating and developing new sources of supply, in situations where information may be difficult to obtain (eg inaccessibility for site visits and performance monitoring) and where quality standards and regulatory regimes may differ (and offer inadequate compliance assurances)
- High transaction costs, given the complexity of international transaction documentation, time zone differences, the need for detailed contracting, specification and contract management and so on. (These will be mitigated to some extent by e-procurement and e-commerce technologies – but this, in itself, represents an extra investment and technology risk.)
- Costs caused by transport risks and delays, caused by distance, lead times in transit, and the potential for deterioration, damage and loss of goods in handling, storage and transit. There will be additional costs of risk management measures to mitigate these risks, such as special packing, refrigeration, insurance, expediting systems and so on.
- Exchange rate risk, as a result of fluctuations in the value of buyer-side or supplier-side currencies (discussed in Chapter 5) and currency management costs (obtaining foreign currencies, arranging letters of credit and so on).
- Payment risk, with reduced confidence for suppliers of being paid owing to distance (especially bearing the risk of non-delivery, loss of goods or rejection of goods paid for in advance) and the complexity of risk management measures (eg letters of credit and bills of exchange: the details of these payment mechanisms should be familiar to you from your Level 4 studies).
- Costs associated with tariff and non-tariff barriers to trade, such as onerous customs procedures and documentation; import duties and taxes; import quotas and so on.

Risks relating to quality standards

5.4   Quality risks arise from a number of factors.

- The difficulty of obtaining verified supplier pre-qualification information (eg via site visits or financial statements) at a distance or with different reporting regimes
- The difficulty of monitoring suppliers' quality management systems, or sampling verified outputs, at a distance

- The difficulty of 'drilling down' through suppliers' own supply chains, in situations where there may be poor supply chain documentation and lack of communication infrastructure
- Perceived emphasis on price competition encouraging a 'cutting of corners'
- Differences in regulatory regimes in regard to consumer protection, labelling and other quality issues (eg the inclusion of poor-quality materials or ingredients)
- Differences in quality standards, and related factors such as vocational education and management development, technology infrastructure, access to quality inputs, awareness of quality management standards and techniques, working conditions, investment in quality, and culturally-conditioned values and perceptions of quality.

5.5   The emphasis in managing such risks may be on: rigorous supplier pre-qualification and monitoring; rigorous specification of quality requirements, tolerances, service levels and KPIs; contract incentives and penalties to support quality performance; the use of grievance mechanisms to trigger problem-solving and dispute resolution; and the use of third party local agents or consultancies to perform supplier appraisal and performance management tasks.

International supply risks

5.6   Supply risks in international supply markets and supply chains may include any of the following.

- Potential disruptions to supply, and risk of supplier failure, caused by factors such as political instability, civil unrest, war or terrorism, trade policy changes (such as the imposition of export or import quotas), industrial unrest or natural factors (eg drought, flood, earthquake or disease) in overseas areas
- Transport risks: the risk of loss, deterioration, damage or theft of goods in transit, given the longer distances and lead times involved – as well as the inherent risks of increased handling, storage and transport conditions (dust, pressure, water and so on). Piracy or war damage may be a risk to sea freight or road haulage in some areas of the world. Natural factors may also cause delays: recent examples include snow disrupting road haulage, and the eruption of a volcano disrupting air freight.
- Increased lead times for supply, due to transport distance (particularly if slower modes of transport such as sea freight or road haulage are used); delays due to weather or transport congestion; delays due to customs clearances and inspections; delays due to inefficient transport planning; and so on.
- Risks of misunderstanding of requirements (in relation to quantity, time, place or other matters), due to differences of language or interpretation (different meanings attached to terms and concepts in different cultures) in negotiation, specifications or supply contracts.
- Problems caused by communication delays (eg because of slow communication infrastructure or time zone differences).

5.7   The management of such risks will generally focus on measures such as the following.

- Proactive demand forecasting and procurement planning, taking into account realistic lead times for international supply
- Proactive transport planning, in order to maximise the security and efficiency of deliveries, customs clearances and so on
- Rigorous risk identification, monitoring and assessment, including the regular updating of supply risk registers
- Contingency planning: developing action plans and mitigating measures for unlikely but foreseeable risk events (including, where appropriate, developing alternative local 'back-up' sources of supply)
- The purchase of appropriate insurances to cover likely and/or high-impact contingencies, and the use of incoterms to establish buyer and supplier responsibilities for insurances, and liability for risk events during storage, transport and handling
- Collaborating with suppliers to minimise identified risks – and/or to help with disaster recovery and supply continuity (eg Toyota supporting its supply network in rebuilding after an earthquake or tsunami)

11

- Using third party service providers (eg agents, freight forwarders or logistics providers), in order to access international expertise and local offices – and share or transfer responsibility for risks
- The use of incoterms to minimise contract ambiguities; establish liability for risk, cost and insurance at all stages of transit; and establish the points at which risk passes from the seller to the buyer.
- The use of local agents or consultants, or translation and interpretation services, in negotiating and developing contracts and agreements.

Compliance, legal and reputational risk

5.8   A further category of risks in international sourcing may arise from the following factors.

- Differences in legal frameworks (eg on contract law, health and safety, employment, environmental protection and intellectual property protection).
  Such differences may cause direct commercial and project risks: eg loss of intellectual assets; breach of the supply contract and costs of litigation or arbitration; the use of unsafe materials or components (with the buyer ultimately liable for loss or damage to consumers, as in Mattel's massive product recall of toys made in China with illegal lead paint).
  There may also be reputational damage to the buyer as a result of exposure of poor labour standards or adverse environmental impacts by its supply chain.
- Issues around 'applicable law': the determination of which country's legal system will have jurisdiction over disputes between parties to international contracts. Efforts are being made, especially within trading blocs, to harmonise legal frameworks and establish international arbitration systems.
- Differences in ethical standards and the cost and complexity of managing them, eg by ethical monitoring of suppliers. As well as impacting directly on business practices (eg costs and ethical conflicts relating to bribes or 'grease money'), ethical issues pose the risk of reputational damage, given increasing public concern about human rights, ethical trading and so on.

5.9   Some risks can be managed operationally: through supplier monitoring; the inclusion of grievance mechanisms in contracts and relationship management planning; insurances; the use of incoterms; and so on. At a more strategic level, sourcing professionals will need to establish policy guidelines (eg on ethics and risk management) and implement ongoing environmental monitoring and research. They will also need to make key strategic decisions about the configuration of the supply network: eg using agents, freight forwarders, logistics lead providers, strategic alliances or local strategic business units (or divisions) to help manage international supply chain relationships.

The use of incoterms

5.10   Incoterms are a set of contractual conditions or terms that can be adopted into international contracts, which are designed to be understood and interpreted on a worldwide basis. *Incoterms 2010* sets out agreed explanations of many of the terms used in international trade to define the obligations of seller and buyer. The document is regularly updated in line with developments in commercial practice.

5.11   The use of incoterms in a contract can save pages of detailed negotiation. When adopting incoterms into the contract, the detailed specifications relating to the relevant incoterm will apply, defining areas of risk and responsibility. Areas detailed within incoterms specify the obligations of buyer and seller at each stage of delivery, and can therefore be used as a framework for checking and managing performance of the contract.

International grievance mechanisms

5.12   The legal systems in the buyer's and supplier's countries may well be different, and the parties to an agreement must agree on two important matters.

- Which country's law should apply in the event of a dispute under the contract?

- In which country's courts should any dispute be conducted?

5.13 In the UK, the Contracts (Applicable Law) Act 1990 gave statutory effect to the Rome Convention on the Law Applicable to Contractual Obligations 1980. The Rome Convention allows the contracting parties to choose the law that will govern the contract between them. The choice must be made expressly within the contract documentation. Where the parties, for whatever reason, do not make a choice on the law of the contract, then Article 4(1) of the Rome Convention states that the law of the country with which it is 'most closely connected' will govern the contract.

5.14 Arbitration is the most commonly used form of dispute resolution for international disputes. There are well established frameworks for international dispute arbitration, using the International Chamber of Commerce (ICC) court of arbitration, or the United Nations Commission on International Trade Law (UNCITRAL) arbitration code. Arbitration brings a measure of neutrality, so that no party is unfairly disadvantaged by the location of the proceedings, the language used, the procedures applied and so on.

5.15 The parties to the contract have to agree to arbitration before it can be applied. The parties can agree to this either before or after the dispute has arisen, but good risk management processes would ensure this is considered prior to entering into an international purchase contract.

5.16 Although the adoption of incoterms into a contract will mean that courts will imply the standards of incoterms in law, the ICC will arbitrate on disputes. If this course of action is considered worthwhile the ICC recommends inclusion of the following term in the contract.

'All disputes arising in connection with the present contract shall be finally settled under the Rules of Conciliation and Arbitration of the International Chamber of Commerce by one or more arbitrators appointed in accordance with the said Rules'.

5.17 Grievance mechanisms may also be used as a tool for establishing open, transparent and equitable communication channels between **business and communities**, as part of a responsible organisation's approach to sustainable development and community relations.

5.18 They can offer a channel for local communities to voice and resolve concerns related to development projects (such as labour rights or environmental concerns), and a way for companies to address those concerns. At the same time, such mechanisms and forums support the company in systematically identifying emerging issues and trends which may create risks in international development projects, as the basis for proactive issues management and reputational defence.

5.19 The World Bank argues that: 'Locally-based grievance resolution mechanisms provide a promising avenue by offering a reliable structure and set of approaches where local people and the company can find effective solutions together'. Such grievance mechanisms would typically recognise a range of internationally recognised human rights, labour and environmental standards, as the basis for desired outcomes and remedies.

6 Model form contracts

Model form contracts

6.1 Model form contracts are published by third party experts (such as trade associations and professional bodies), incorporating standard practice in contracting for specific purposes within specific industries, and ensuring a fair balance of contractual rights and responsibilities for buyer and seller.

6.2 They are often used in particular industries to establish conditions of contract between buyer and seller which become an acceptable and familiar commercial and legal basis upon which business is usually conducted. Model form contracts can usually be adapted to suit particular circumstances and relationships.

The NEC (New Engineering Contract)

6.3   The Institution of Civil Engineers has produced a model form contract, standardising terms used across the construction industry. The **New Engineering Contract (NEC)** is intended for use for civil, engineering, building and electrical or mechanical works. It was originally developed in the early 1990s with the aim of introducing a non-adversarial contract strategy which would enhance the smooth management of projects.

The FIDIC (International Federation of Consulting Engineers) Contract

6.4   The International Federation of Consulting Engineers (*Fédération Internationale Des Ingénieurs-Conseils* or **FIDIC**) represents the global engineering industry. It has developed a range of model form contracts for use by the construction industry worldwide, including:

- The Construction Contract (contract for construction for building and engineering works designed by the employer) or Red Book
- The Plant & Design-Build Contract (contract for electrical and mechanical plant and for building and engineering works designed by the contractor) or Yellow Book
- The Short Form of Contract, or Green Book
- The Design-Build-Operate (DBO) Contract
- Forms of agreement for the engagement of consultants: the Client/Consultant Model Services Agreement (or White Book); Sub-Consultancy Agreement; and Joint Venture Agreement.

6.5   The FIDIC contracts include clauses on risk, responsibility, liability, indemnity, insurance and *force majeure*.

Provisions for use of risk registers and notices

6.6   The NEC 3 contract incorporates a **risk register**. This is intended to support the management of project risk in a collaborative and proactive manner. The contract (Clause 11) defines the risk register as 'a register of the risks *listed in the Contract Data* and the risks which the Project Manager or the Contractor has *notified as early warning matters.'*

6.7   Each party lists the risks that they see within the contract (broadly price, time and quality risks), which they want to see managed. The minimum content requirement is a description of the risk, plus a description of the action(s) required to avoid or reduce the risk. Risks that were unforeseen at the time of contracting can be added to the register at a later date.

6.8   Clause 16 further provides for a **warning procedure**. If an unforeseen risk emerges, the project manager or the contractor must notify the other party of any issues that impact upon price, time or quality. If necessary, a **risk reduction meeting** can then be called, so that the parties can co-operate in developing plans to overcome the newly identified risk. The project manager has a duty to update and revise the risk register to reflect the issues as discussed, and any decisions taken.

Provisions for compensation events

6.9   The risk register, warning procedures and risk reduction meetings are important in the NEC because of the possibility of 'compensation events'. Compensation events are a mechanism in NEC contracts through which contractors can submit **claims** (for additional time and/or cost) to compensate them for the negative effect of contingencies.

6.10   If the risk of an event happening is owned by the employer, under the contract, and if the event materialises and the contractor suffers negative effects (such as higher costs), the contractor can treat the event as a compensation event, and submit a claim for extra time or money.

6.11   The inclusion of this mechanism was intended to limit the number of disputes arising during projects. The events that are permitted to give rise to a claim are limited to those which have been specifically identified as compensation events within the contract. If a specific event is not included, no claim may be submitted by a contractor in respect of that event – even if the event has, in fact, delayed the contractor during the execution of the works, or given rise to additional costs and expenses.

6.12   If a new risk arises that ultimately results in a claim by the contractor (as a compensation event), the claim may be reduced in value if it is deemed that the contractor could or should have given early notice of the situation and its potential impacts (using the warning procedure or risk reduction meeting) but failed to do so. In other words, the contractor will have failed in its duty to mitigate the loss, by bringing the matter to the attention of the project manager at a sufficiently early stage, when action could have been taken to eliminate or reduce its effect.

6.13   Where an issue *has* been raised as being a risk to the project, but no mitigation plan is made, or the project manager does not consider that mitigating action is required, this is recorded in the risk register. If the issue subsequently escalates into a compensation event, the register can be used to show that due warning was given: this will help the contractor to substantiate its claim and avoid penalties for failure to mitigate.

6.14   Contractors will have to determine whether or not they have a valid claim – while the project manager must carefully evaluate any claims received from a contractor, in order to decide whether it needs to be assessed or dismissed. A valid compensation event is one in which:

- The event does not arise from a fault of the contractor
- The event is one of the compensation events stated in the contract
- The event has happened
- The event has had an effect on the contractor's costs, key dates or completion date
- The claim for additional time or cost is made within the deadline provided for in the contract

Chapter summary

- An important aspect of risk mitigation is careful drafting of contracts with suppliers. This should clarify the obligations of all parties and the means of proceeding if things go wrong.
- It is common to define (and perhaps limit) the liability of contracting parties by specific terms covering indemnity, insurance and limitation of liability.
- Typical contractual clauses relating to performance will cover testing and inspection, passing of title, price, time of performance, subcontracting and assignment, liquidated damages and *force majeure*.
- It is usual to protect intellectual property rights by means of contractual clauses. These would cover inventions, designs, trade marks, and confidentiality.
- It is increasingly common for projects to be organised on an international scale, but this adds particular risks such as those arising from cultural differences, foreign exchange and different legal systems.
- Model form contracts are published by third party experts and incorporate standard practice within a particular industry.

Self-test questions

Numbers in brackets refer to the paragraphs where you can check your answers.

1 Distinguish between (a) express terms and implied terms, and (b) conditions and warranties. (1.3)

2 List possible remedies for an injured party if a contract is breached. (1.10)

3 What is meant by an indemnity clause? (2.5)

4 What is meant by an exclusion clause? (2.13)

5 Describe the types of clause that may prevent a supplier from increasing his quoted price during the course of a contract. (3.6)

6 Distinguish between a liquidated damages clause and a penalty clause. (3.17)

7 List types of asset that may be protected by a clause covering intellectual property rights. (4.2)

8 List benefits that may be sought from a policy of international sourcing. (5.1)

9 What risks arise in relation to price and cost when international sourcing is adopted? (5.3)

10 In the context of NEC contracts, what are compensation events? (6.9)

CHAPTER 12

Third Parties in Risk Management

Assessment criteria and indicative content

3.2 Analyse the use of outsourced third parties in risk management in supply chains

- The use of outsourced third party providers for credit rating and other business services
- The use of outsourced third party providers for auditing risks in supply chains
- The use of outsourced third party providers for disaster recovery services

3.3 Evaluate the use of insurances for protection against risks in supply chains

- The use of insurance in hedging against risk
- The main categories of insurance: employers and public liability; professional indemnity; product liability; and trade credit
- Legal principles of insurance
- Underwriting and claims

Section headings

1. Business services for risk management
2. Risk auditing services
3. Disaster recovery services
4. The use of insurance
5. Types of insurance

Introduction

In this chapter we turn to another generic approach to risk management: the use of third party services and resources.

In the first sections of the chapter we look at the various third party service providers who may be contracted or otherwise utilised to undertake various aspects of an organisation's risk management activity: the syllabus highlights credit rating, risk auditing and disaster recovery (although this will be discussed in more detail in Chapter 13). The syllabus specifies the outsourcing of such risk management functions to third party providers, but in fact the range of third party resources and services may not always be amenable to outsourcing. (There are more cost-effective and flexible, at-need models for accessing services, in some cases.)

In the final sections of the chapter we turn to a generic mitigation measure often mentioned in this Course Book, in relation to a range of risks: insurance.

1 Business services for risk management

1.1 A range of third party business services may be used to assess and reduce risk, as part of supply chain risk management.

The use of third party credit rating services

1.2 Credit reporting and business risk management agencies may offer a menu of services to businesses wishing to access credit and financial information about other businesses as part of their due diligence prior to entering into contracts or business partnerships. Credit rating information is available via a number of websites. The financial director of the buying firm may be able to access such reports on behalf of the procurement function.

1.3 A buying organisation will frequently use such services (in addition to its own analysis of financial data and reports) when pre-qualifying a supplier for a tender, appraising a supplier prior to contract award, or carrying out vendor rating on a current supplier with a view to keeping them on the approved supplier list. Credit rating checks are a standard part of supplier financial appraisal: analysis of the supplier's financial status and stability; sources of financial risk (such as an excessive debt burden or ineffective management of debtors or creditors); efficiency; cost structure and profitability; and so on.

1.4 A marketing organisation will also use credit rating services as part of its assesment and management of credit risk: establishing the creditworthiness of potential customers, as the basis for negotiating open account trading, credit terms and credit limits. Suppliers face the risk that the buyer will be unable or unwilling to pay when the debt falls due. In order to minimise this risk, suppliers will generally screen potential customers before granting them credit. It should be standard practice to seek references from the potential customer's bank and from other trade creditors. In some cases, it may be appropriate to get a full-scale credit reference from a specialist credit agency (such as Dunn & Bradstreet). An appropriate credit limit should then be set.

1.5 Dun and Bradstreet, for example, offers the following services

- **Business information reports** on a named company, giving a comprehensive business credit check, including: a business summary, payment history and organisation chart; industry trends and public report filings; financial statements; and a credit limit recommendation (on the basis of creditworthiness)
- **Comprehensive insights reports** on a named company, for a complete business credit check and financial insights, including: business summary payment history and organisation chart; public report filings; industry comparisons; financial statements; credit limit recommendation; D&B credit rating; and commercial credit and financial stress scores
- **Credit evaluator reports** on a named company: a summary credit report, usually used to support business credit decisions, including report monitoring, credit limit recommendation and industry payment benchmarks.

Other business services in risk management

1.6 A range of other business services may be helpful in different aspects of risk management.

- Employment agencies, covering unanticipated human resource requirements (eg unanticipated demand, loss of staff through illness or accident, industrial action)
- Information assurance consultants, specialising in information systems risk management (as discussed in Chapter 3)
- Premises security services, providing security staff (eg warehouse guards, reception security), systems (eg alarms, surveillance systems, ID card systems), and risk assessments

- Other security-based services and consultancies, providing services such as: advice on travel risk or political risk; protective and security (eg body-guarding, defensive driving) services; 'kidnap for ransom' consultancy; corporate internal investigations (into security risks and breaches); and computer and/or financial forensic investigations
- Brokerage and agency services, contributing specialist expertise and/or 'local' knowledge to mitigate business risk for an organisation entering new product or supply markets, or international markets
- Legal services, contributing specialist expertise to assess, minimise and mitigate contractual, legal and compliance risk
- Insurance services

2 Risk auditing services

2.1 External risk auditing services may be bought in from (or outsourced to) a number of sources, according to the particular risk profile of the organisation.

- External auditors
- Risk consultants and security advisors
- Research companies
- Mystery shoppers
- External auditors

2.2 Specialist external auditors (typically working for firms of accountants) are engaged to carry out independent investigations into the corporate finances and internal controls of public companies. A similar role is taken in the public sector by the National Audit Office and the Audit Commission. In the UK private sector, external audit is a legal requirement for companies with annual turnover above a defined threshold, and must be carried out annually. The auditors report directly to the shareholders, by-passing the Board of Directors.

2.3 The role of external auditors in corporate governance and financial reporting is to:

- Express an opinion on whether financial statements give a 'true and fair' view of the financial position of a business: if not, eg if statements are thought to be affected by fraud or error, the audit report is qualified accordingly.
- Design audit procedures so as to have a 'reasonable expectation' of detecting mis-statements due to fraud or error
- Document any findings which indicate that fraud or error may exist, and report them to management. (If the matters needs to be reported to external authorities, in the public interest, the external auditors will request that the directors make that report. If the directors do not do so, or if the fraud casts doubt upon the integrity of the directors, the auditors should make the report themselves.)

2.4 The external auditor will normally investigate the systems of internal controls operating in the organisation. The outcome of this review will often include identification of areas of potential vulnerability and unmanaged risk.

2.5 One of the key benefits of using external auditors is their **independence:** that is, as third parties, they are outside the systems and operations they are called on to evaluate, and so less likely to be subject to conflicts of interest. There are limits to the independence of external auditors in practice, however.

- Although in theory the auditors are appointed by the shareholders, in practice it is the directors who select the audit firm.
- Auditors are only human. They may, for example, be subject to intimidation by directors, or fearful of the consequences of pressing concerns forcefully.
- Audit firms invariably perform other non-audit work for their audit clients: tax advice, consultancy. They naturally wish to retain such business, and may therefore be reluctant to 'rock the boat' with an

unfavourable audit report. (Many countries have placed restrictions on the amount of non-audit work that the external auditor can perform for a client.)

2.6 The work of the external auditor is perceived as a useful check on the accuracy of a company's accounts, and on the company's systems of internal control. However, the external auditor is *not* specifically required to detect or report on risk or fraud issues, *except* in so far as they lead to a material mis-statement of the accounting figures. Errors below a certain threshhold will be regarded as immaterial to the 'true and fair view' – even if they come to light. External auditors have to plan their work entirely on a sampling basis, and it would be impractical to check all transactions. The main reason the auditor is interested in internal controls is that, if internal control systems are effective, less testing is needed in order to arrive at an audit opinion: the auditor has some assurance that the accounting figures can be relied on.

Risk consultants and security advisors

2.7 There are many commercial risk consultancy services, often specialising (or offering access to specialist expertise) in identified risk categories, such as: international risks; kidnap, hostage and extortion risks; health and safety risks; premises security; fire and flood; and environmental impact assessment.

2.8 Government agencies (such as the UK's Health and Safety Executive), trade associations, insurance providers, third-sector organisations (such as environmental research and pressure groups) and police, fire and emergency services also offer risk appraisals and advice in regard to relevant risk categories. Some of this assistance may be offered free of charge, or on a low-cost basis, in order to further the mission of the providing organisation – and such options should arguably be pursued before commissioning a commercial (profit-seeking) consultancy.

2.9 The appointment of external risk consultants has several benefits.

- They bring a 'fresh set of eyes' to the organisation or supply chain, without the constraining effect of existing norms, assumptions and vested interest in the *status quo.*
- They offer independent judgement, without the constraints that an internal consultant or line manager may face (in terms of criticising colleagues, say, or criticising a system they helped to plan and implement).
- They bring specialist expertise and wide experience of the risk category and issues, which may enable them to pinpoint risks more accurately and quickly than insiders (of a generalist bent and limited experience) could do.
- They may offer specialist resources and competencies for managing risks: for example, the installation of security systems or the provision of security staff, or environmental clean-up services.

2.10 There is also a downside of using external consultants.

- The costs of consultancy and service provision
- Potential disruption to operations during the audit and change processes
- Time and resources required to brief the consultants on the particular circumstances, culture and risk factors of the client organisation
- Potential stakeholder resistance and conflict, as a result of the perception that 'outsiders' are being used to judge the adequacy of current performance, or to force through unwelcome changes on behalf of management (but enabling management to distance itself from the responsibility).

Research companies

2.11 The organisation may commission third party research providers to conduct environmental scanning, market and competitor intelligence gathering, consumer or industry trend analysis and other forms of risk-focused research. Alternatively, it may purchase generic published reports from such organisations (eg on industry, market, political or commodity risk). A company planning to expand into a new overseas market, for example, might commission dedicated research on market conditions, the local economy, the activities of competitors, existing consumer perceptions of the brand (if any) and so on. Alternatively, it might purchase or subscribe to published reports on the country and market.

2.12 A range of research reports and briefings is also available from organisations such as the government departments, Chambers of Commerce, industry associations and other organisations designed to support trade, industry and exports.

2.13 Specialist consultancies may be used for the gathering of **competitive intelligence**, and **competitor analysis,** which may be a key issue in strategic risk. The focus of such research will be on:

- Identifying the key competitors of the firm: not just obvious players in the market, but likely new entrants (both domestic and international)
- Identifying the competitive strengths and weaknesses of existing and potential competitors; their distinctive strategic competencies and resources; their sources of competitive advantage (in relation to the strengths, weaknesses and resources of the focal firm)
- Comparing available competitive criteria (eg market share)
- Analysing key benchmark areas, to learn from the competitor's strengths: eg through reverse engineering (analysing competitor products and processes to see how they are achieved), comparing cost structures and supply chain relationships and so on.

2.14 Competitive intelligence consultancies use public news sources, often held in online databases; interview ex-employees of the target organisation; and – where possible – interview current employees and stakeholders (such as suppliers and customers) of the target organisation. It should be obvious that such activities are fraught with ethical issues, since the most valuable information for competitive analysis would be regarded as confidential or sensitive by the target competitor. The Society of Competitive Intelligence Professionals (SCIP) has a strict code of ethics to ensure that information is legally and ethically obtained.

Mystery shoppers

2.15 In the retail and service sectors, specialist research services may be used to audit marketing and reputational risks. Mystery shoppers, for example, may be employed by marketing research agencies, to act anonymously as customers: testing, observing, recording and reporting on the customer experience of an organisation's business processes. The purpose of such an exercise, in risk management, is to identify areas of vulnerability, negative encounters and attributes (such as price or quality), and the comparative performance of competitors.

3 Disaster recovery services

3.1 Disasters are major natural or human-induced events which cause significant damage to the infrastructure critical to an organisation or supply chain, and therefore significant disruption to its operations. Examples include war or terrorist attack, sabotage, floods, hurricanes, earthquakes, fires and so on – and also, depending on the nature of a business, events such as power failures and systems failures. We will discuss disaster recovery planning in detail in Chapter 13, as a discipline of contingency planning.

Third-party resources for disaster recovery

3.2 Third party resources from whom disaster recovery services can be obtained, or to whom they can be outsourced, include the following.

- Commercial services providing for off-site back-up storage of data and documents (including 'cloud computing' services and off-site archival facilities)
- Specialist services for the recovery of ICT systems and data centres, using specialist disaster recovery hardware and software components

- A range of commercial services to whom business-critical operations can be outsourced or contracted on short-term recovery (or ongoing) basis, with advance pre-qualification of outsource providers a priority for business continuity planning. This may include the use of: call centres (to maintain customer service); IT services (to maintain systems and data management); procurement services (to maintain procurement and supply); logistics, transport and warehousing services; and so on
- Sources of alternative premises, facilities or work accommodation, if the organisation's premises are damaged or rendered unsafe
- Public emergency services: eg for evacuation, clean-up and maintenance of public services (eg in the event of flood, fire, earthquake and so on, which may affect whole cities or regions)
- Grants and financial assistance (eg from government and government agencies, industry associations or trade unions) for disaster recovery.

3.3   If premises, vehicles or equipment are damaged in a disaster, various business services may be used in disaster recovery.

- Alternative premises, facilities and/or operations may be maintained or provided by third-party disaster recovery services. Back-up office facilities are often designated as 'cold' (eg alternative space to house the staff); 'warm' (space plus equipment); or 'hot' (space, equipment, plus software and back-up data files, enabling the business to resume operations immediately). It should be obvious that maintaining a hot back-up site is a costly process, in terms of up-front investment and management.
- Alternative premises or resources may be 'lent' or provided by other business units or sites, of the firm, or by supply chain partners or major corporate customers. The disaster recovery plan may require sufficient spare space to be kept available in designated branch offices or plants, for example.
- Alternative premises, equipment, vehicles and other resources can be *hired* from external providers, on a short-term basis (to allow for recovery).
- Serviced offices may be rented as required.

Incentives to outsource disaster recovery

3.4   There may be strong incentives to retain specialist disaster recovery services at times of natural disaster.

- Staff and managers of the business may be personally affected and traumatised by events, and may not be in the best position to respond effectively (even if the organisation did not wish to project a humane empathy for their situation).
- Specialist services have the expertise, trained personnel, equipment and other resources to respond effectively to the conditions and hazards presented by the disaster. It would be unlikely that a business case could be made for the organisation to invest in these kinds of resources and capabilities itself, given the low probability of many disaster risks.

3.5   In regard to the specialist area of data centre or IT systems disaster recovery, *e-Week.com* suggests the following 'ten compelling reasons for outsourcing disaster recovery'.

- Data centre diversity. Most data centres include new and old equipment from multiple vendors. Working with a DR provider helps leverage a shared pool of current and older ('legacy') equipment. The provider can also bring an expert recovery services team, skilled in working in complex IT environments.
- Scope of service: providers understand and can fulfil a range of critical service requirements, such as different operating platforms, communication services and integrated applications.
- Recovery systems readiness. A business cannot afford to have recovery systems standing idle in anticipation of disaster. A DR provider can have hundreds of servers available at a single site: shortening recovery times – at a fraction of the cost of maintaining the same equipment internally.
- Focus on the DR business: dedicated support, resources and expertise – without 'distractions' from other business priorities.
- Robust infrastructure: servers with the capability to ensure that hosted applications are available on a 24/7 basis – and can expand and upgrade as business needs change.

- Recovery experience. IT staff rarely have experience of a full recovery exercise: a DR provider can offer people skilled in recovery methodologies and best practices.
- Knowledge bank. Working with a DR provider gives access to knowledge acquired from thousands of recovery tests and events – beyond what could be predicted and trained for in-house.
- Compliance. Data centres need to be compliant with a range of regulations and standards, and DR providers have expertise in accreditations and compliance.
- Employee support. DR providers offer support services to affected employees, including flexible options and workspaces for employees to work in a safe environment, either on-site or remotely.

3.6   You might also use this as a checklist for appraising and selecting a DR services provider.

4   The use of insurance

4.1   Insurance is a form of risk management used to 'hedge' against the risk of a contingent, uncertain loss, or a loss which may not occur.

4.2   In technical terms, 'hedging' is a technique of taking a position (making an investment) in one market which is specifically intended to offset or balance the losses that may be incurred by another position or investment. Various forms of risk can be protected against with a hedge, including commodity price risk, credit risk, currency or foreign exchange risk, interest rate risk, equity risk and volumetric (customer demand) risk. Hedges can be constructed using a range of financial instruments, including forward exchange contracts for currencies (as discussed in Chapter 5 on the mitigation of exchange rate risk); futures contracts, options and derivatives (eg to hedge against movements in commodity or share prices); and insurance. In more general terms, 'hedging' (as in 'hedging one's bets') is used as a synonym for 'insuring oneself against loss.'

4.3   Insurance is defined as 'the equitable transfer of the risk of a loss from one entity to another, in exchange for payment'.

4.4   Premiums (amounts charged for a certain amount of insurance coverage) are paid by the insured party (or insurance policy holder) to an insurer (the company selling the insurance). This builds up a reserve of funds, from which – if the covered risk event occurs – the policy holder's losses can be compensated by the insurer. In other words, the insurer pools funds from *many* policy holders, in order to cover the losses that only *some* policy holders may incur.

4.5   A wide range of insurance covers are available, for risks such as the following.

- Theft and fraud
- Damage to property
- Fire and flood
- Marine (shipping), aviation (air) and motor (road haulage) transit insurance
- Public liability (if a member of the public suffers an injury on the insured party's premises)
- Product liability (if a member of the public suffers injury through use of a product)
- Employer's liability (if an employee suffers injury or illness at work).

Benefits of insurance

4.6   Insurance does not address the underlying risks, hazards or vulnerabilities – and is therefore certainly *not* a substitute for robust risk assessment and mitigation. However, insurance:

- Reduces the financial impact of a risk event. (This is sometimes called 'hedging' against risk.)
- Aids recovery, by providing funds to replace lost or damaged assets
- May satisfy customers, suppliers and other key stakeholders: funds are available to mitigate any losses to them (eg through liability insurance) or which would otherwise be passed on to them (eg insuring

goods in transit)

- May be required by the contract of purchase or sale (eg to ensure that a supplier is able to cover its liabilities to the buyer)
- May be required by law. (Employer's liability insurance, for example, is a statutory requirement in the UK.)

The legal principles of insurance

4.7 In legal terms, the insured party assumes a guaranteed, known and relatively small loss (in the form of contracted payments to the insurer) in return for the insurer's promise to **indemnify** (or compensate) it in the case of financial loss. The **insurance policy** is a contract, which details the conditions and circumstances under which the insured will be indemnified.

4.8 Many different types of risks can potentially be insured, and the insurance policy will set out in detail which 'perils' (insurable risk events) are covered – and which are not. The risk insured against must, however, meet certain qualifications in order to be considered an effectively **insurable risk** (Robert I Mehr & Emerson Camack, *Principles of Insurance*).

- The insurer must be able to charge a sufficient premium to cover all expenses of the risk (in other words, the risk cannot be so large that no insurer could hope to pay for the loss) but the premium must also be affordable (in other words, the risk cannot be so large as to put the premium beyond the ability of any client to pay). The premiums need to cover the expected cost of losses, plus the insurers' costs of issuing and administering the policy, investigating and adjusting the loss and maintaining capital to assure ability to pay claims.
- The nature of the loss must be definite (taking place at a known time, in a known place and from a known cause) and financially calculable.
- The size of the loss must be meaningful from the perspective of the insured party, in order to justify the payment of premiums. On the other hand, the loss must not be large enough to bankrupt the insurer (catastrophically large loss): capital constrains insurers' ability to sell earthquake insurance, for example.
- The loss should be random or accidental in nature: that is, not something the insured party has advance information about, and not something that is under the control of the insured party.
- The loss should be 'pure': resulting from an event for which there is *only* downside risk. Speculative risks (such as business risks) are generally not considered insurable.

4.9 Some of the key legal principles of insurance are as follows.

- **Contract.** An entity seeking to transfer risk becomes 'the insured party' once risk is assumed by the 'insurer' by means of a contract, called an 'insurance policy'. The insurance contract typically includes: identification of the participating parties (insurer, insured, beneficiaries); the premium; the period of coverage; the particular loss event(s) covered; exclusions (events *not* covered); and the amount of coverage (the amount to be paid to the insured or beneficiary in the event of loss). When the insured party experiences a loss for a specified risk, the coverage entitles it to make a claim against the insurer for the covered amount of loss, as specified by the policy.
- **Indemnity**. The insurance company guarantees to indemnify, or compensate, the insured, in the case of losses, up to a certain amount (the 'insured's interest'). Indemnity implies reinstating the indemnified party, as far as possible, to the position that it was in prior to the occurrence of a specified event.
- **Insurable interest**. The insured party must have an interest or stake in the loss or damage to the persons or property insured (eg by virtue of ownership or liability), so that the insured party suffers directly from the loss.
- **Proximate cause** *(causa proxima)*. The cause of loss (the risk event) must be covered under the policy, and the dominant or main cause of loss must not be an exclusion under the policy.
- **Mitigation**. The asset owner has a duty to attempt to keep the loss arising from the risk event to a

minimum, as if the asset was not insured.

- **Subrogation**. The insurance company acquires legal rights to pursue recoveries on behalf of the insured, in order to mitigate the loss: for example, the insurer may sue those liable for the insured's loss.
- **Utmost good faith** *(uberrima fides)*. The insured and insurer are bound by a good faith bond of honesty and fairness. All material facts relevant to the risk and contract must be disclosed.

Insurance in practice

4.10 An insurer will usually be a large financial services organisation, with sufficient asset backing to assure payment of claims. Insurance companies make their money by underwriting risks (selecting which risks to insure, and deciding how much to charge for accepting those risks), and collecting more in premiums (and investment income) than is paid out in losses.

4.11 Clients often deal with expert intermediaries called **insurance brokers**, whose role is to advise clients as to the most suitable policy and best cover available, and to act as an agent of the client to negotiate the insurance contract (with favourable premiums) with insurers. Brokers are usually paid commission by the insurer with whom the contract is placed.

4.12 The cost to the insured (in the form of **premiums**) is calculated by the insurer's actuary, on the basis of the statistical probability of the risk event. There is usually an amount (called the **excess**) which the insured party will have to pay out of pocket: that is, the insured party agrees to bear the first part of any loss suffered. The excess can generally be varied, in exchange for lower or higher premiums: the insured party may agree to a higher excess (bearing more of the loss if the risk event occurs) in exchange for lower premiums (maximising value if the risk event *doesn't* occur) – or a lower excess (more of the loss is compensated, if the risk event occurs) in exchange for higher premiums (bearing a higher cost of insurance, if the risk event *doesn't* occur).

4.13 The insurer may enter a contract of **re-insurance**, sharing the risk (and premium income) with other insurer(s), in order to reduce its own exposure – particularly in the case of catastrophically large risks. However, in such circumstances, the insured party's contract is entirely with the original insurer. The contract of reinsurance is between the insurance companies, and does not affect the insured party.

Underwriting

4.14 Underwriting is the process whereby one party (such as a bank or insurance company) agrees to accept some of the risk of another party, in exchange for a premium. The term is derived from the Lloyd's of London insurance market. Bankers, who agreed to accept some of the risk of a venture (originally, often a trading voyage by sea, with the risk of shipwreck) in exchange for a premium, would write their names under the risk information on a Lloyd's record slip.

4.15 Underwriting by insurance company underwriters involves the following procedures.

- Evaluating the risk exposure of the potential client
- Deciding whether the insurance company should accept the risk of insuring the client, and how much coverage the client should receive
- Determining a premium (how much the client will pay for the insurance) that will be commensurate with the insurance company's risk exposure
- Protecting the insurance company's portfolio of risk ('book of business') from risks that are likely to make a loss. One of the main ways in which insurers make money is by selecting which risks to insure and how much to charge for accepting those risks.

4.16 Each insurance company has a set of guidelines for underwriters, to assist in determining:

12

- Whether and to what extent the company will accept a given risk
- What kinds of information will be used to evaluate risk exposure (eg for employee health insurance, the underwriter may need to asses the applicant's age, occupation, health status and medical history).

4.17 Price setting for policies is based on actuarial calculations, using statistics and probabilities to forecast the rate of future claims, based on a given risk. This means looking at the frequency and severity of insured hazards, and the expected average payouts resulting from them. Historical loss data will be collated, calculated at its 'present value' (ie its value in today's currency), and compared to the value of premiums, in order to evaluate the adequacy of premium coverage. Underwriting performance is measured by the 'combined ratio': the ratio of expenses and losses to premiums. (A combined ratio of less than 1 represents an underwriting profit, while a ratio of more than 1 represents an underwriting loss.)

4.18 The factors that underwriters use to classify risks should be: objective (as far as possible); related to the degree of exposure and the cost of providing coverage; practical to administer; compliant with applicable law and regulation; and, ultimately, such as to protect the long-term sustainability and viability of the insurance programme (*Actuarial Standards of Practice No 12*).

Claims

4.19 Claims may be filed directly with the insurer, or through the insurance broker or agent. If the insured party suffers loss arising from an insured event, it makes a claim for financial compensation: this is, in effect, the insurance 'product' which has been paid for.

4.20 The insurance company will investigate the claim to ensure that it is valid: in other words, to ensure that the loss has occurred and that it arose directly from a risk covered by the insurance contract. Incoming claims are classified based on severity, and are assigned to **claims adjusters** or **loss adjusters,** who investigate the claim (usually in co-operation with the insured), calculate the monetary value of the claim, and authorise payment.

4.21 In cases of liability insurance claims (where a third party is involved), adjustment may be particularly complex, because the plaintiff (the injured party) – unlike the insured – has no contractual obligation to co-operate with the insurer, and may be seeking the maximum possible compensation. In such cases, the adjuster must obtain legal counsel for the insured party, monitor litigation, and participate in the final settlement conference.

4.22 An insured party may hire its own third party adjuster to negotiate the settlement with the insurance company on its behalf. (It may also take out a separate 'loss recovery insurance' policy, which covers the cost of employing an adjuster, for policies that are likely to result in complex claims.)

4.23 The general process for making a claim can therefore be summarised as in Figure 12.1.

Figure 12.1 *The claims process*

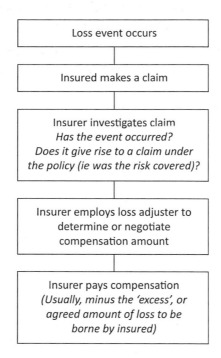

4.24 In many ways, the selection of an insurance provider or broker will be subject to the same criteria as the selection of any other service provider. (You might think of Ray Carter's 10Cs: competence, capacity, cost, commitment to quality, control of processes, cash, consistency of service, compatibility, compliance and CSR.) However, there may be additional factors in the decision.

- Whether the insurer specialises in key areas of industry risk – and whether this is desirable
- Whether the insurer is prepared to be flexible in insuring special risks (eg innovative processes)
- Whether the insurer is willing to negotiate on premiums and excess amounts
- The insurer's risk appetite
- The insurer's track record on speed of claim assessment, payment of claims, claim disputes and so on
- The insurer's willingness to collaborate, or offer ancillary services, for risk identification and assessment

Self insurance

4.25 Self insurance is where a firm elects:

- *Not* to purchase insurance from an external provider, but to establish and maintain its own reserves, emergency funds or contingency funds to cover any future losses
- To purchase insurance, with a large 'excess' on any claims, in return for reduced premiums: the excess to be borne by the internal reserve fund.

4.26 The key benefits of such an approach are as follows.

- Reduced 'up-front' insurance costs (avoiding paying insurance premiums to external insurers)
- Securing coverage for risks which cannot otherwise be insured (and where operating cash reserves are unavailable to meet contingencies)
- The flexibility of the reserve fund to cover a wide range of contingencies

4.27 The main disadvantage of this approach is the opportunity costs of funds dedicated to the reserves, which could be invested for more immediate return or benefit elsewhere. There is also the risk that the organisation will suffer a loss greater than can be covered by available reserves – since the reserve will generally be smaller than may be maintained by a large financial services provider.

12

4.28 Firms with a common risk profile (eg an industry association, or a group of local government authorities) may set up joint or pooled reserves for self-insurance, as another way of sharing risk.

Captive insurance

4.29 Captive insurance is a variation of self-insurance whereby a firm or industry association forms or acquires an insurance company, dedicated to insuring its own risks. A captive insurer is in many ways the same as an external insurer: participating companies pay premiums and make claims as required. This is a more formal approach than self-insurance, in that the captive company will be bound to observe all the disciplines of a specialist insurer.

4.30 Where feasible, a captive insurance approach has several benefits.

- Reduced insurance premiums
- Profits from the provision of insurance services retained within the business or group
- Influence over the types of risk covered, benefitting from specialist awareness of industry conditions and so on
- Tax advantages (particularly if the insurance provider operates off-shore).

5 Types of insurance

5.1 As we have noted, many types of risk can potentially be insured. A single insurance policy may cover risks in more than one category: for example, vehicle insurance typically covers both property risk (covering theft or damage) and liability risk (covering legal claims arising from an accident).

5.2 Some of the main types of insurance that may be purchased by a business in the UK, as part of its risk management portfolio, are described in Table 12.1.

Table 12.1 *Types of insurance in the UK*

Casualty insurance	A broad category of insurance which might also embrace some liability insurances (such as employer's liability). • Crime insurance covers the organisation against the criminal acts of third parties (such as losses arising from theft or fraud). • Political risk insurance covers the organisation for losses arising from political instability or conflict in areas of operation. • Kidnap and ransom insurance covers the organisation from losses arising from kidnap, extortion, wrongful detention, hijacking and other hazards of operating in high-risk areas.
Property or indemnity insurance	A broad category of insurance covering losses arising from damage to property. This includes specialised forms of insurance such as: fire, flood and earthquake insurance; terrorism insurance; equipment breakdown insurance (accidental damage to equipment or machinery); builder's risk insurance (physical loss or damage to property during construction); pollution insurance (contamination of insured property due to the sudden and accidental release of hazardous materials, covering clean-up and liability); and aviation and marine insurance (for airlines and shipping companies).
Liability insurance	A broad category of insurance covering losses arising from legal claims against the insured party. An organisation may be liable to pay damages (or the costs of other remedies) where the courts uphold a claim of breach of contract; negligence resulting in damage, injury or economic loss to another party; breach of a statutory duty (eg under the Health and Safety at Work Act); or provision of defective goods (under the Consumer Protection Act). Liability policies offer indemnification (payment by the insurer on behalf of the insured) with respect to legal claims. However, they typically cover claims arising only from the *negligence* of the insured party – not wilful or intentional acts resulting in loss or damage. • *Public liability insurance* covers a business for losses arising from claims made by members of the public for personal injury or damage/loss of property (on the organisation's premises, or as a result of its operations or actions) • *Employer's liability insurance* covers a business for losses arising from claims by employees who have sustained injury, illness or incapacity as a consequence of their employment) • *Professional indemnity insurance* covers insured professionals (such as architects, lawyers and medical professionals) against losses arising from claims of negligence brought by their clients • *Product liability insurance* covers an organisation for losses arising from claims of injury or damage/loss of property arising from the use of goods supplied, repaired or tested by the organisation)
Credit insurance	Credit insurance repays some or all of a debt or loan, when certain circumstances prevent payment by the borrower. • *Trade credit insurance* is a form of business insurance covering the insured party's accounts receivable: that is, the outstanding amounts owed to it by debtors. The policy pays the insured organisation for covered accounts receivable, if the debtor defaults on payment.
Business interruption insurance	Business interruption insurance covers an organisation for the loss of income, and the expenses incurred, after a covered risk event (peril) interrupts normal business operations. This would normally form part of a business continuity plan.

Chapter summary

- A range of third party resources can help to mitigate organisational risk. These include credit rating agencies, employment agencies, premises security services etc.
- In different ways, both external auditors and risk consultants can help to mitigate risk. Some organisations also use research companies for environmental scanning.
- Third party resources can also be vital in disaster recovery. For example, they can provide off-site data back-up, or alternative premises.
- Perhaps the most common use of third parties in mitigating risk is the process of insuring organisational assets. However, some organisations choose to do this by means of self-insurance or captive insurance.
- Typical uses of insurance are to cover casualties, property, liabilities, credit risk, and business interruption.

Self-test questions

Numbers in brackets refer to the paragraphs where you can check your answers.

1   List the types of service that may be provided by a credit reference agency. (1.5)

2   List different types of external risk auditing services. (2.1)

3   How in practice is the independence of external auditors limited? (2.5)

4   What are the benefits of appointing external risk consultants? (2.9)

5   List disaster recovery services that may be provided by third party suppliers. (3.2)

6   List reasons why it is advisable to outsource disaster recovery. (3.5)

7   What are the benefits of taking out insurance? (4.6)

8   List the procedures involved in the process of underwriting. (4.15)

9   List stages in the process of making an insurance claim. (Figure 12.1)

10 What types of liability insurance might an organisation adopt? (Table 12.1)

CHAPTER 13

Contingency Planning

Assessment criteria and indicative content

3.4 Analyse the use of contingency plans to overcome risks in supply chains
- The implications of a contingency plan
- The components of a business continuity plan and disaster recovery plan

4.4 Develop a strategy to mitigate risks in supply chains
- Preparing a contingency plan
- Preparing a business continuity plan and disaster recovery plan

Section headings

1 Contingency planning
2 Business continuity planning
3 Disaster recovery planning

Introduction

In this final chapter we turn to another generic process that has frequently been mentioned in this Course Book as an essential discipline of risk management: contingency planning. Contingencies are, basically, 'events which may (or may not) happen' – and in a sense, this is what all risk management is about: planning for events of a greater or lesser degree of uncertainty. However, the discipline of contingency planning has been highlighted as a key mitigation strategy for risks which are inherently low probability – but high impact. While the low probability might tempt the organisation to tolerate the risk, the high impact makes it imperative to have a 'Plan B' in place.

There is considerable confusion in general usage between the terms 'contingency planning', 'business continuity planning' and 'disaster recovery planning' (and also 'crisis management', a term which is not used in this syllabus). Essentially, **contingency planning** is developing a Plan B (work-around, fall-back position or back-up plan), in case Plan A is derailed by a risk event.

Business continuity planning (BCP) is a proactive planning process aimed at minimising catastrophic risks to business-critical resources, functions and processes: ensuring that the business can maintain the flow of key business deliverables in the face of supply chain risk. **Disaster recovery planning** (DRP) is a proactive contingency planning approach, whereby the organisation plans its emergency and recovery responses to a catastrophic event. Where BCP is about 'keeping things running', DRP is about 'getting them back up and running'. Both processes, however, contribute to the *resilience* of the business and supply chain: its ability to withstand (BCP) or 'bounce back' (DRP) from damaging shocks. Both processes will typically include a corporate communications, public relations or reputational defence component.

1   Contingency planning

1.1   **Contingency planning** is planning to mitigate the impacts of risk events, variances and failures, by making secondary plans, work-arounds, fall-back positions or 'Plan Bs' in case things go wrong or the original plan fails. In other words, contingency planning asks: 'What will we do if...?'

1.2   A simple example might be planning for the possibility that a new e-procurement system fails to go live on time, as planned. The contingency plan (Plan B) may involve measures such as maintaining the old system in parallel running, reverting to manual procurement processing, and/or contracting out e-procurement operations to a pre-selected, pre-briefed service provider. Such a plan might also include how Plan A will be got back on track: what is the next opportunity to switch systems, and how can we ensure that the process delays or glitches have been solved? It will also include plans for stakeholder communication about the delay, the back-up plan, work-around arrangements, and so on.

1.3   Another simple example, with which you may be familiar, is the planning of emergency evacuation procedures in factories and office buildings, in the (generally unlikely) event of fire, bomb threat or terrorist attack. All organisations will have such procedures in place, and they will be the subject of staff training and instruction, and regular maintenance and testing (through evacuation drills or practices). If or when 'the real thing' happens, in theory all necessary resources and procedures will be in place, and stakeholders will know exactly what to do. Immediate provisions will be made for evacuation, the securing of data and premises, and so on.

1.4   In such crisis level contingencies, immediate emergency-response plans will also be linked to more comprehensive plans.

- To maintain **business continuity**: that is, to enable essential processes and services to continue through the risk event (eg by triggering pre-planned arrangements for temporary alternative working accommodation, access to ICT infrastructure and data, communication with key stakeholders, and deploying additional HR resources if required)
- To begin **disaster recovery**: that is, to begin to restore data, assets, infrastructure and functions lost as a result of the risk event (eg by restoring data, replacing systems and equipment, developing new working accommodation and so on).

The role of contingency planning

1.5   Contingency planning is important because of three of the fundamental principles of risk, discussed right back in Chapter 1.

- **Many risks cannot be completely eliminated.** They may be caused by factors outside the organisation's control (such as natural disasters, the outbreak of disease, terrorist attack or third party action). Or the elimination of risk may require such tight programming and restriction of organisational activity as to be dysfunctional: eliminating discretion, flexibility, innovation and opportunity. Contingency planning is based on the recognition that 'bad things happen'.
- **Risks may be low-probability but high impact.** A risk may be too unlikely to justify continual or costly measures to *prevent* its occurrence – but sufficiently high impact to justify planning for mitigation measures (minimising costs and consequences) if it *does* occur. Contingency planning is based on 'thinking positive – but planning for the worst'.
- **Risk mitigation is more effective when proactive than when reactive**. Risk mitigation requires systematic planning, resource deployment and lead time for implementation – all of which may be in short supply once a risk event has occurred, or is in the midst of occurring. Contingency planning is based on having plans and resources ready and waiting to be put into action when triggered.

1.6   An article in *Supply Management* in October 2006, however, suggested that 'a large number of companies still have no contingency plan to deal with disruption to their supply chain'. According to the *Annual Global*

Survey of Supply Chain Progress (Computer Sciences Corporation), 44% of firms lack a written contingency plan. Similar research from the Chartered Management Institute suggested that 49% of companies lack plans in place to ensure they will be able to keep running if disaster strikes.

1.7 Rene de Sousa, interviewed in *Supply Management* (25 May 2006), emphasised that it is part of procurement's responsibility to ensure continuity of supply – and that this requires contingency planning. 'It is really vital. You must identify where the constraints are and put procedures in place, whether you are in the private or public sector. The consequences of not doing it can undo a lot of good work in your business, especially if you look at your reputation as well – your customers expect you to manage this.'

Formulating contingency plans

1.8 A general process for contingency planning is outlined in Figure 13.1

Figure 13.1 *The contingency planning process*

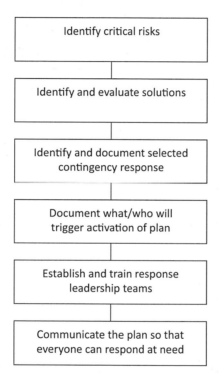

2 Business continuity planning

2.1 **Business continuity planning** (BCP) is designed to identify potential threats to the critical activities or success factors of an organisation, and to ensure that these can be reduced or responded to in such a way as to maintain business functions and processes through risk events. It is about maintaining the essential business deliverables of an organisation during a disruption, or through ongoing processes of change.

2.2 BCP is thus a branch of contingency planning, specifically focused on the critical factors which threaten continuity of operations, and on maintaining (or restoring) business functions in the face of potentially disruptive events, problems or failures. If contingency planning asks 'What's Plan B if contingency X occurs?', business continuity planning asks: 'What are the contingencies that could shut us down, and how do we keep our core functions going if they happen?'

2.3 The Business Continuity Institute (BCI) defines business continuity management (BCM) as: 'a holistic management process that identifies potential impacts that threaten an organisation and provides a framework for building resilience, with the capability for an effective response that safeguards the interests of its key stakeholders, reputation, brand and value-creating activities.'

2.4   WE Naef *(Infocon,* October 2003) reports that following a major office or factory fire, 44% of businesses fail to re-open, and 33% of those that do fail to survive beyond three years. 'The bottom line is that businesses need to have plans in place to cope with incidents (whether they be major terrorist attacks or a minor hardware problem) and thereby avoid major business interruptions.'

2.5   Business continuity planning provides a framework:

- To ensure the resilience and continuing viability of a business
- To respond to enterprise-level risk assessments
- To prevent loss, damage, failure or disruption in the business-critical processes and resources (including data and knowledge, systems, talent and supply chains) which underpin continuing output of core business deliverables
- To ensure continuity of service to key customers, and protect related revenue streams, in the face of disruptive events.

2.6   BCP involves the processes and procedures for the development, testing and maintenance of a plan (or series of plans) that will maintain core business functions against critical threats. It includes measures such as:

- Management succession planning (ensuring continuity of direction and managerial 'talent')
- Knowledge management (protection and preservation of business-critical knowledge)
- Supplier transition planning (minimising supply disruption and risks to assets, intellectual property and/or delivery performance as a result of supplier 'switching')
- Technology or systems changeover planning
- Disaster recovery planning (DRP): a suite of plans for the recovery of specific operations, functions, sites, services or applications following major crisis events, natural or human-caused disasters, or failures.

The BCP process

2.7   Business continuity management is an enterprise-level risk management exercise. It is therefore important to gain the involvement and 'buy-in' of key stakeholders throughout the organisation and supply chain. The Board of Directors should initiate a BCP programme, as this will:

- Ensure a strategic orientation, focused on enterprise-level risks and business-critical factors
- Ensure top-down support or 'championship' for the programme.

2.8   A cross-functional BCP team should then be formed, with responsibility for initiating and driving the planning process. A timescale and budget for BCP delivery should be formulated (as for any project).

2.9   The general process or project lifecycle for a BCP exercise is summarised in Table 13.1.

Table 13.1 *The BCP process*

Project initiation and management	Establishing the need for BCP; gaining management support and 'buy in'; and establishing the BCP management structure, budgets and timescales.
Business risk assessment (BRA)	Determining the events and internal or external environmental factors that can adversely affect the organisation with disruption and/or disaster; focusing on critical success factors and business deliverables, to identify business-critical threats and vulnerabilities.
Business impact analysis	Identifying the business impact of identified disruptions and disaster scenarios, and quantifying the potential loss or consequences arising from them. This also helps to identify critical business functions, their recovery priorities and inter-dependencies – which will be a priority for contingency planning and recovery planning. • What personnel or roles are essential to organisational functioning (and/or to immediate post-disaster recovery)? • What technology and systems does the organisation need to be able to function adequately? • What are the key deliverables of the business? • What stakeholders depend on the organisation? • What contractual, legal and regulatory obligations must be maintained?
Business continuity strategy	Evaluating alternative strategies for protection and/or recovery of operations
Business continuity action plans	Some continuity plans will be proactive and ongoing (eg for succession planning, knowledge management, information assurance and supplier management). Others will be contingency plans, emergency response plans (responding to and stabilising the situation following a major risk event) or disaster recovery plans (restoring operations to defined levels within defined timescales). These will be implemented only when triggered by clearly identified threat indicators or the occurrence of the risk events.
Testing	Contingency and disaster recovery plans, in particular, need to be tested, under realistic conditions, to ensure their feasibility and adequacy. This may involve 'table top exercises' (eg using simulations or computer models) and/or, where possible, real-life drills, communication tests and 'full rehearsals'.
Stakeholder involvement	Implementing communication and training programmes, so that all participant stakeholders are aware of the plans (and take the need for them seriously) and resourced to carry out their part in the plans (and ongoing continuity management process) as required
Maintenance	Periodically reviewing, testing and evaluating existing plans to ensure that they meet changing needs and threats – and maintaining the planning cycle, with periodic business risk assessment. The BCP may need to be updated, for example, after new systems implementation, the upgrading of equipment, the replacement of a strategic supplier, or changes in supply chain management strategy.

2.10   The Business Continuity Institute has developed a five-stage process model, intended as a generic framework which will be applicable across industries and sectors.

- Business risk assessment and business impact planning
- Plan development
- Document
- Test
- Maintain

2.11   A comprehensive business continuity plan will embrace the 'seven Ps'.

- People – roles and responsibilities, awareness and education
- Programme – proactively managing the process
- Processes – all business processes, including supply and information management
- Premises – building and facilities
- Providers – the supply chain and outsource providers
- Profile – brand, image and reputation
- Performance – benchmarking, evaluation and audit

13

Succession planning

2.12 As we mentioned in Chapter 3, one of the major sources of operational risk faced by an organisation is change of personnel – and specifically, the departure from the organisation of key personnel who have specialist knowledge vital to business continuity and/or to the management of risk.

2.13 There is a risk that important knowledge about business operations and task requirements (including risks and risk management plans in a particular area) may be lost to an organisation:

- When skilled and knowledgeable personnel move on from the organisation through retirement, resignation, dismissal or redundancy or
- When activities carried out by the organisation are outsourced to external service providers, so that internal units are downsized or discontinued, and internal knowledge banks are no longer maintained.

2.14 Succession planning is the process whereby the organisation proactively identifies potential leaders, or replacements for key positions, and prepares them (through systematic career, skill and personal development) to replace the current leader or key person if they leave or retire.

2.15 Here are some of the risks caused by a lack of systematic succession planning.

- Lack of leader development and leader transition management, creating 'vacuums' of leadership when a leader leaves the organisation, loss of strategic direction and momentum, potential for conflict and adversarial leadership transitions, poor performance due to hurried or unevaluated appointments, and loss of stakeholder confidence in the leadership. One example would be the traumatic, unplanned leadership transitions at Marks & Spencer between 1998 and 2004.
- Loss of continuity of leadership, and consistency of brand and organisational values, owing to lack of forethought in the succession and grooming of potential leaders.
- Lack of strategic innovation and capability for cultural change, because of an unquestioned tradition of internal promotion, and failure to plan for 'new blood' in key positions.
- Leaders – or other personnel in key roles – taking over positions for which they are insufficiently prepared or developed, or with insufficient internal support
- Loss of critical knowledge possessed by departing specialist staff, which has not been handed over to pre-identified successors (or stored in some form of knowledge bank, so that it is available to successors when required)
- Loss of critical skills possessed by departing specialist staff, which have not been passed on to pre-identified successors.

2.16 A systematic approach to succession planning might include the following activities.

- Identify **key positions**, transitions in which are an area of vulnerability for the organisation because of knowledge and skills that are strategic, essential for operational continuity, or rare.
- Review the **job description and person specification** for a key position, or conduct job analysis to establish the key tasks, responsibilities and knowledge requirements of the position.
- Use the **performance appraisal** system of the organisation to identify individuals with *potential* to be promoted or transferred to the post in future (including skills, aptitudes, motivation, aspirations and so on).
- Develop and implement **talent management plans** for identified potential successors: appraise their current skills, experience and knowledge and identify training needs; appoint a mentor to guide the potential successor through the transition process; plan education, training and other developmental activities (project or committee work, job 'shadowing', coaching and so on) to prepare the potential successor for the position.
- Implement internal **management development programmes**: career development planning, management education and training, mentoring and so on.
- Review **recruitment policies** to ensure that there is a preference for internal recruitment and promotion (and related succession planning) for key positions.

- Implement **transition plans** (as for supplier transition): where possible, utilising the resource represented by outgoing personnel to brief and coach their successors; to ensure that their knowledge is documented; and to ensure that any work in progress is well-organised, documented and prepared for handover.
- Conduct **exit interviews** with outgoing key personnel, aimed at determining reasons for leaving (to reduce staff turnover in future) and securing information necessary for smooth transition.

Knowledge management

2.17 Knowledge management may be defined as 'the systematic process that supports the continuous development of individual, group and organisational learning; involving the creation, acquisition, gathering, transforming, transfer and application of knowledge to achieve organisational objectives' (John P Wilson, *Human Resource Development).* Mullins identifies knowledge management both with organisational learning and with the ability of the organisation 'to make effective use of its intellectual assets'.

2.18 Knowledge management is closely linked to organisational learning. It recognises that learning and doing are important to organisational success and that knowledge gained in developing products and processes, monitoring and reviewing projects etc should not be lost to the organisation. Knowledge sharing can reduce the likelihood of a risk event occurring by ensuring that mistakes will not be repeated.

2.19 MP Kerr ('Knowledge Management'; *Occupational Psychologist)* identifies seven drivers for knowledge management in organisations.

- Business pressure for innovation
- Inter-organisational enterprises (eg mergers, takeovers)
- Networked organisations (including supply chains), and the need to co-ordinate geographically dispersed groups (eg in virtual organisations)
- Increasingly complex products and services with a significant knowledge component
- Hyper-competitive global markets (with decreasing product lifecycles and time to market, putting pressure on innovation and responsiveness)
- The digitisation of business environments and the ICT revolution (including an explosion of available knowledge, and tools for managing knowledge)
- Concerns about the loss of organisational knowledge, due to increasing downsizing, outsourcing and staff mobility.

2.20 Different organisations and sectors will have their own particular issues with knowledge management. You might be aware, for example, of the current struggle of music, film, software and consumer electronics companies to protect their business-critical intellectual property (copyright, patents and designs). Generally, organisations may struggle to find a balance between the need to *protect* knowledge (confidentiality and intellectual property: requiring a culture of protection and control) and the need to *capture, share and disseminate* it (requiring a culture of trust and transparency).

2.21 A systematic approach to knowledge management involves the following processes.

- *Acquiring* knowledge (eg from environmental scanning, market research, procurement research, benchmarking, modelling, networking and so on)
- *Generating or creating* knowledge, through processes such as ideas generation (eg brainstorming and think-tanks); research and development; stakeholder consultation (eg suggestion schemes, quality circles, early supplier involvement); lesson learning (eg project reviews and learning capture); and cultivating supplier and workforce diversity (for diverse perspectives and information)
- *Transforming* information into new knowledge (eg by compiling, combining, analysing, interpreting or re-formatting)

13

- *Capturing* unspoken, internal (tacit) knowledge to convert it to open, stated (explicit) knowledge, so that it can be communicated, shared and used
- *Storing* knowledge effectively in information and knowledge management systems
- *Sharing* or disseminating knowledge throughout the organisation (eg via ICT networks, cross-functional teams)
- *Protecting* distinctive, value-adding knowledge for competitive advantage (eg via access controls, confidentiality agreements and intellectual property protections)
- *Applying* knowledge to develop core capabilities (such as innovation or agile supply) which cannot easily be imitated by competitors.

Systems transition planning

2.22   We have already discussed the management of risk in the introduction of new technology and systems, as an operational risk, in Chapter 5. Some business continuity measures to ensure a smooth transition may include the following.

- Clear lines of responsibility for implementing and following up the change: the change agents (eg systems developers or IT managers) should work closely with the operational managers who will assume responsibility for use of the new system
- Comprehensive documentation of new policies, systems and procedures: user manuals, policy statements, procedure flowcharts and so on. Ideally, these should be developed in collaboration with users, so that questions can be addressed and documentation designed for ease of user understanding.
- Initial education and training of users. Training needs are likely to be significant in the case of new systems.
- Acceptance testing. Users should, if possible, be given the chance to operate the new system, and to report on how far it meets their needs and how its results compare with old methods and with the stated deliverables of the change project. The system can then be adjusted, if necessary, prior to acceptance and full implementation.
- Mechanisms for follow-up, support and assistance, where needed: technical support services may be available on an ongoing basis or during the initial period.

2.23   The introduction of new technology or systems is often managed by phased implementation, to minimise the risks of teething troubles and to allow time to embed and adjust the system.

- **Direct changeover** is a comparatively simple, but risky, approach, where an old system is completely replaced by a new system in one step. It may be the appropriate solution where two systems are very different. New systems are often introduced during down time – such as a bank holiday weekend or business closure – to minimise disruption.
- A less risky approach is to use **phased (or incremental) implementation**, where one discrete change (or part of the overall change programme) is made and bedded in before moving on to the next. Changes may be made to one process, product category or supplier at a time, say.
- **Parallel running** allows old and new systems to be run in parallel for a period of time. Results can be cross checked, to evaluate the new system, and the risks of disruption are minimised, as the old system provides a back-up. Parallel running will have to be carefully planned to avoid confusion and inefficiency.
- **Pilot programmes** may be used in selected units of the organisation, or for selected suppliers, so that the new systems can be tested live (or online) while limiting the risk of disruption in the event of problems. This allows bugs to be ironed out and gives users practice in the new system: staff involved in the pilot programme can then be used to coach others.

Supplier transition planning

2.24 The adoption of a new supplier, or the replacement of one supplier with another, represents a significant change where the product or service supplied is important to the buying organisation or where the supply contract represents significant expenditure. There are a number of key issues, which should be familiar to you from your studies.

- Negotiation and preparation of product or service specifications, service level agreements and supply contracts, so that there is clear understanding of the expectations of both parties and how the relationship between them will be managed (in terms of communication and collaboration, quality and performance management, dispute resolution and so on).
- The contract should include a negotiated transition plan, detailing the risks and responsibilities of both parties in the changeover process, including the identification and ironing out of unforeseen problems or issues. There should also be provision for **acceptance testing** (measuring the quality and service provided against requirements specifications) prior to adoption of the contract, perhaps during a trial period or pilot programme.
- Readiness of stakeholders, systems and infrastructure for the implementation of the new contract. Buying and supplying organisations must have plans, controls, systems and resources in place to handle the logistics, inventory, quality and other operational implications of the contract. Staff in both organisations need to be aware of the new relationship and their responsibilities within it. Customers may need to be made aware of any implications for quality or delivery.
- Different changeover approaches may be used. A trial period or pilot programme, for example, allows buyer and supplier organisations to test their readiness, identify issues and iron out problems prior to acceptance or full implementation. Direct or phased implementation may be used, depending on whether there are discrete sub-sets of the service that can be phased in incrementally. Some variation of parallel running may be used, where the outgoing supplier's activity is progressively reduced or 'ramped down' while the incoming supplier's is 'ramped up'. A ramp-up/ramp-down phase gives all parties a chance to adjust with minimal disruption (and the chance to measure the new supplier's performance against the old).
- Contract management and review, to ensure that: co-operative working relationships are built with the new supplier; shortfalls on agreed specifications or service levels are followed up; any changes to contract terms are systematically documented and managed; and continuous improvements are built into supplier performance over time. (This will be particularly important for outsourced services, in order to retain control over the activity.)

2.25 In any change of supplier, there is a risk that the current supplier may attempt to disrupt the transfer of business to new suppliers for a new contract period, or may simply lose motivation to provide the required service levels. A range of contractual provisions may be used to minimise this risk, covering: the outgoing supplier's co-operation in the transition period; handover of work in progress, assets and documents; and the sharing of any data and reports required to facilitate transition or minimise disruption to routine operations.

2.26 Incentives may be used, in the form of loyalty or performance-related bonuses or positive supplier rating, to motivate the supplier to provide quality service right to the end of the existing contract. Where necessary, however, sanctions may be applied to enforce the terms of the contract and service level agreement for the full duration of the contract.

3   Disaster recovery planning

3.1   Disaster recovery planning (DRP) is a subsidiary discipline of business continuity planning which specifically focuses on the advance planning and preparations necessary to recover the essential operations, sites, functions, systems and resources of the organisation, in the event of catastrophic failure or disruption – such as fire, flood, strategic supplier failure, major product recall or IT systems failure.

3.2   Where business continuity planning focuses on 'keeping the business running', disaster recovery planning focuses on 'getting it up and running again'. A corporate business continuity plan may incorporate a range of specific DRPs for particular types of disaster and/or for particular sites, operations or systems of the business. Much of what we have said about the process of BCP (eg in Table 13.1) also applies to DRP: particular emphasis will be placed on the **testing** of recovery plans (evacuation drills, communication tests, stress tests of new systems and so on.)

The benefits of effective DRP

3.3   The benefits of effective disaster recovery planning can be summarised as follows.

- Identification of business-critical systems, processes, resources and related vulnerabilities, to support risk management (and the prioritisation of recovery resources)
- Identification and definition of roles and responsibilities for response action, providing ownership, focal points for communication – and clarity in an emergency situation
- Support for a swift, co-ordinated response in an emergency situation (where time and clarity may not be available to start formulating responses)
- Determination of the resources and timescales required to restore minimum acceptable levels of operation and service (ie critical business deliverables and success factors)
- Reduction of the consequential or secondary risks arising from unplanned action and panic responses
- Reduction of reputational and commercial risks from disrupted service to customers (and/or lack of a transparent and responsible response to the crisis)
- Opportunities for proactive input from suppliers and other key stakeholders to the recovery process (eg contingency planning, pre-commitment of recovery resources and support)
- Time to develop resources and skills for recovery which are currently lacking (eg lead time for supplier development, information assurance protocols, or the building of reputational strength)
- Imposing rigour on system, product and process, and relationship design and development, with a view to building in resilience (the ability to survive shocks)
- Increasing organisational risk awareness.

Contents of the DRP

3.4   Some basic generic elements of a disaster recovery plan are listed in Table 13.2.

Table 13.2 *Basic elements of a DRP*

Roles and responsibilities	Identify who needs to take responsibility for each action, including deputies to cover key roles (since key personnel may be affected by the disaster).
	Identify an emergency response and recovery team and co-ordinator.
Incident checklists for key staff	Action checklists are easy to follow in emergency conditions
First stage	There should be clear, direct instructions (or a separate checklist) for the crucial first hour following an incident: identified as an emergency response plan
Follow-up stages	There should be a separate checklist of measures that can wait until after the first hour: this ensures a focused emergency response and clear priorities
Document review	Agree how often, when and how you will check the plan, to ensure that it is current.
	Update the plan to reflect changes in the organisation and risks.

3.5   A template for action, following the lifecycle of a generic crisis or disaster, is summarised in Table 13.3.

Table 13.3 *The disaster recovery lifecycle*

1	Commence disaster log	Commence a record of timings, decisions (and by whom taken) and actions taken from the onset of any disaster event. The record keeper should sign each entry. Such a record may be required at any subsequent internal or external inquiry, hearing or investigation into the disaster.
2	Emergency services	If the emergency services are involved, contact should be channelled through an appointed Liaison Officer. Co ordination with public authorities may be required to access recovery resources and services, work within wider recovery efforts (where relevant), and ensure compliance with relevant law, regulation and emergency guidance.
3	Record of damage	Carry out a damage assessment and document: • Injury to staff, visitors or members of the public • Damage to property and loss of stock • Damage to buildings, machinery, equipment and vehicles • Assess the extent of the disruption to business
4	Assemble the recovery team	Emergency response and business recovery teams should be clearly identified (with contact telephone numbers) in the DRP, including alternates
5	Look after, support and brief staff	Immediate priority should be given to: • Removing staff to a place of safety (where relevant) and ensuring that all staff are accounted for • Accessing on-site or off-site medical assistance for injured staff (where relevant) – and informing family members • Appropriate welfare provision for staff members affected (eg trauma counselling, relocation assistance) • Keeping all managers and staff fully briefed on the status of the disaster, and if/when/where to report to work (eg by text message or help line) – and maintain records of all briefings.
6	Inform stakeholders	Inform customers, suppliers and contractors: maintain records of all communications
7	Public and media relations	Crisis communication plans should be in place to inform the media and public during crisis situations. A prepared 'holding' statement may be required as a first emergency response, until information is available: the priority will soon shift to clear, transparent, responsible communication.
8	Debrief and learning	Arrange a full debrief and review for stakeholders, as soon as possible after the emergency is over. Disseminate positive feedback and lessons learned on the handling of the crisis. Assign responsibility, actions and timelines for any corrective or preventive actions required in relation to the cause of the crisis.
9	Review the DRP	The DRP – and wider BCP – should be reviewed and adjusted in the light of the current disaster (was the risk correctly identified and assessed?) and the way in which it was handled (was the DRP adequate to the task?)

3.6   We will now look briefly at how this may play itself out in some specific disaster or crisis scenarios.

Computer system failure

3.7   A disaster recovery plan for computer systems failure might include elements such as the following.

- Design and testing of systems to minimise risks and maximise resilience
- Use of a **telephone cascade** (a call list, via which each member notified of an event is responsible for calling others) to inform all relevant staff as fast as possible of the need to trigger emergency recovery measures
- Restore equipment to working order, via emergency repair or replacement (eg triggering a high-priority call-off on a pre-prepared supply contract), or drawing on back-up disaster recovery services (eg an off-site IT service with duplicate systems and data)
- Retrieve back-up devices from (pre-planned) off-site storage – or access back-up data from virtual storage servers
- Re-install software and data
- Re-enter data from the period since the last back-up
- Notify business contacts and other stakeholders, as appropriate, if there are likely to be data gaps or systems glitches

13

Supplier failure

3.8   A disaster recovery plan for supplier failure (as part of a supply continuity plan) might include elements such as the following.

- Advance planning for contract termination and transition (exit strategy)
- Contract, performance and relationship management to minimise risk (and/or give early warning) of supplier financial or operational problems
- Supply chain mapping and environmental (STEEPLE) monitoring for early warning of supply vulnerabilities
- Pre-identified and pre-qualified back-up sources of supply
- Pre-negotiated framework contracts, with emergency ('hot start') call-off facilities
- Establishment of direct contacts with lower-tier suppliers (in case of first-tier failure)
- Pre-authorised procurement card or cash payment facilities to enable the payment of emergency suppliers (while credit arranged)
- Use of telephone cascade, intranet or email to inform all relevant staff of the need to trigger the emergency response plan, on notification of supplier failure or supply disruption
- Trigger supplier transition arrangements and termination clauses: smooth handover guarantees; protection of intellectual property and confidential data; sharing of transition costs; ownership of assets involved in the contract etc
- Notify business contacts and other stakeholders as appropriate

Fire/flood emergency and damage to premises

3.9   A disaster recovery plan for fire, flood, earthquake, terrorist threat, explosion or other emergencies might include elements such as the following.

- Fire, emergency and evacuation procedures, equipment, alarms and practice drills
- Trained emergency officers (eg fire wardens) to co-ordinate emergency procedures
- Pre-planning of staff welfare provision: medical treatment, crisis counselling, briefings
- The use of remote-access ICT systems (laptops, mobile phones, text messaging) to co-ordinate activity
- The proactive use of off-site data back-up and storage facilities and/or IT services
- The preparation of alternative accommodation and work site arrangements
- Contracts in place to enable the call-off of stand-by services to cover disruption (eg IT services bureau, call centre)
- The triggering of fast-track emergency procurements or existing order expediting (if stock has been damaged)
- Notification of insurance providers
- Notification of business contacts and other stakeholders as appropriate
- Implement crisis management plan for corporate communications